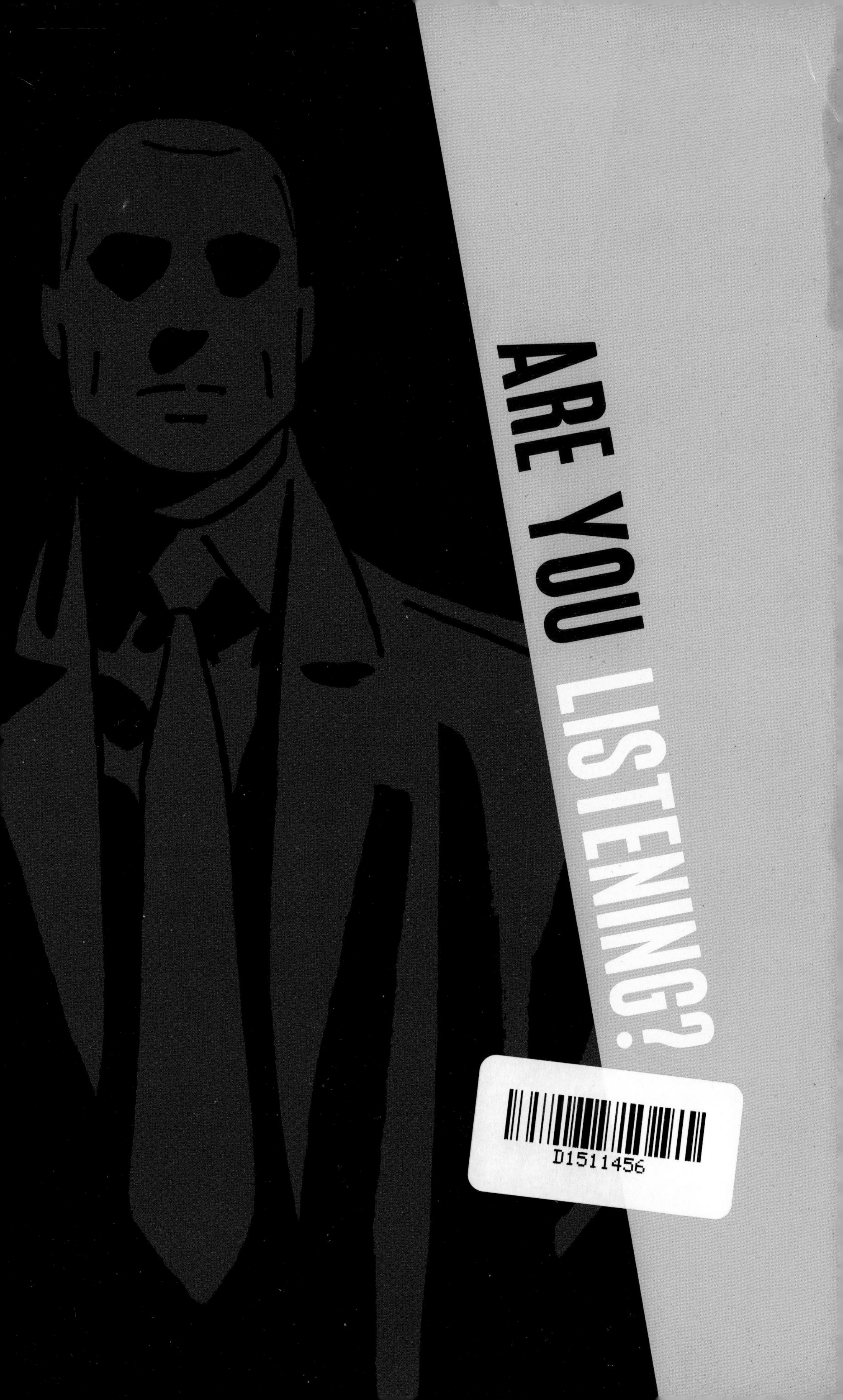
ARE YOU LISTENING?

WHO IS

IMAGE COMICS, INC.

Robert Kirkman - chief operating officer
Erik Larsen - chief financial officer
Todd McFarlane - president
Marc Silvestri - chief executive officer
Jim Valentino - vice-president

Eric Stephenson - publisher
Todd Martinez - sales & licensing coordinator
Sarah deLaine - pr & marketing coordinator
Branwyn Bigglestone - accounts manager
Emily Miller - administrative assistant
Jamie Parreno - marketing assistant
Kevin Yuen - digital rights coordinator
Tyler Shainline - production manager
Drew Gill - art director
Jonathan Chan - senior production artist
Monica Garcia - production artist
Vincent Kukua - production artist
Jana Cook - production artist

www.imagecomics.com

Book design by Jeff Powell

WHO IS JAKE ELLIS? Vol. 1. First Printing. October 2011. Published by Image Comics, Inc. Office of publication: 2134 Allston Way, 2nd Floor, Berkeley, California 94704. Copyright © 2011 Nathan Edmondson and Tonci Zonjic. All rights reserved. Contains material originally published in magazine form as WHO IS JAKE ELLIS? #1-5. WHO IS JAKE ELLIS?, the Who Is Jake Ellis? Logo, and the likenesses of all characters herein are trademarks of Nathan Edmondson and Tonci Zonjic. Image Comics and the Image Comics logos are registered trademarks of Image Comics, Inc. No part of this publication may be reproduced or transmitted, in any form or by any means (except for short excerpts for review purposes) without the express written permission of Nathan Edmondson, Tonci Zonjic, or Image Comics, Inc. All names, characters, events, and locales herein are entirely fictional. Any resemblance to actual persons (living or dead), events, or places, without satiric intent, is coincidental. PRINTED IN THE U.S.A. For information regarding the CPSIA on this printed material call: 203-595-3636 and provide reference # EAST – 407909. Representation: Law Offices of Harris M. Miller II, P.C. ISBN: 978-1-60706-459-6.

JAKE ELLIS?

STORY NATHAN EDMONDSON

ART TONČI ZONJIĆ

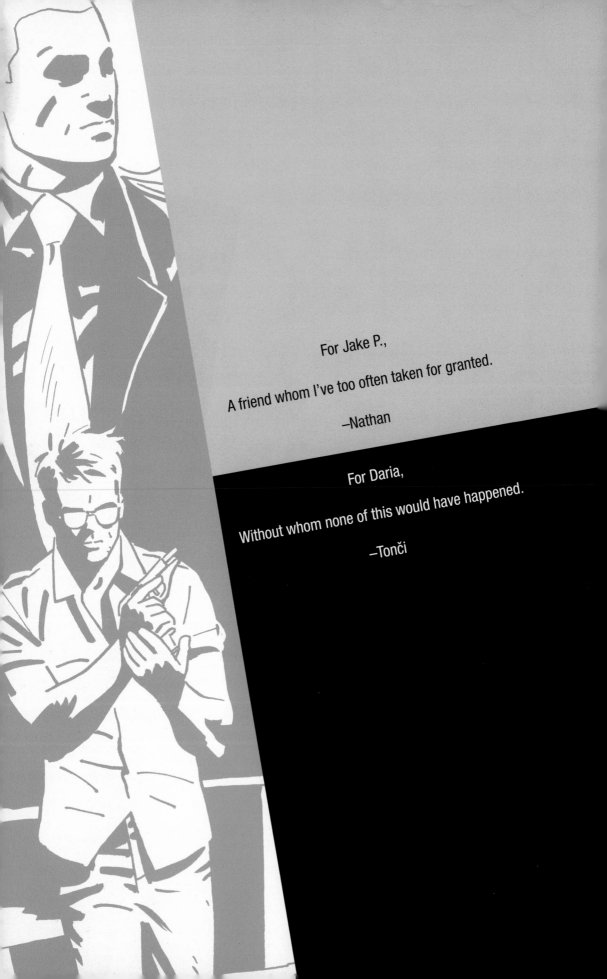

For Jake P.,

A friend whom I've too often taken for granted.

–Nathan

For Daria,

Without whom none of this would have happened.

–Tonči

CHAPTER 1

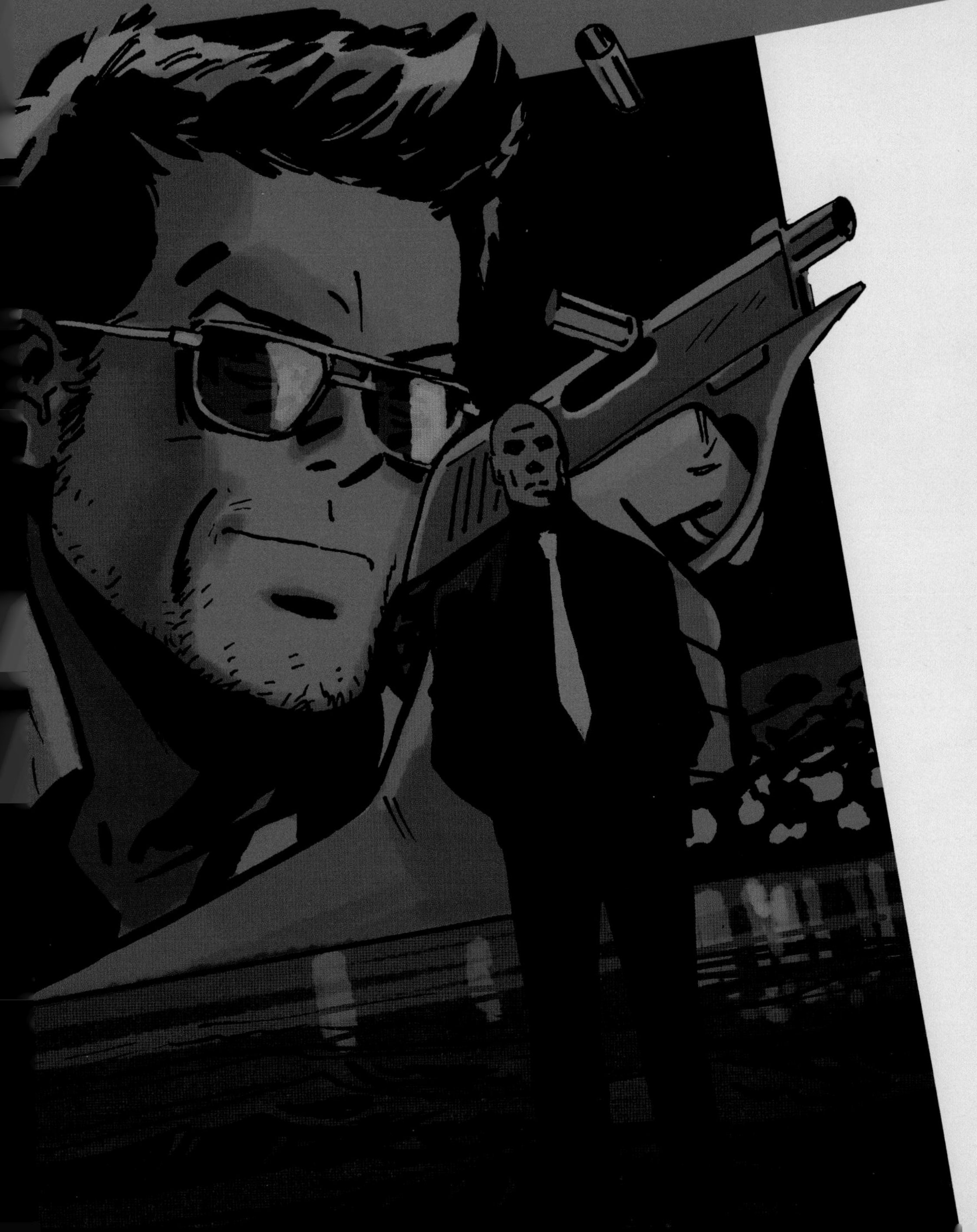

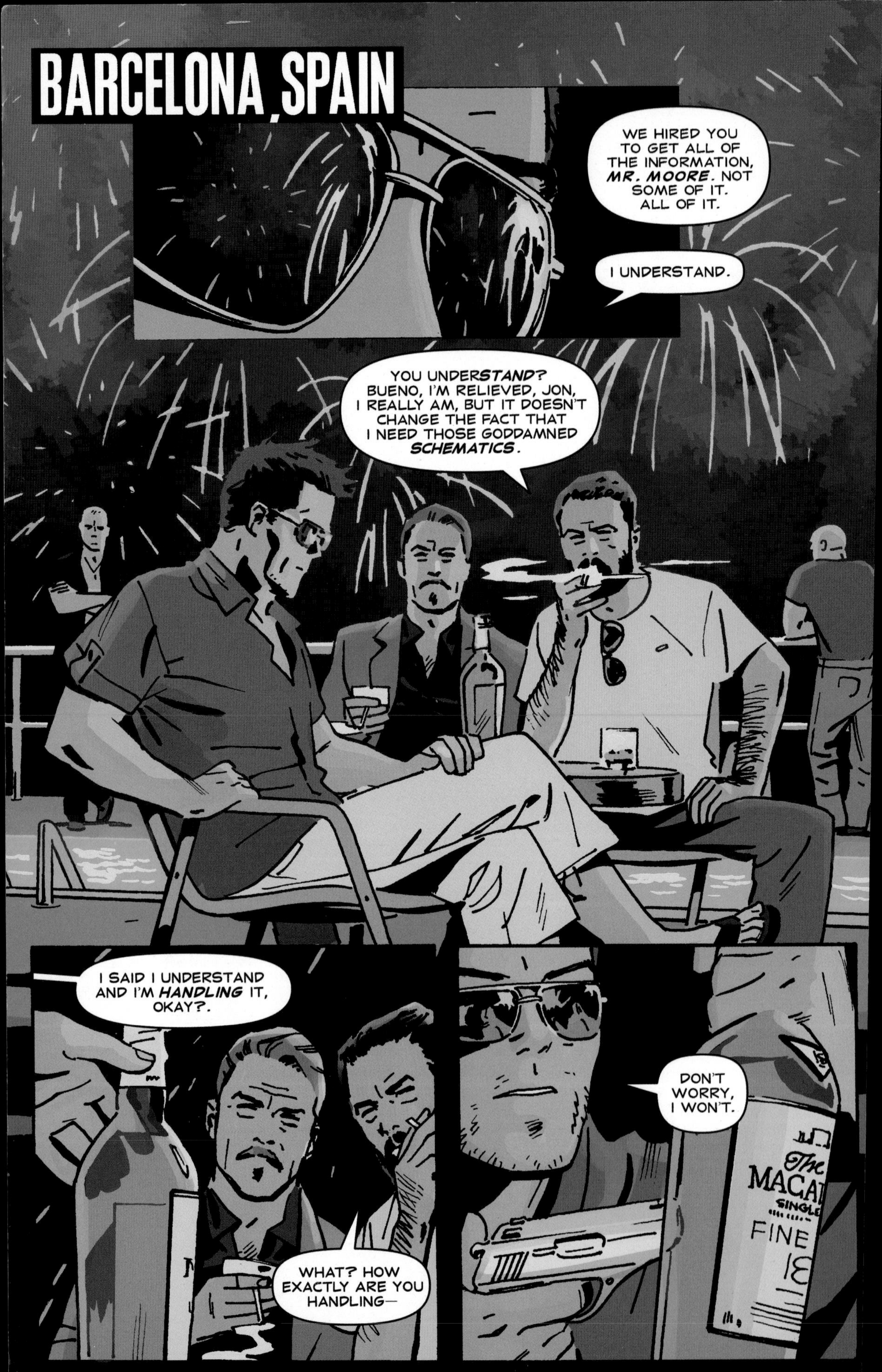
BARCELONA, SPAIN
WE HIRED YOU TO GET ALL OF THE INFORMATION, MR. MOORE. NOT SOME OF IT. ALL OF IT.
I UNDERSTAND.
YOU UNDERSTAND? BUENO, I'M RELIEVED, JON, I REALLY AM, BUT IT DOESN'T CHANGE THE FACT THAT I NEED THOSE GODDAMNED SCHEMATICS.
I SAID I UNDERSTAND AND I'M HANDLING IT, OKAY?.
WHAT? HOW EXACTLY ARE YOU HANDLING—
DON'T WORRY, I WON'T.
The MACA SINGLE FINE 18

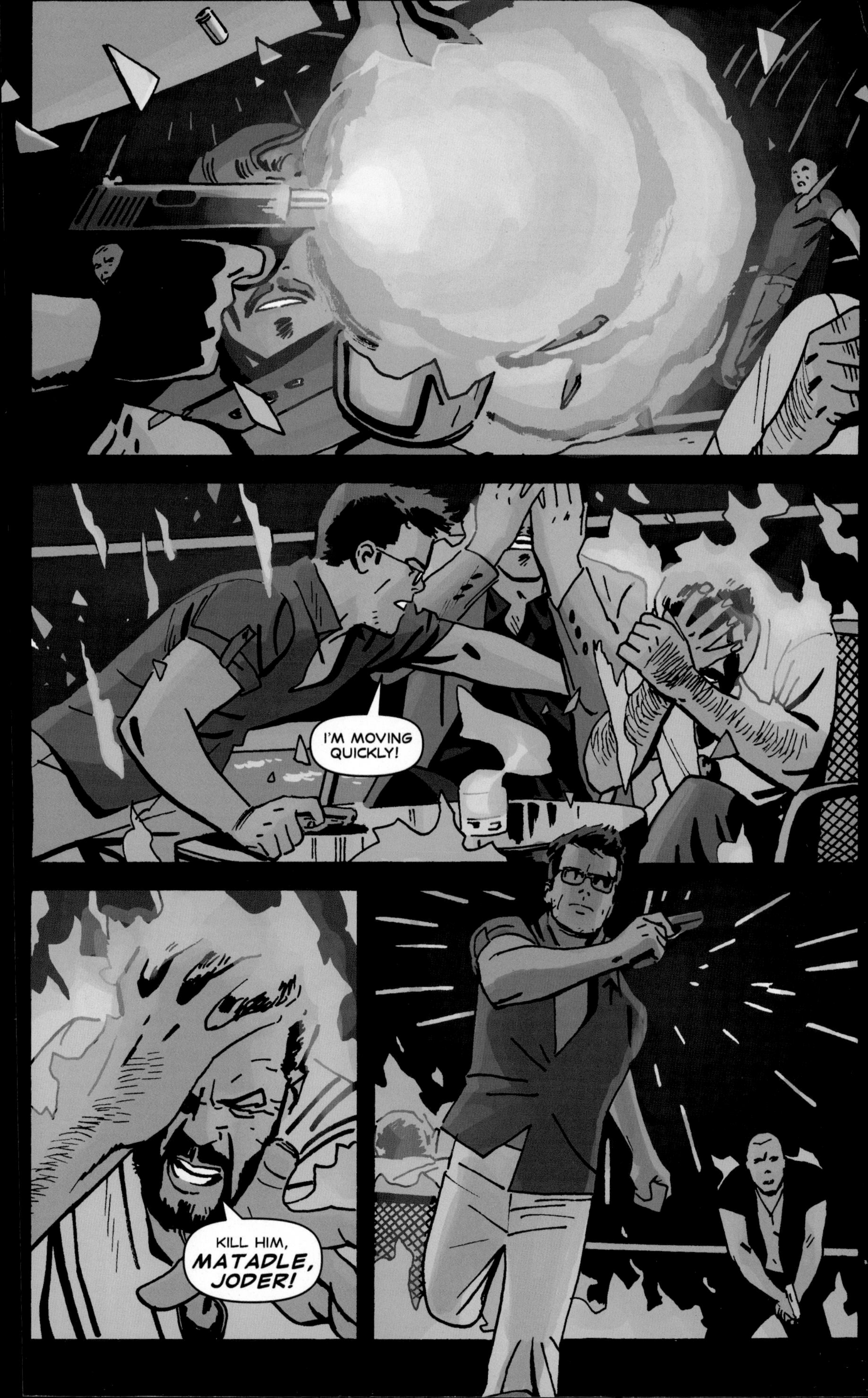
I'M MOVING QUICKLY!
KILL HIM, MATADLE, JODER!

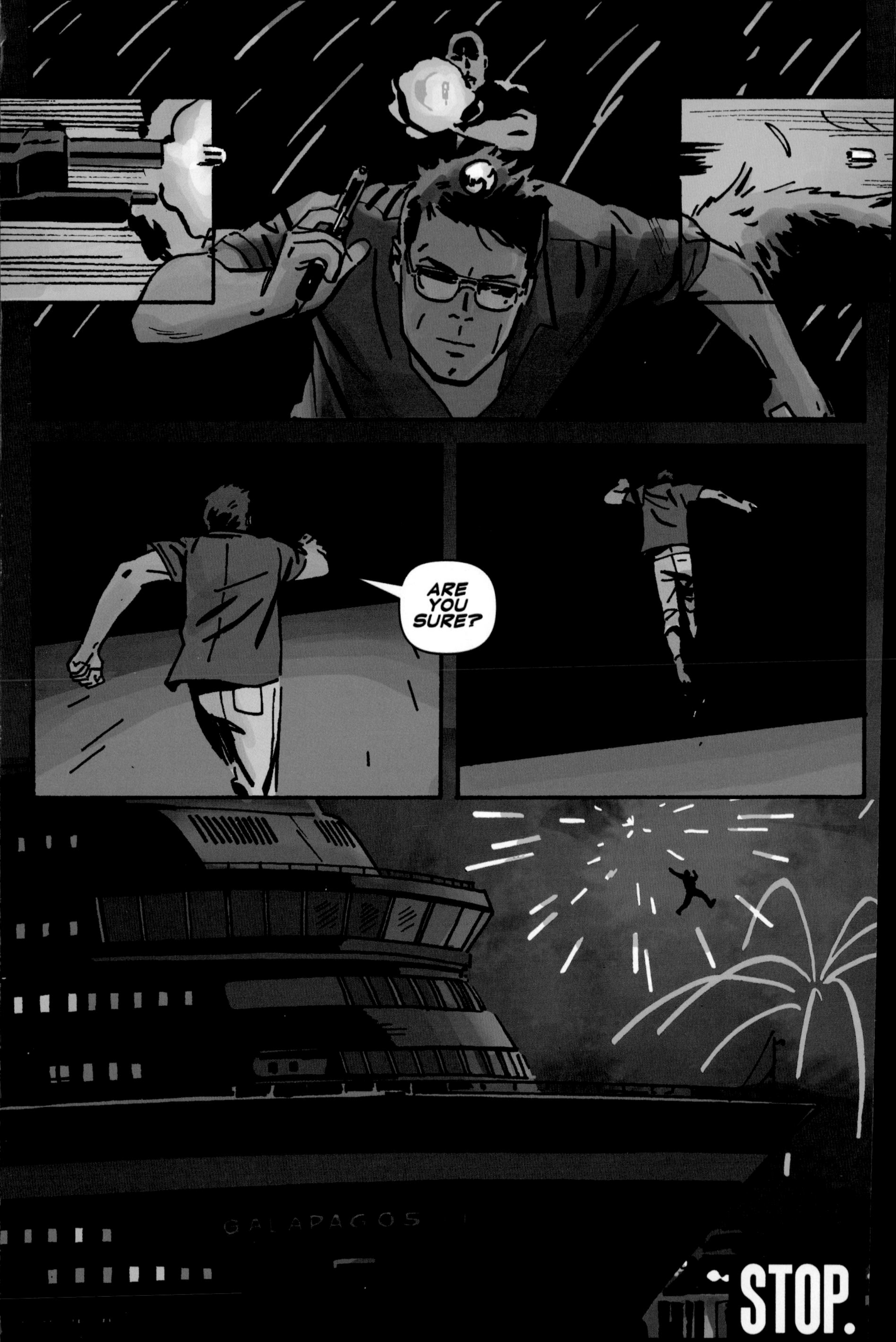
ARE YOU SURE?
GALAPAGOS
STOP.

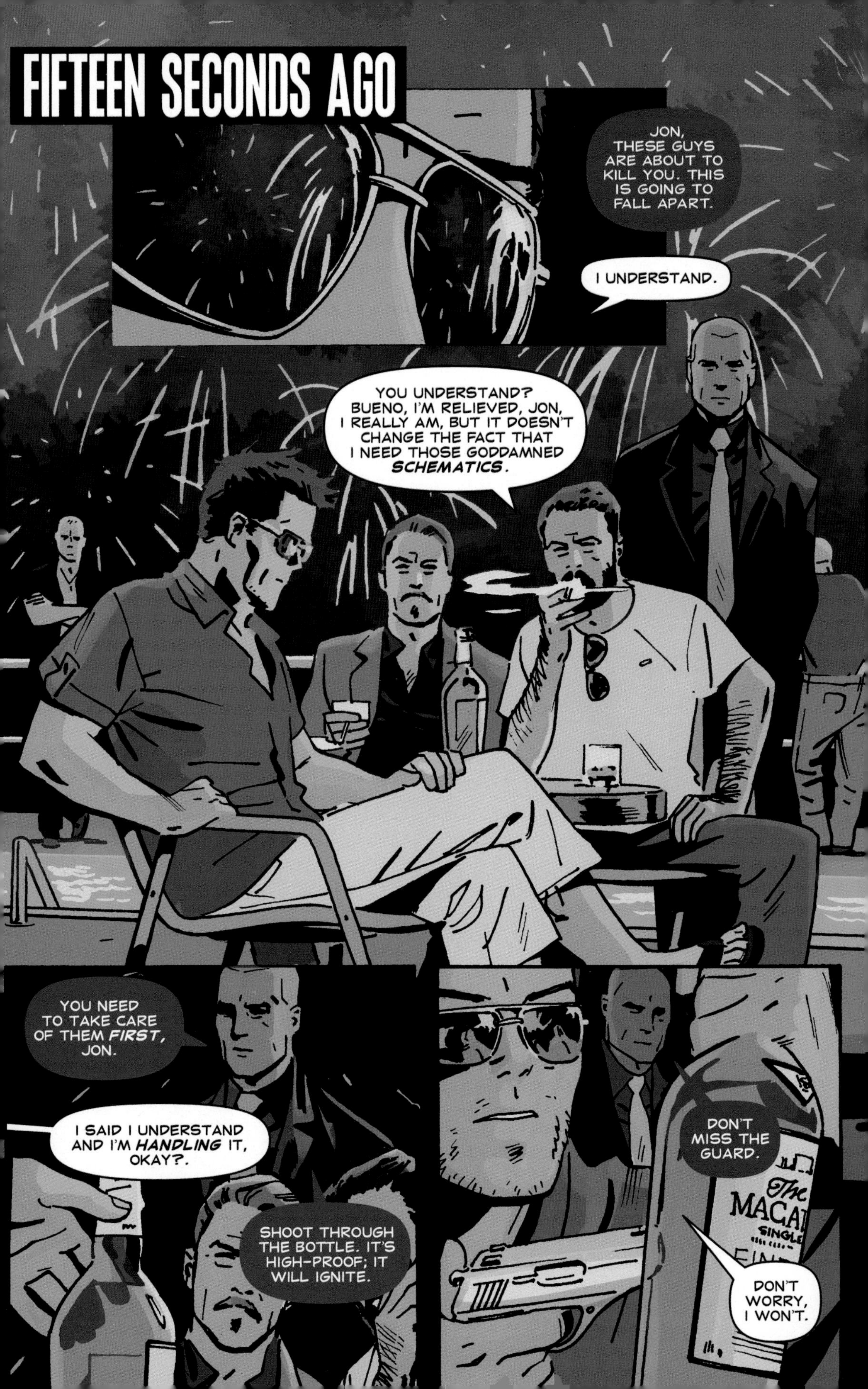
FIFTEEN SECONDS AGO
JON, THESE GUYS ARE ABOUT TO KILL YOU. THIS IS GOING TO FALL APART.
I UNDERSTAND.
YOU UNDERSTAND? BUENO, I'M RELIEVED, JON, I REALLY AM, BUT IT DOESN'T CHANGE THE FACT THAT I NEED THOSE GODDAMNED *SCHEMATICS*.
YOU NEED TO TAKE CARE OF THEM *FIRST*, JON.
I SAID I UNDERSTAND AND I'M *HANDLING* IT, OKAY?.
SHOOT THROUGH THE BOTTLE. IT'S HIGH-PROOF; IT WILL IGNITE.
DON'T MISS THE GUARD.
DON'T WORRY, I WON'T.

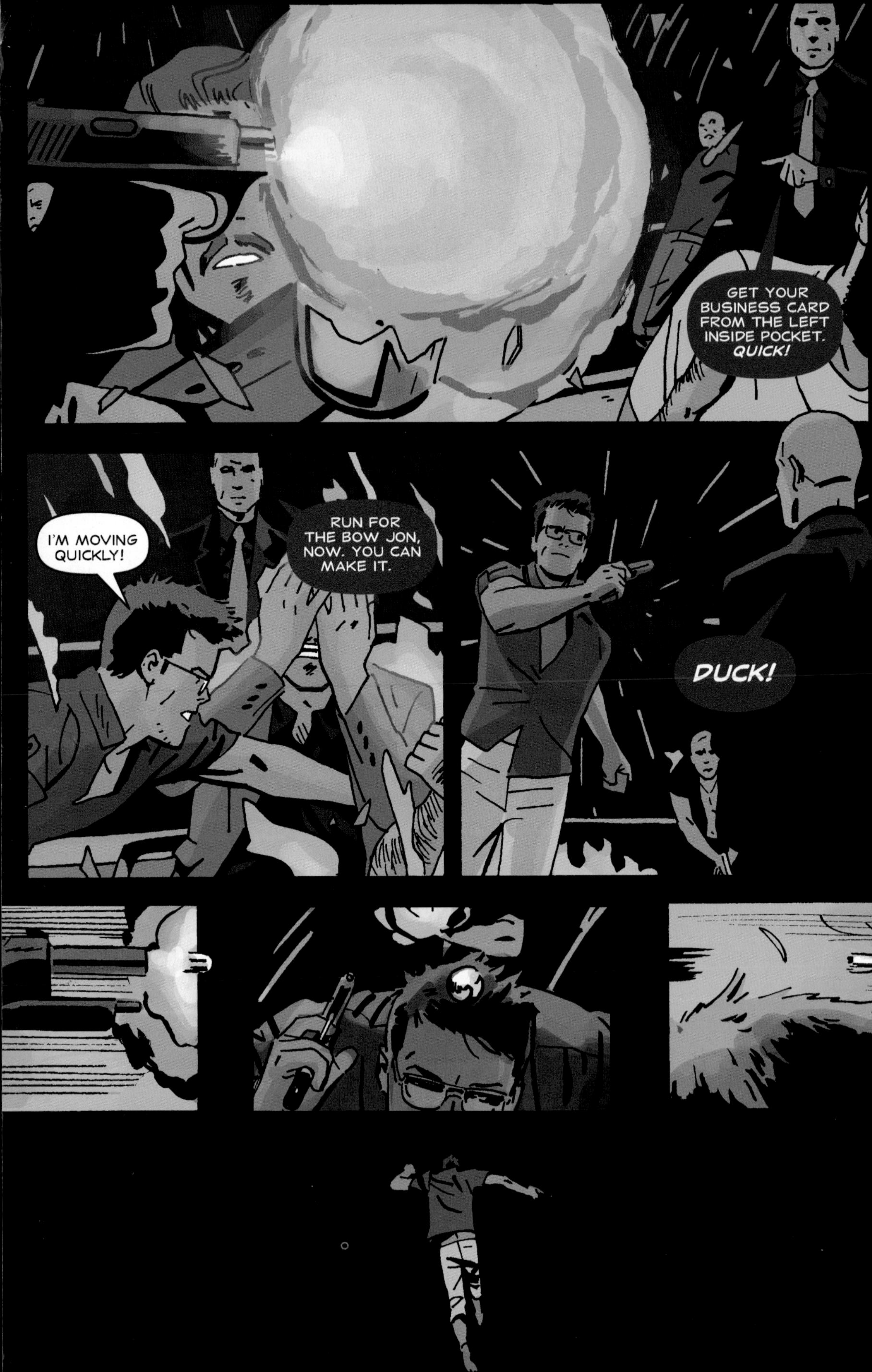
GET YOUR BUSINESS CARD FROM THE LEFT INSIDE POCKET. QUICK!
I'M MOVING QUICKLY!
RUN FOR THE BOW JON, NOW. YOU CAN MAKE IT.
DUCK!

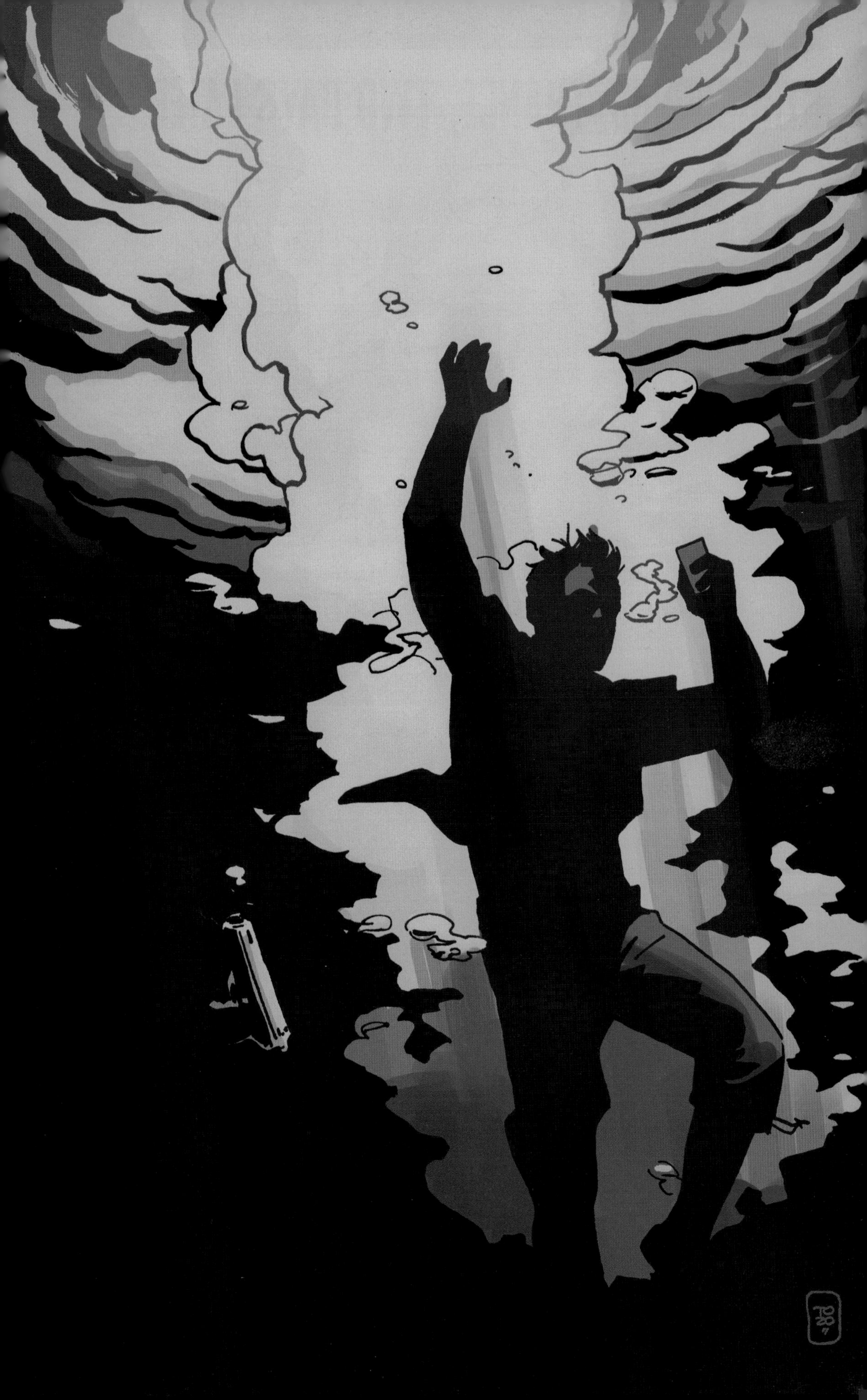

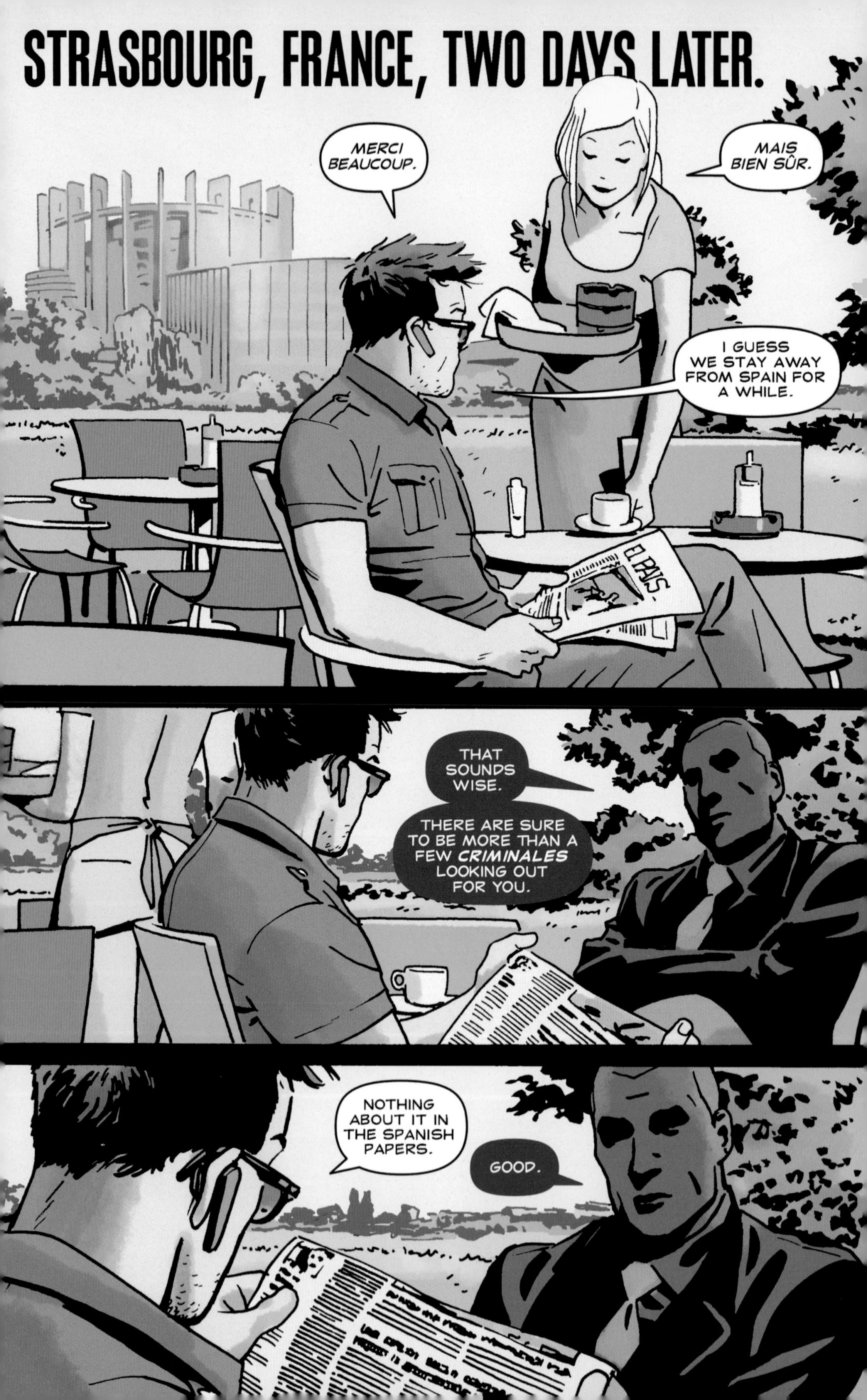
STRASBOURG, FRANCE, TWO DAYS LATER.
MERCI BEAUCOUP.
MAIS BIEN SÛR.
I GUESS WE STAY AWAY FROM SPAIN FOR A WHILE.
EL PAIS
THAT SOUNDS WISE.
THERE ARE SURE TO BE MORE THAN A FEW *CRIMINALES* LOOKING OUT FOR YOU.
NOTHING ABOUT IT IN THE SPANISH PAPERS.
GOOD.

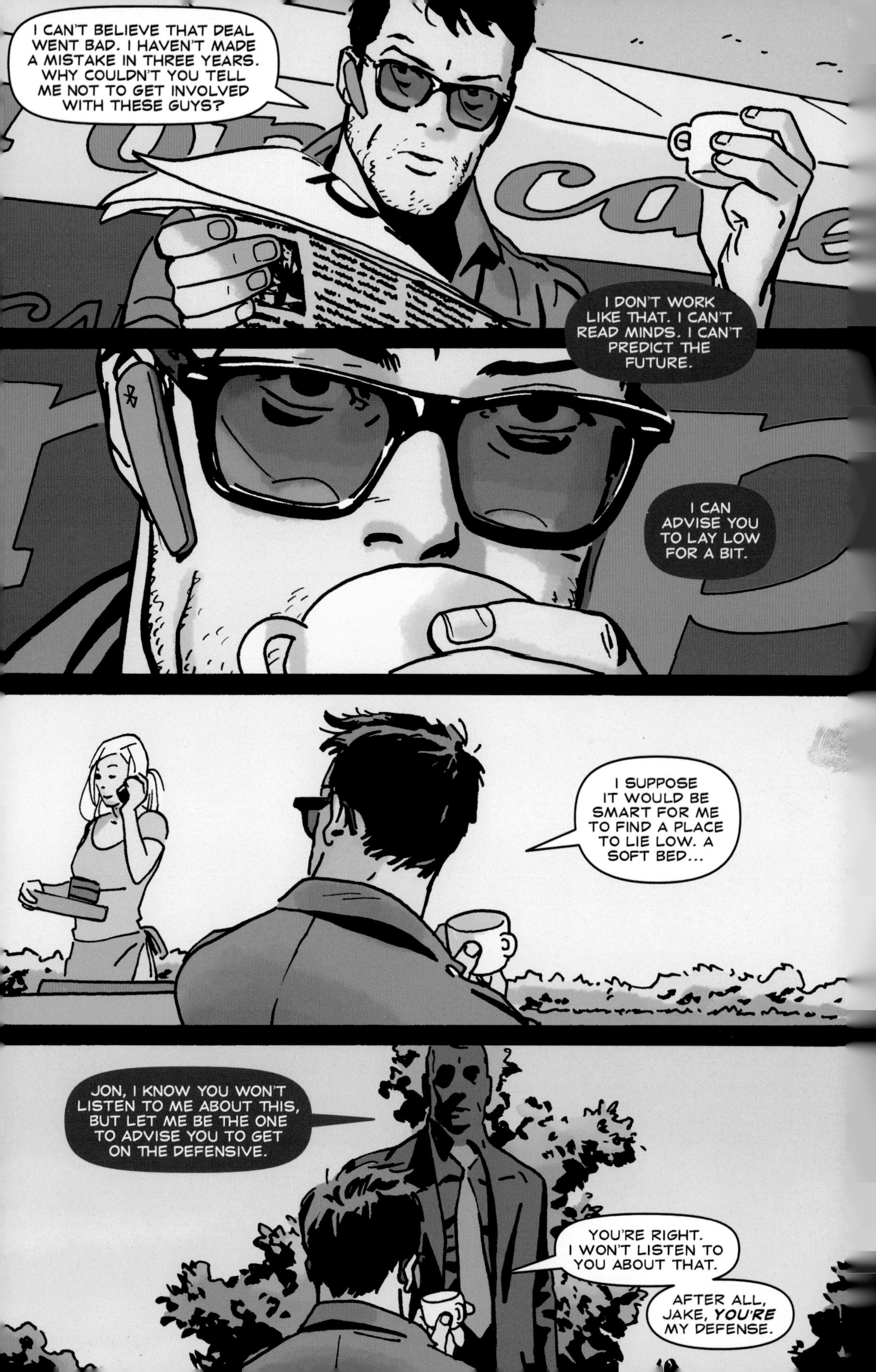
I CAN'T BELIEVE THAT DEAL WENT BAD. I HAVEN'T MADE A MISTAKE IN THREE YEARS. WHY COULDN'T YOU TELL ME NOT TO GET INVOLVED WITH THESE GUYS?
I DON'T WORK LIKE THAT. I CAN'T READ MINDS. I CAN'T PREDICT THE FUTURE.
I CAN ADVISE YOU TO LAY LOW FOR A BIT.
I SUPPOSE IT WOULD BE SMART FOR ME TO FIND A PLACE TO LIE LOW. A SOFT BED...
JON, I KNOW YOU WON'T LISTEN TO ME ABOUT THIS, BUT LET ME BE THE ONE TO ADVISE YOU TO GET ON THE DEFENSIVE.
YOU'RE RIGHT. I WON'T LISTEN TO YOU ABOUT THAT.
AFTER ALL, JAKE, *YOU'RE* MY DEFENSE.

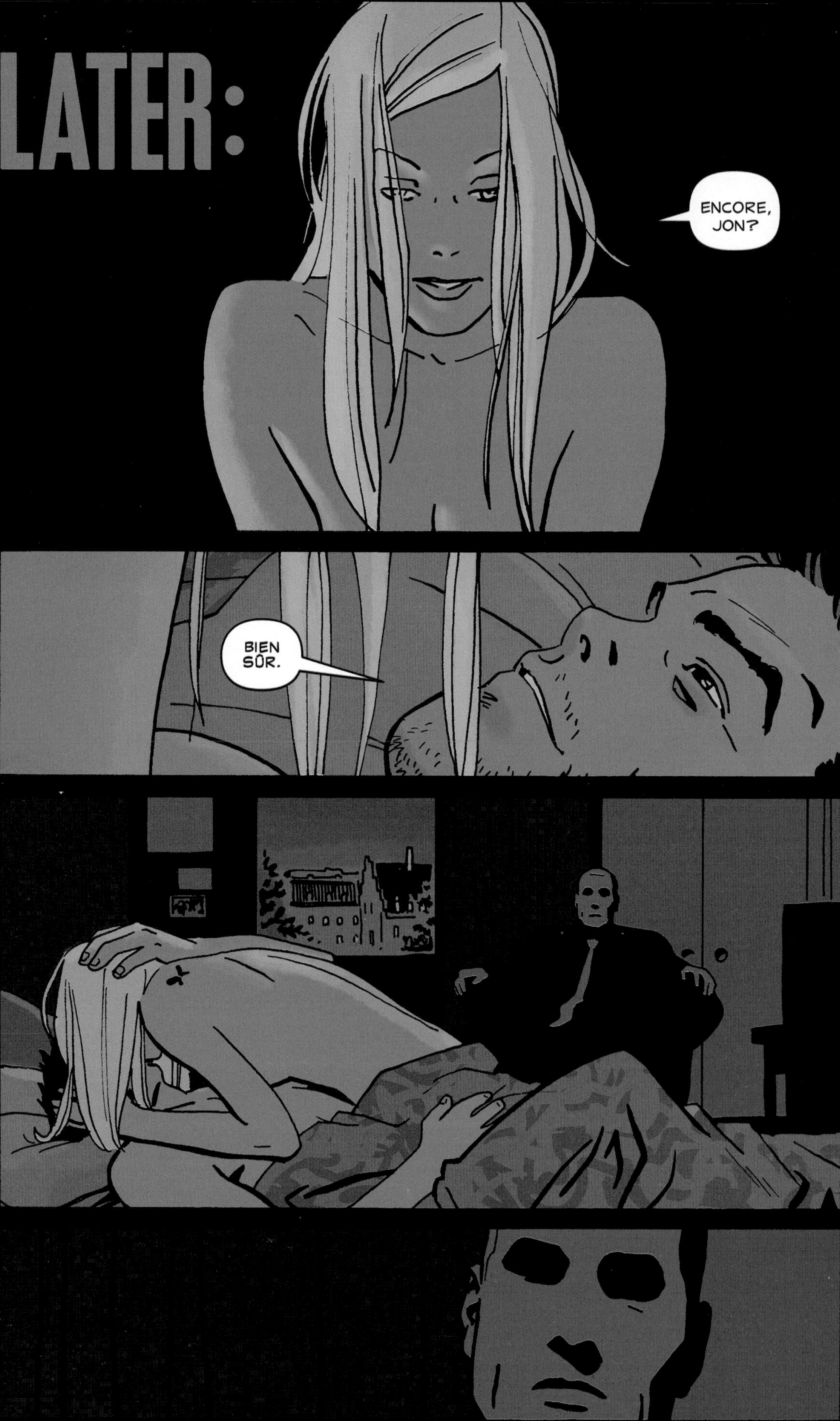
LATER:
ENCORE, JON?
BIEN SÛR.

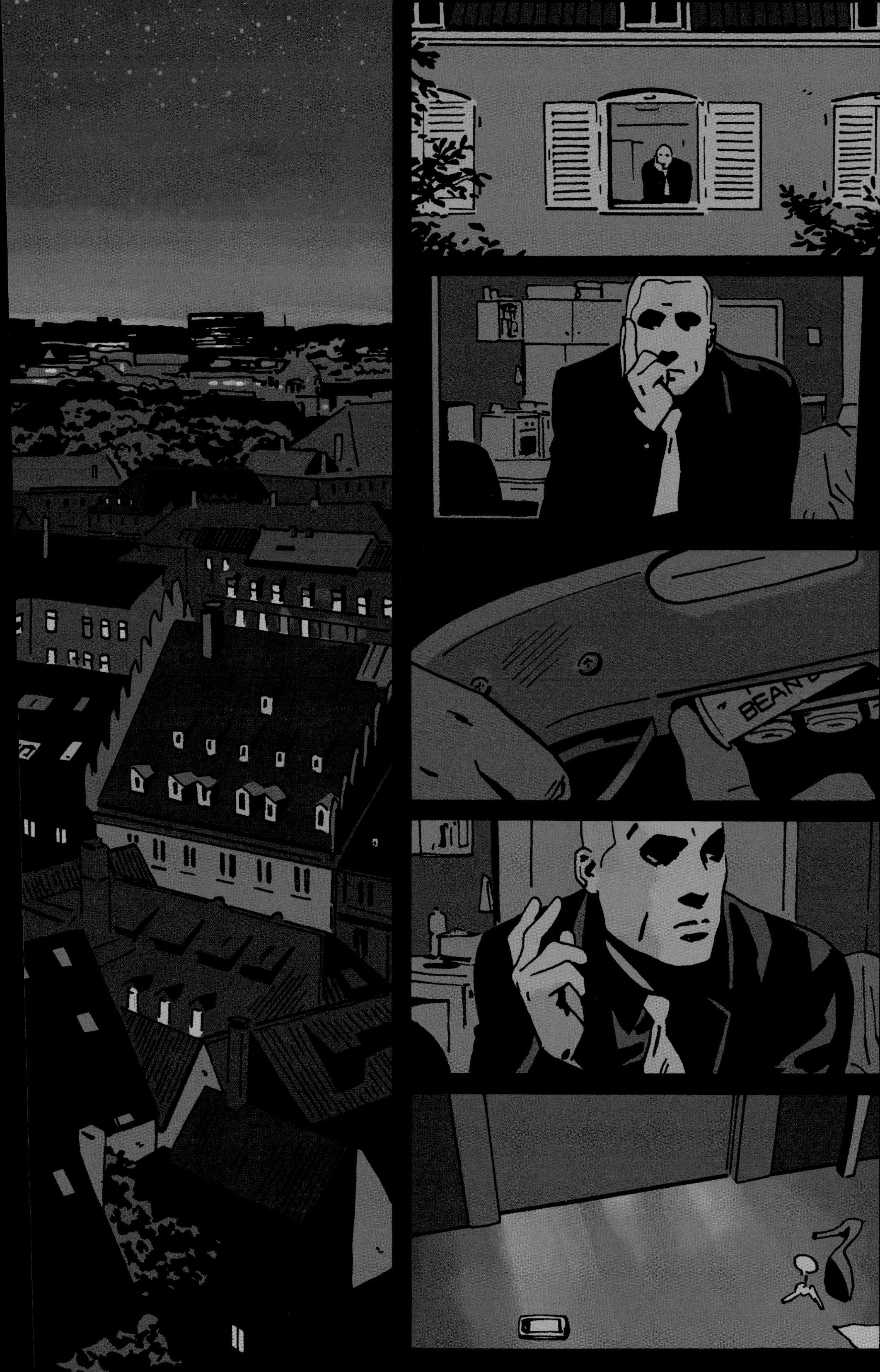
BEAN

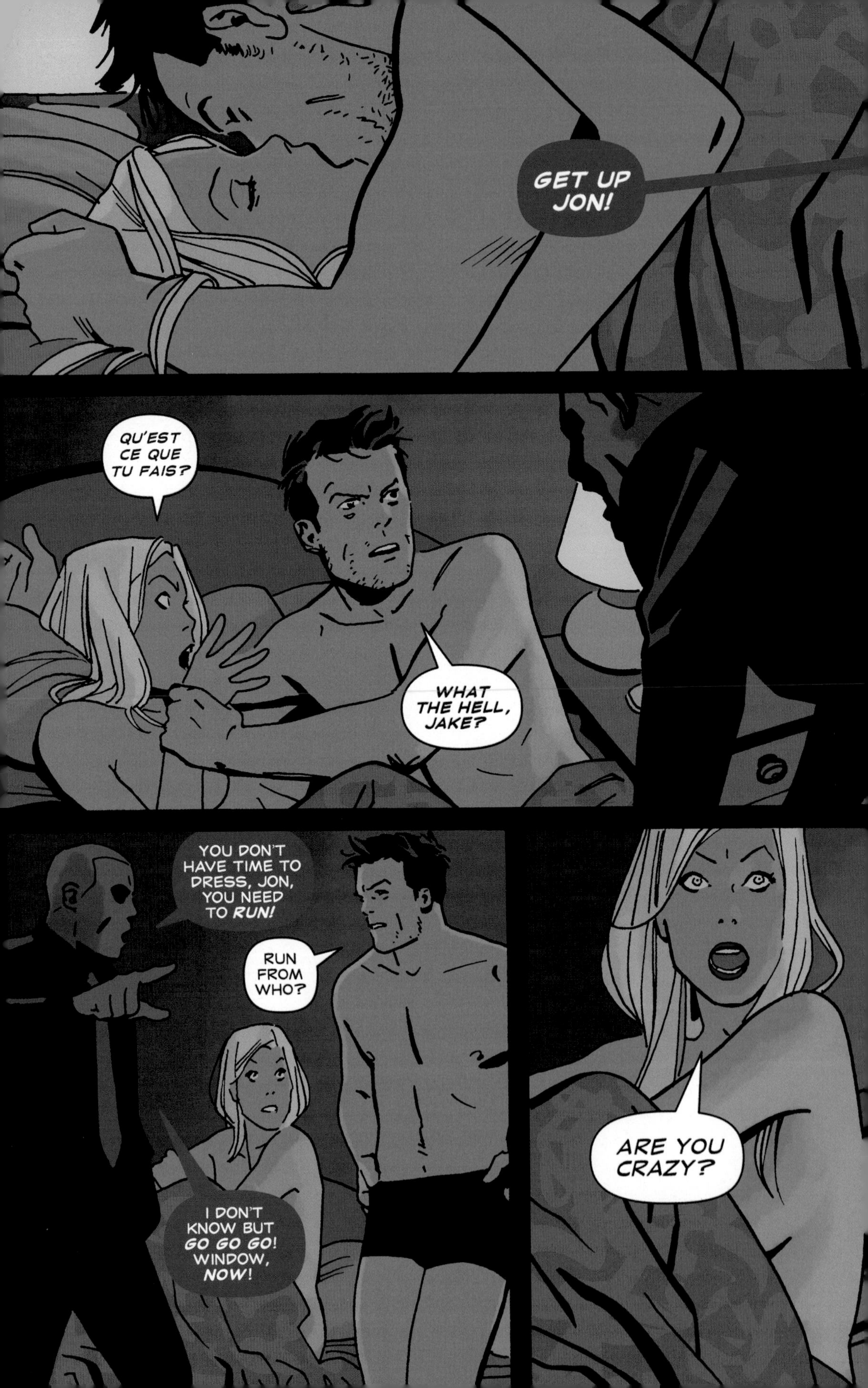
GET UP JON!
QU'EST CE QUE TU FAIS?
WHAT THE HELL, JAKE?
YOU DON'T HAVE TIME TO DRESS, JON, YOU NEED TO *RUN!*
RUN FROM WHO?
I DON'T KNOW BUT *GO GO GO!* WINDOW, *NOW!*
ARE YOU CRAZY?

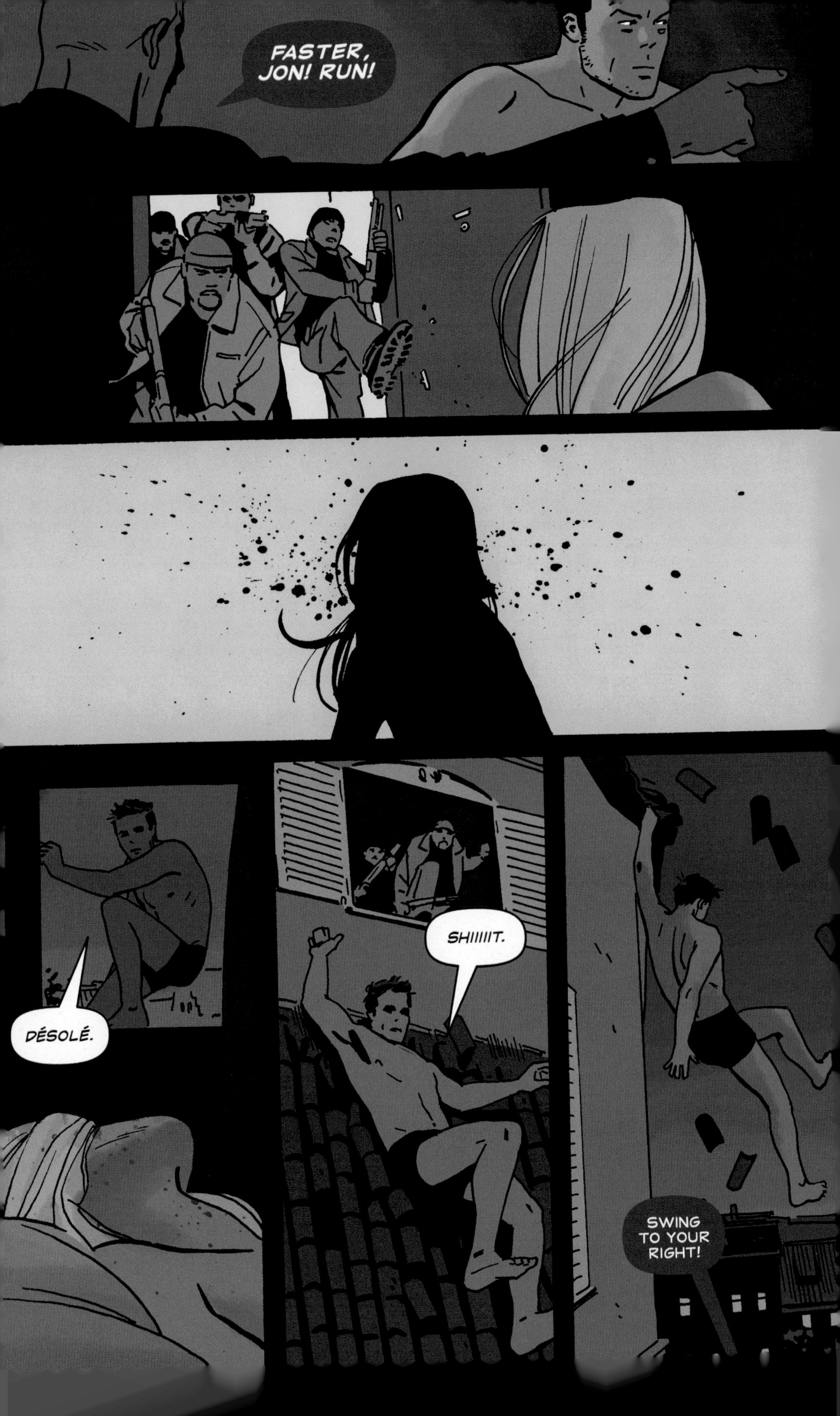
FASTER, JON! RUN!
DÉSOLÉ.
SHIIIIIT.
SWING TO YOUR RIGHT!

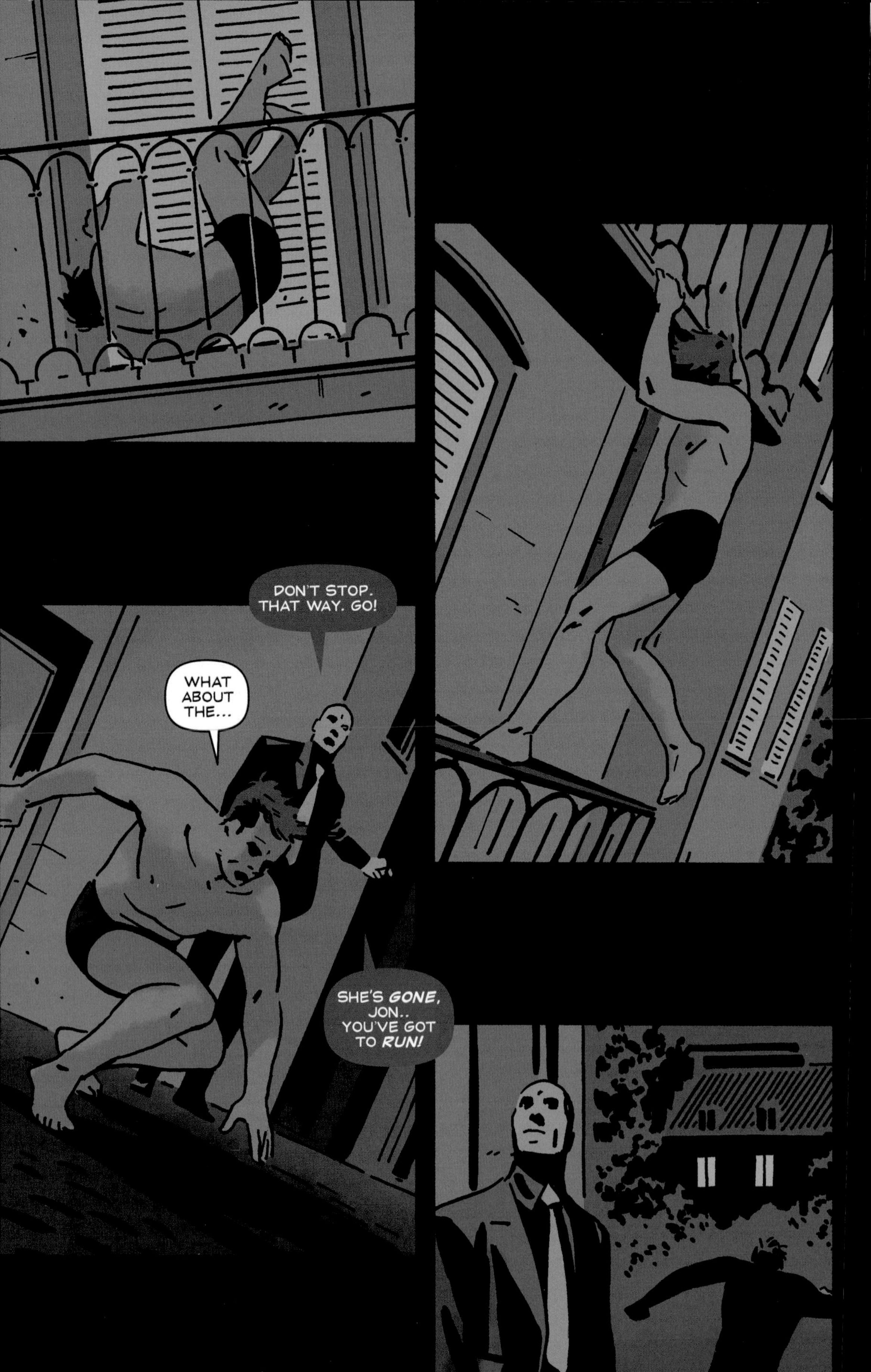
DON'T STOP. THAT WAY. GO!
WHAT ABOUT THE...
SHE'S *GONE*, JON.. YOU'VE GOT TO *RUN!*

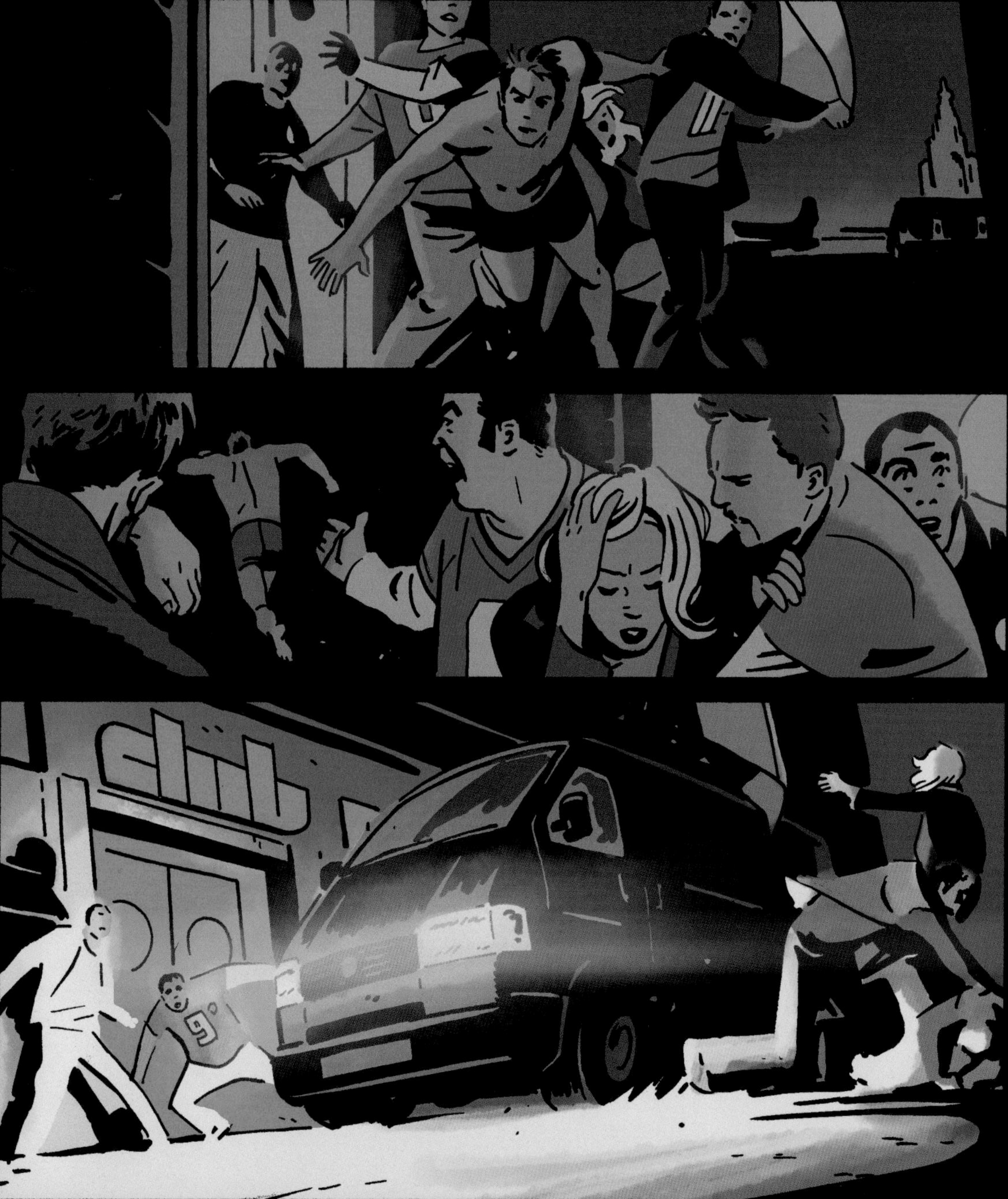
club

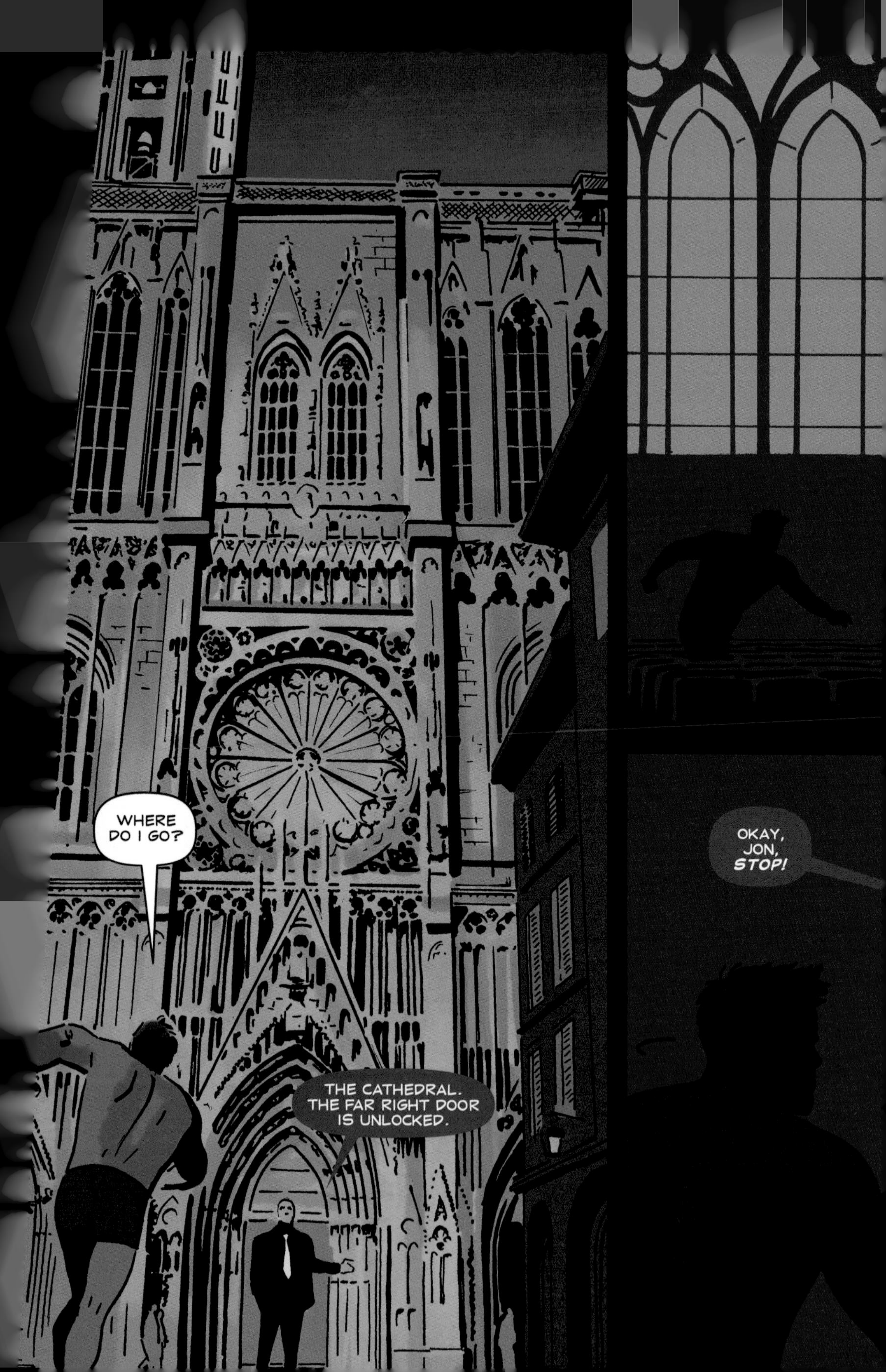
WHERE DO I GO?
THE CATHEDRAL. THE FAR RIGHT DOOR IS UNLOCKED.
OKAY, JON, STOP!

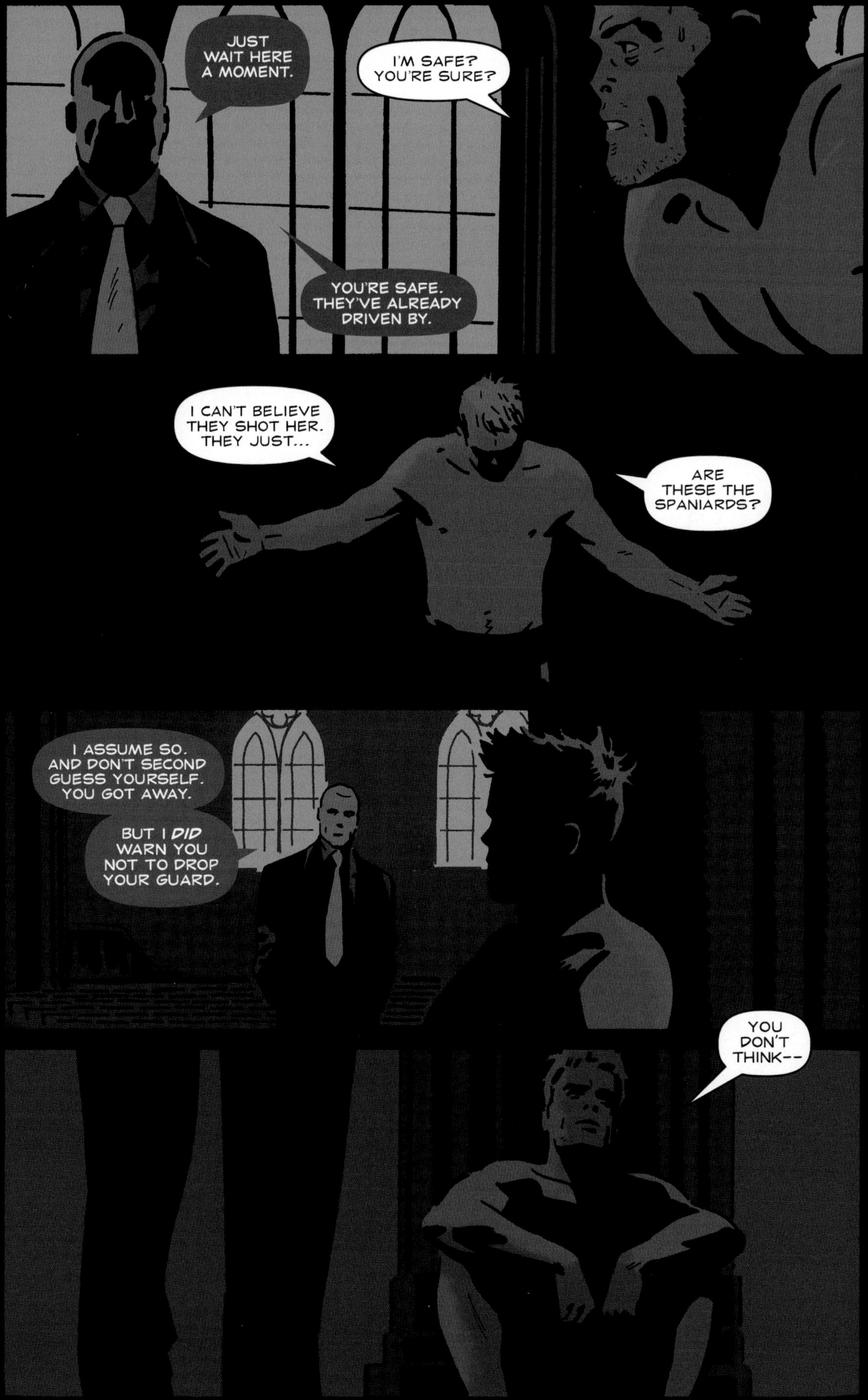

JUST WAIT HERE A MOMENT.
I'M SAFE? YOU'RE SURE?
YOU'RE SAFE. THEY'VE ALREADY DRIVEN BY.
I CAN'T BELIEVE THEY SHOT HER. THEY JUST...
ARE THESE THE SPANIARDS?
I ASSUME SO. AND DON'T SECOND GUESS YOURSELF. YOU GOT AWAY.
BUT I *DID* WARN YOU NOT TO DROP YOUR GUARD.
YOU DON'T THINK--

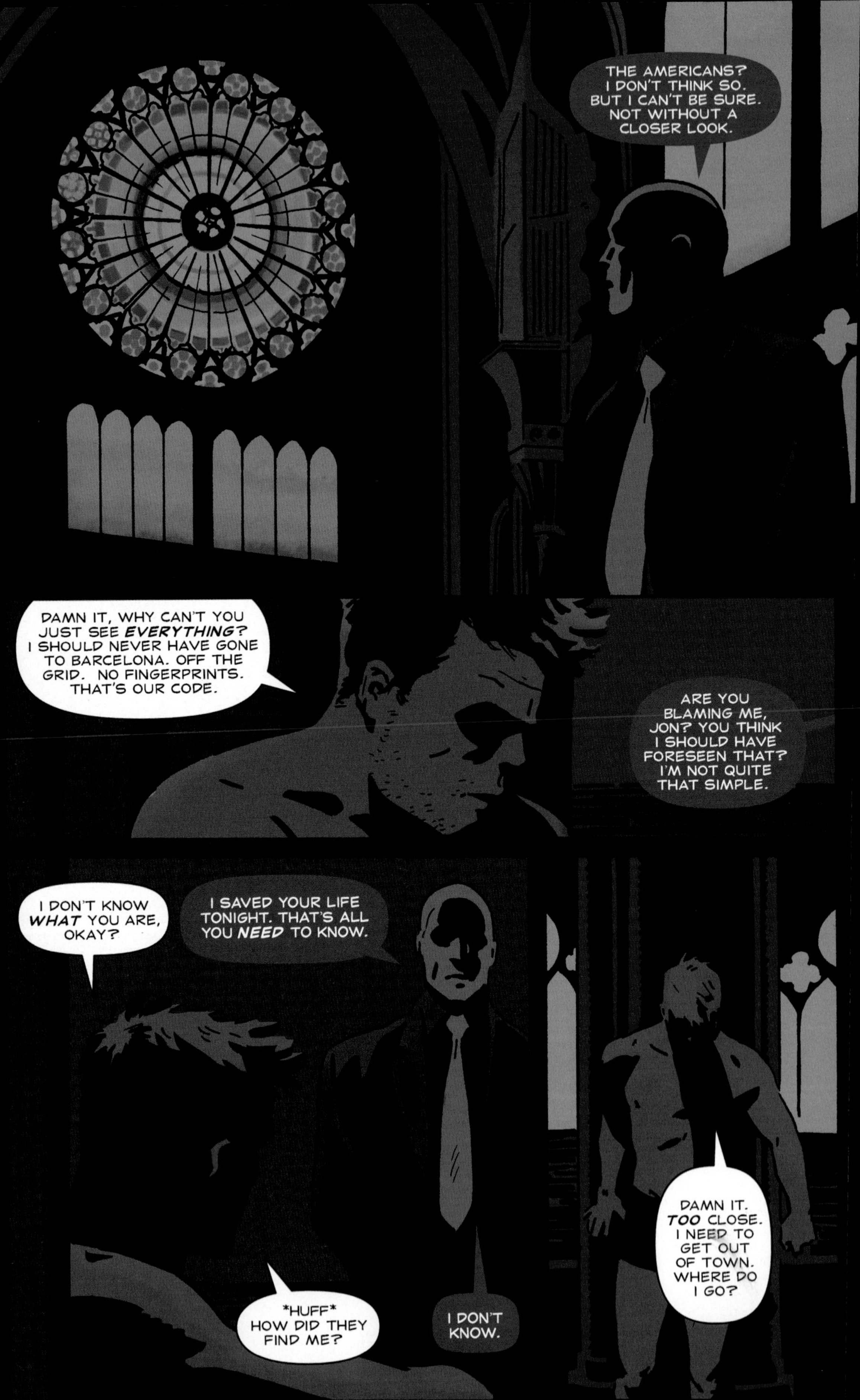
THE AMERICANS? I DON'T THINK SO. BUT I CAN'T BE SURE. NOT WITHOUT A CLOSER LOOK.
DAMN IT, WHY CAN'T YOU JUST SEE EVERYTHING? I SHOULD NEVER HAVE GONE TO BARCELONA. OFF THE GRID. NO FINGERPRINTS. THAT'S OUR CODE.
ARE YOU BLAMING ME, JON? YOU THINK I SHOULD HAVE FORESEEN THAT? I'M NOT QUITE THAT SIMPLE.
I DON'T KNOW WHAT YOU ARE, OKAY?
I SAVED YOUR LIFE TONIGHT. THAT'S ALL YOU NEED TO KNOW.
HUFF HOW DID THEY FIND ME?
I DON'T KNOW.
DAMN IT. TOO CLOSE. I NEED TO GET OUT OF TOWN. WHERE DO I GO?

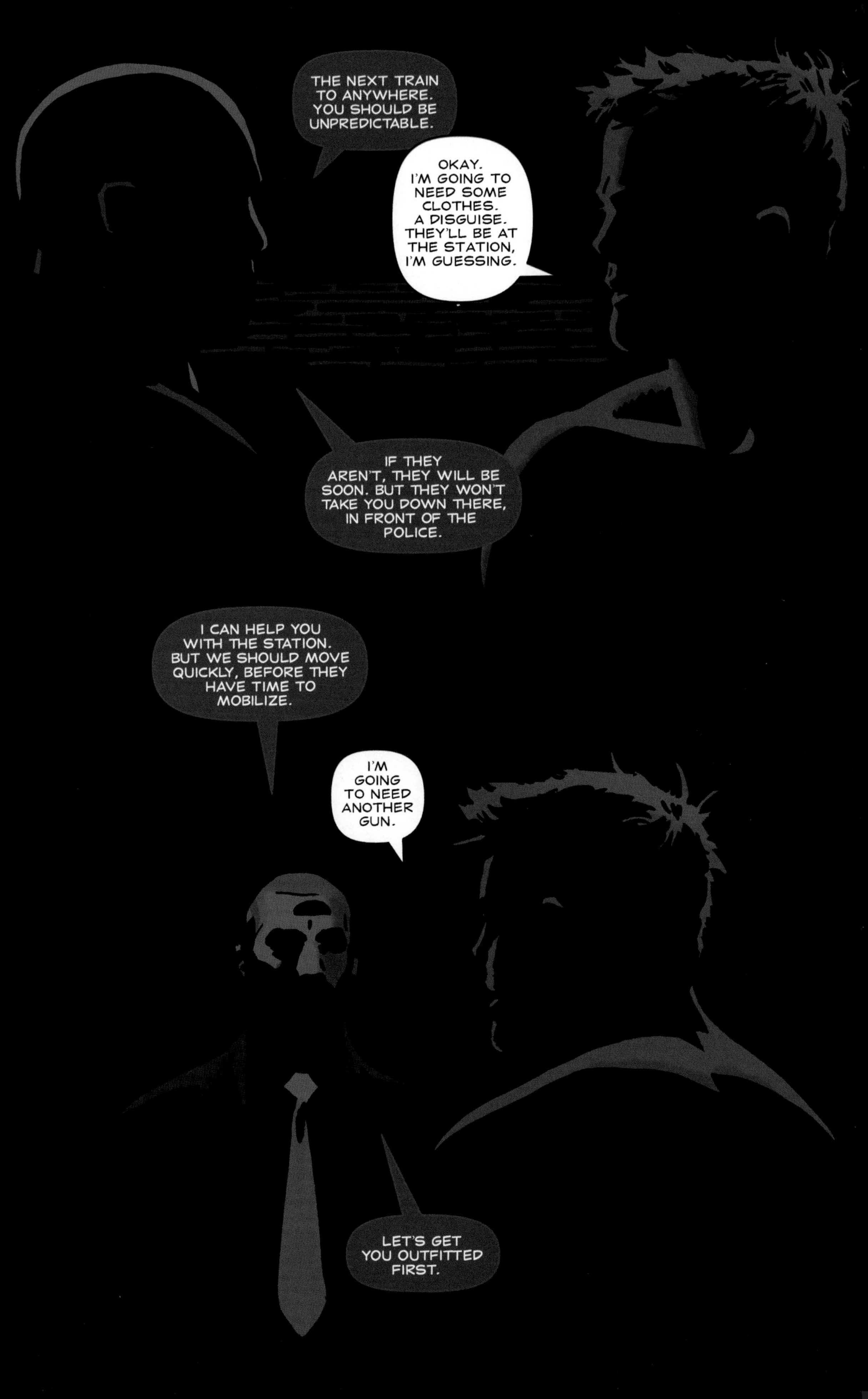
THE NEXT TRAIN TO ANYWHERE. YOU SHOULD BE UNPREDICTABLE.
OKAY. I'M GOING TO NEED SOME CLOTHES. A DISGUISE. THEY'LL BE AT THE STATION, I'M GUESSING.
IF THEY AREN'T, THEY WILL BE SOON. BUT THEY WON'T TAKE YOU DOWN THERE, IN FRONT OF THE POLICE.
I CAN HELP YOU WITH THE STATION. BUT WE SHOULD MOVE QUICKLY, BEFORE THEY HAVE TIME TO MOBILIZE.
I'M GOING TO NEED ANOTHER GUN.
LET'S GET YOU OUTFITTED FIRST.

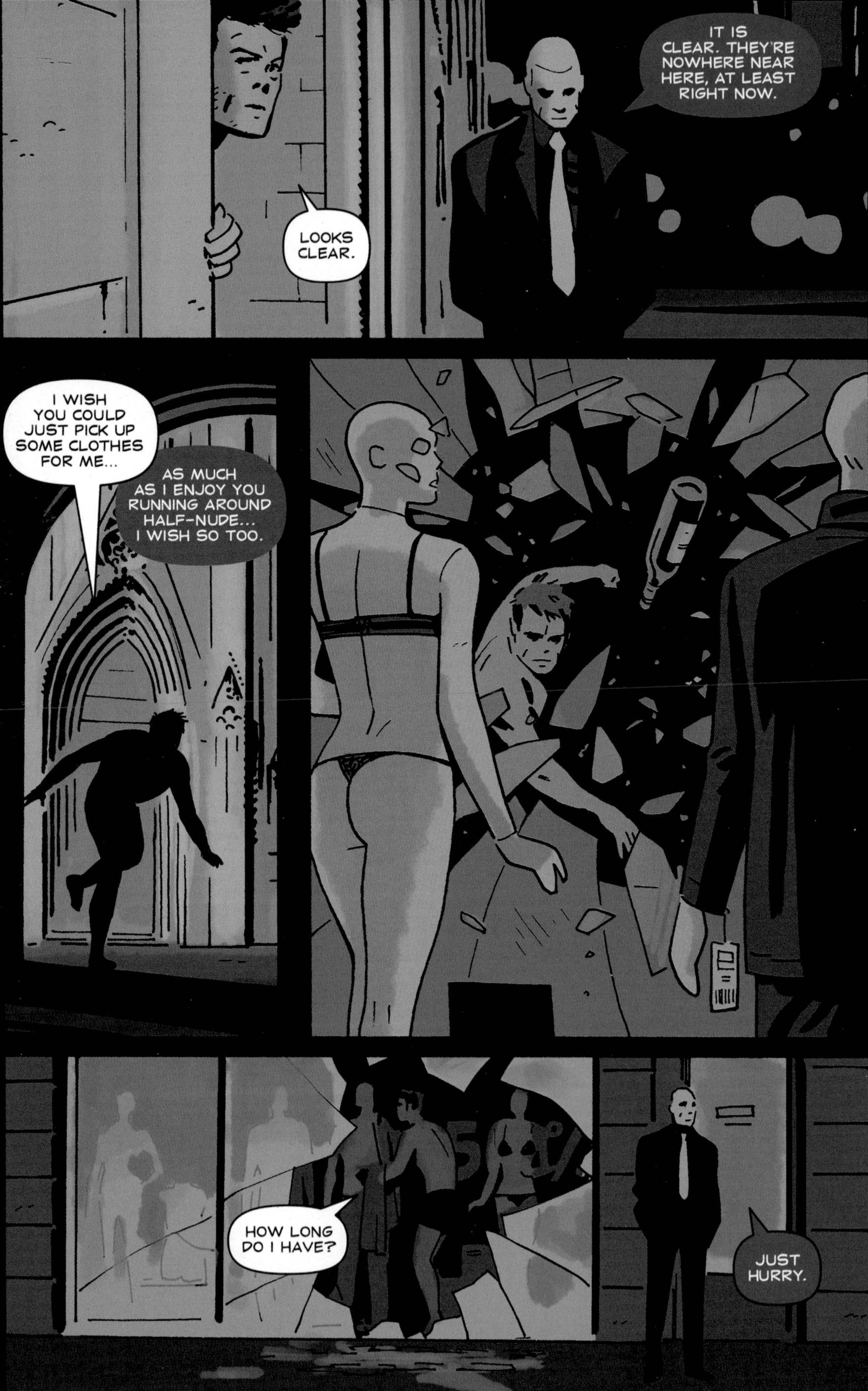

LOOKS CLEAR.
IT IS CLEAR. THEY'RE NOWHERE NEAR HERE, AT LEAST RIGHT NOW.
I WISH YOU COULD JUST PICK UP SOME CLOTHES FOR ME...
AS MUCH AS I ENJOY YOU RUNNING AROUND HALF-NUDE... I WISH SO TOO.
HOW LONG DO I HAVE?
JUST HURRY.

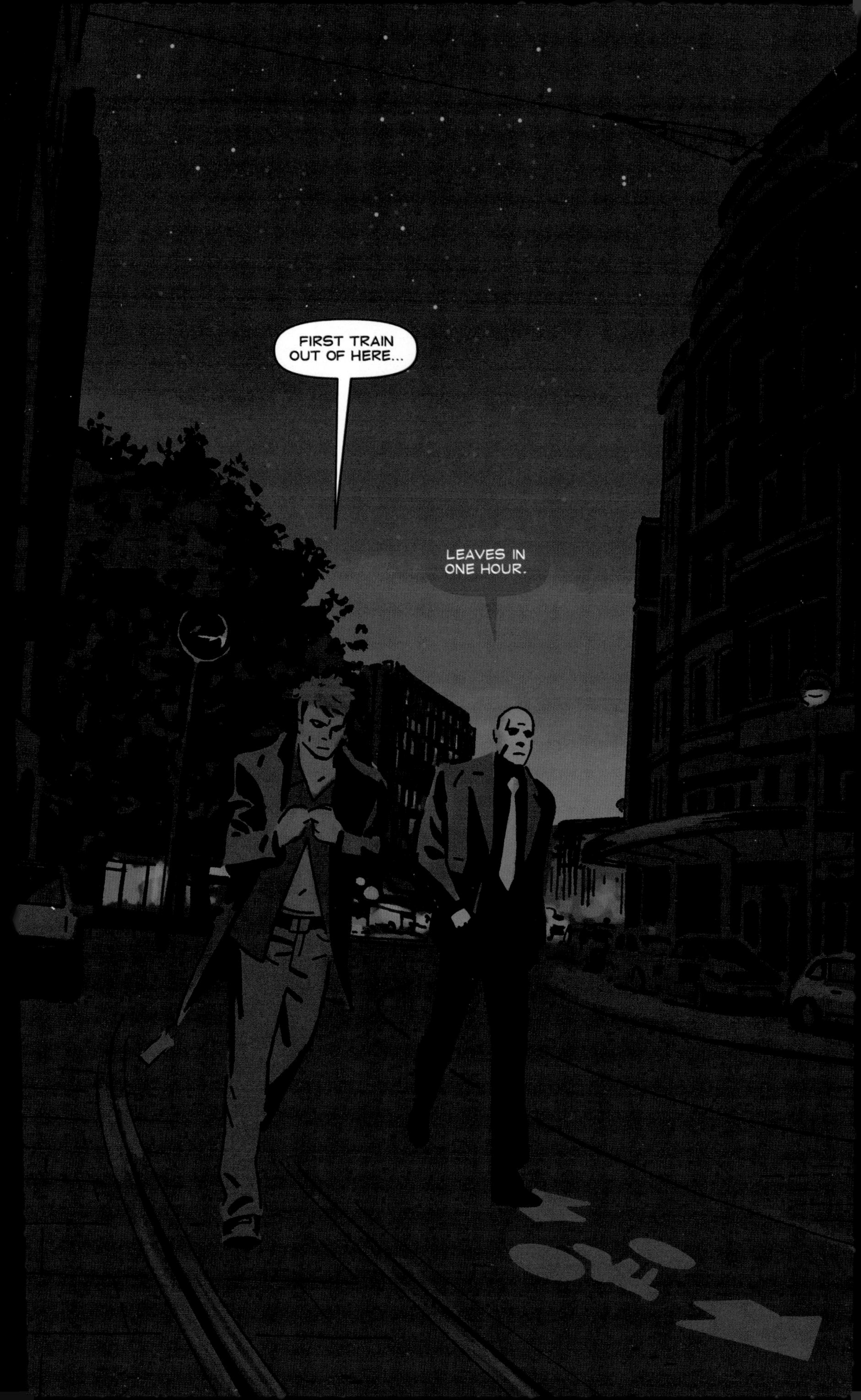
FIRST TRAIN OUT OF HERE...
LEAVES IN ONE HOUR.

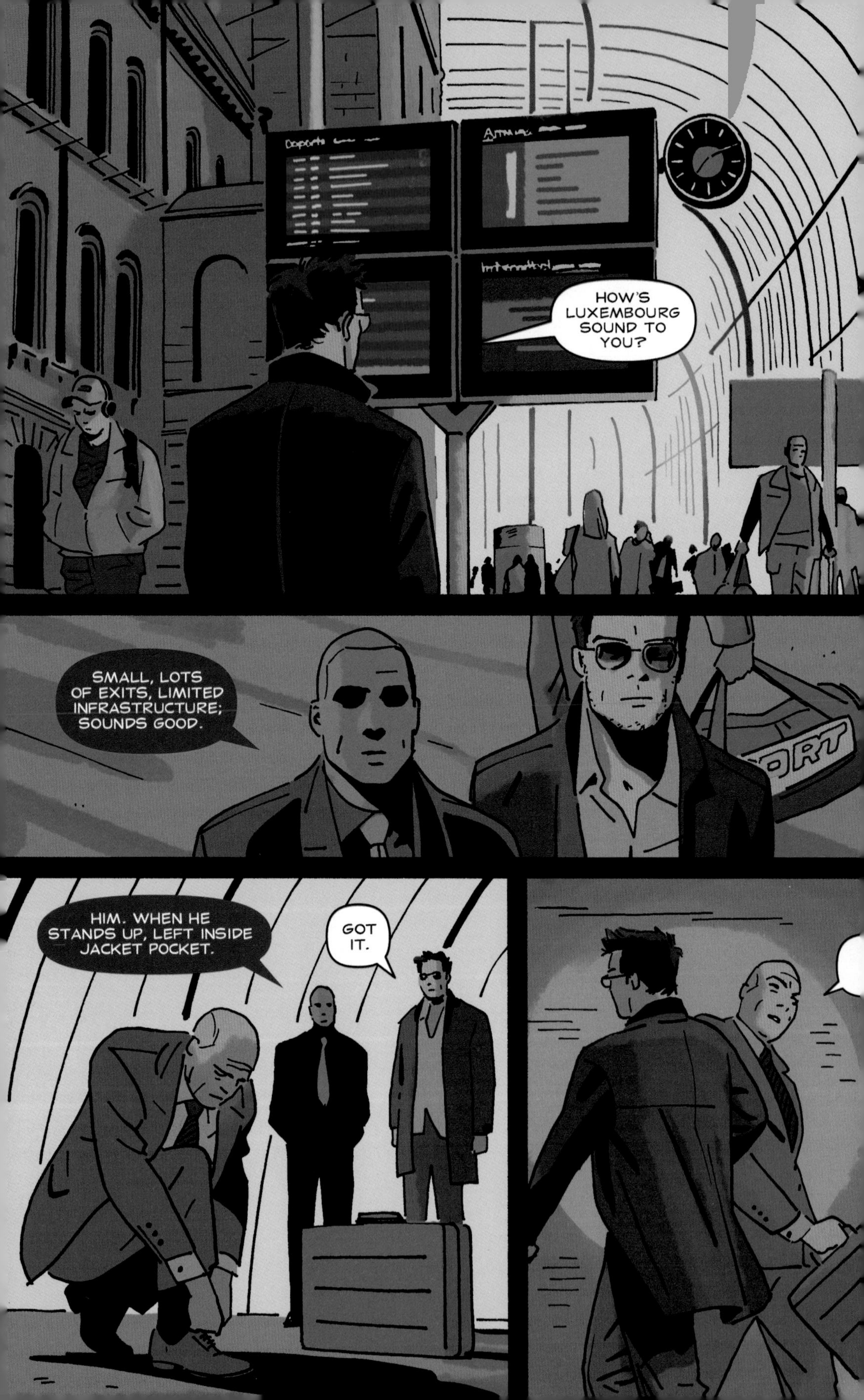

HOW'S LUXEMBOURG SOUND TO YOU?
SMALL, LOTS OF EXITS, LIMITED INFRASTRUCTURE; SOUNDS GOOD.
HIM. WHEN HE STANDS UP, LEFT INSIDE JACKET POCKET.
GOT IT.

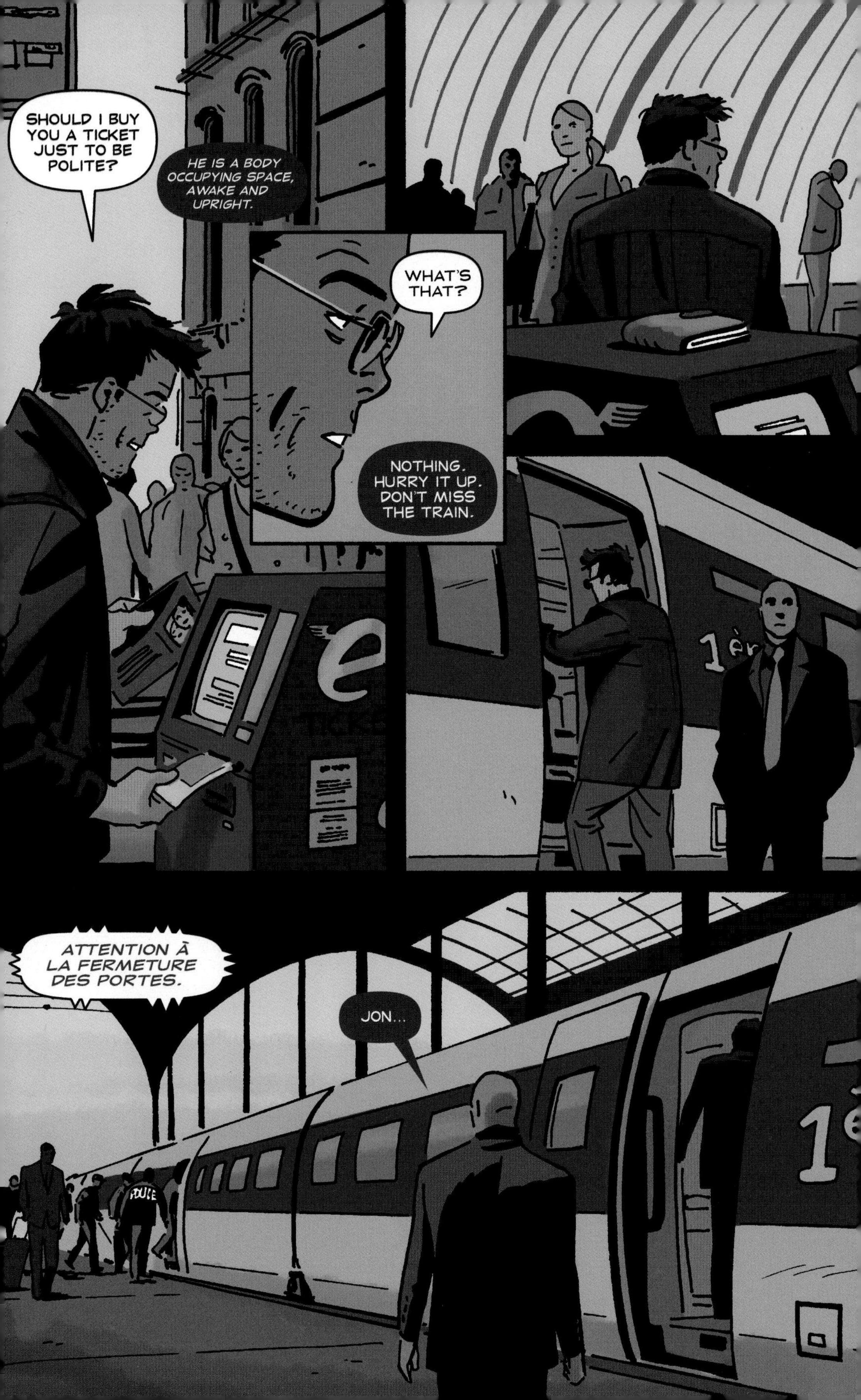
SHOULD I BUY YOU A TICKET JUST TO BE POLITE?
HE IS A BODY OCCUPYING SPACE, AWAKE AND UPRIGHT.
WHAT'S THAT?
NOTHING. HURRY IT UP. DON'T MISS THE TRAIN.
ATTENTION À LA FERMETURE DES PORTES.
JON...

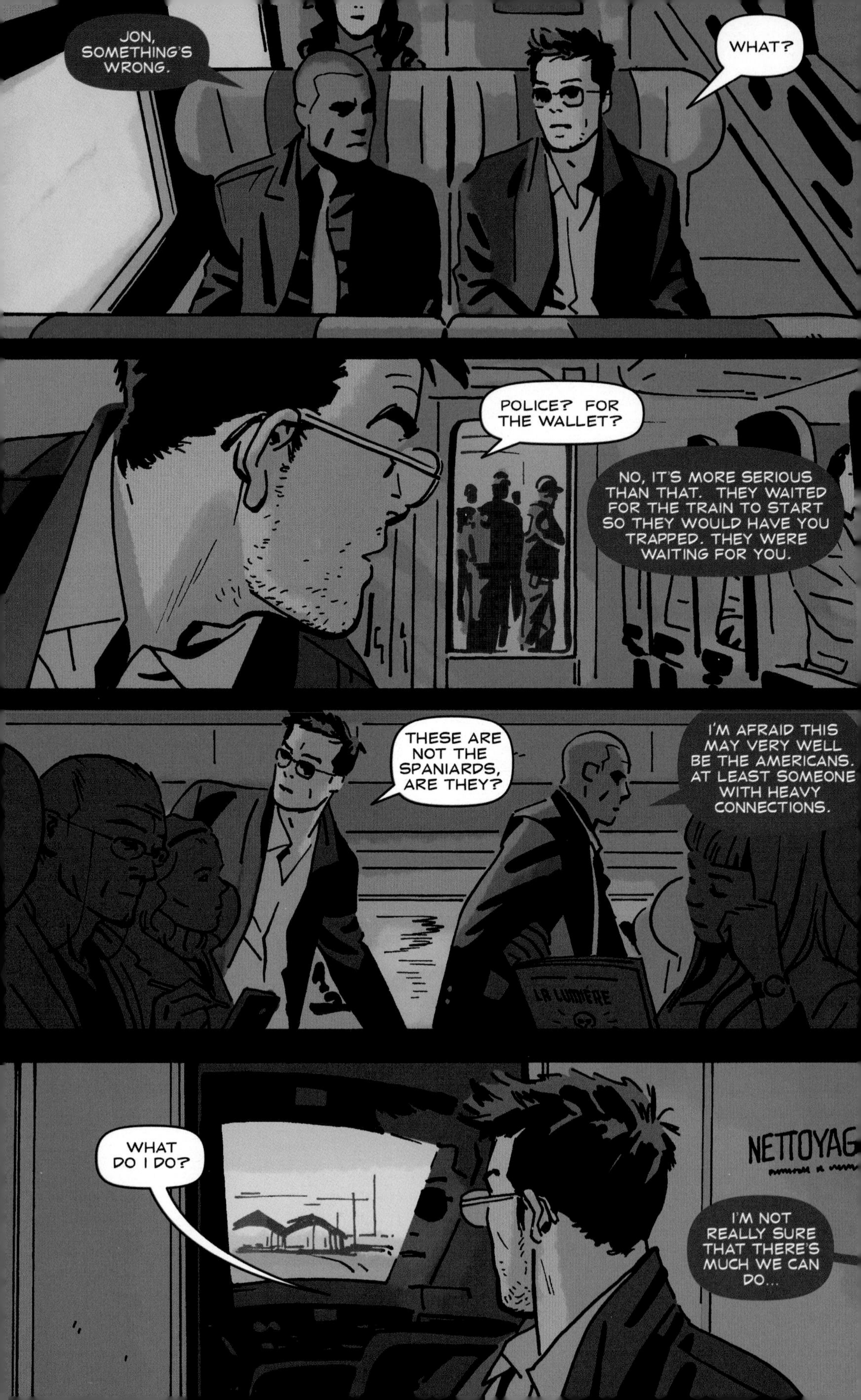
JON, SOMETHING'S WRONG.
WHAT?
POLICE? FOR THE WALLET?
NO, IT'S MORE SERIOUS THAN THAT. THEY WAITED FOR THE TRAIN TO START SO THEY WOULD HAVE YOU TRAPPED. THEY WERE WAITING FOR YOU.
THESE ARE NOT THE SPANIARDS, ARE THEY?
I'M AFRAID THIS MAY VERY WELL BE THE AMERICANS. AT LEAST SOMEONE WITH HEAVY CONNECTIONS.
NETTOYAG
WHAT DO I DO?
I'M NOT REALLY SURE THAT THERE'S MUCH WE CAN DO...

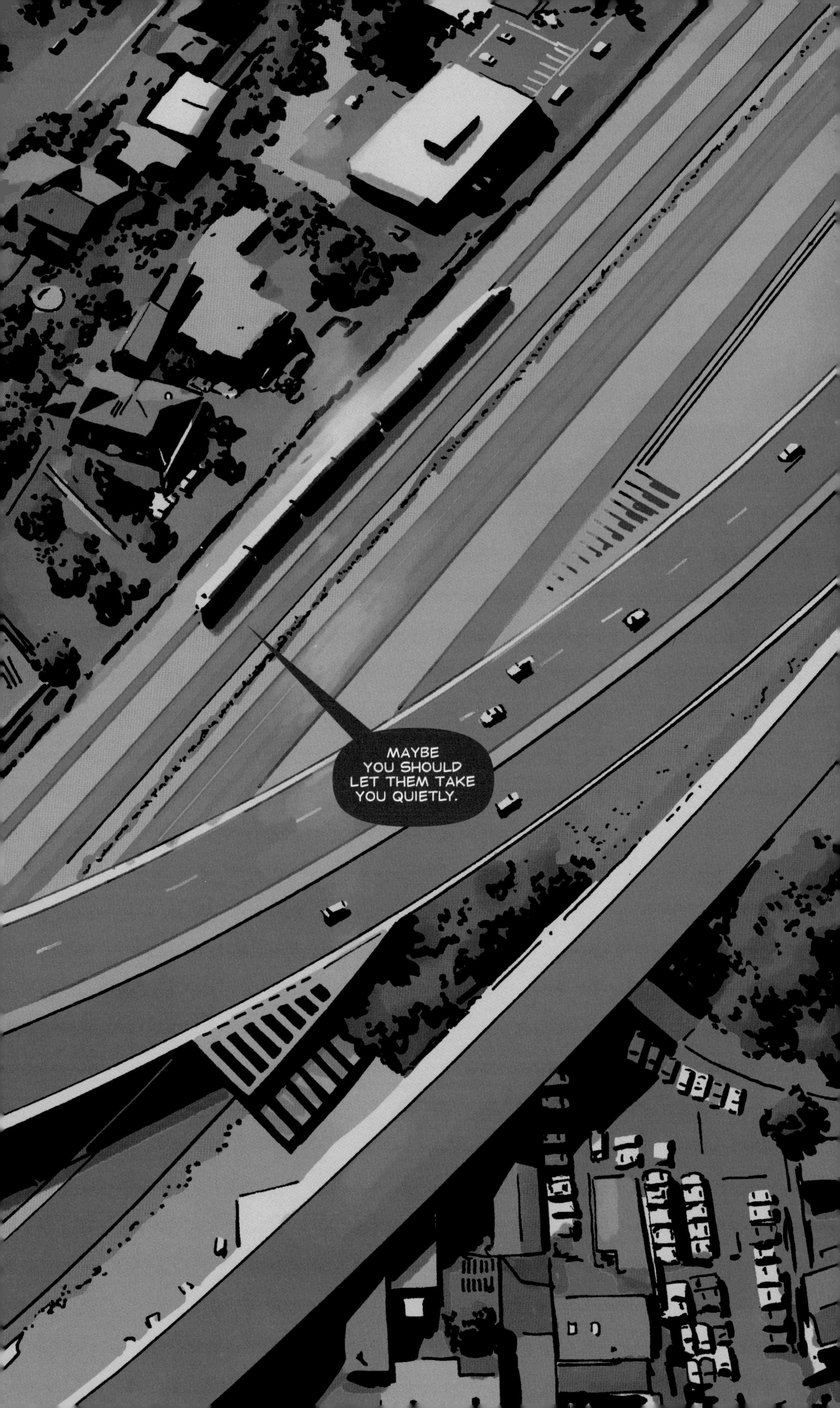
MAYBE YOU SHOULD LET THEM TAKE YOU QUIETLY.

CHAPTER 2

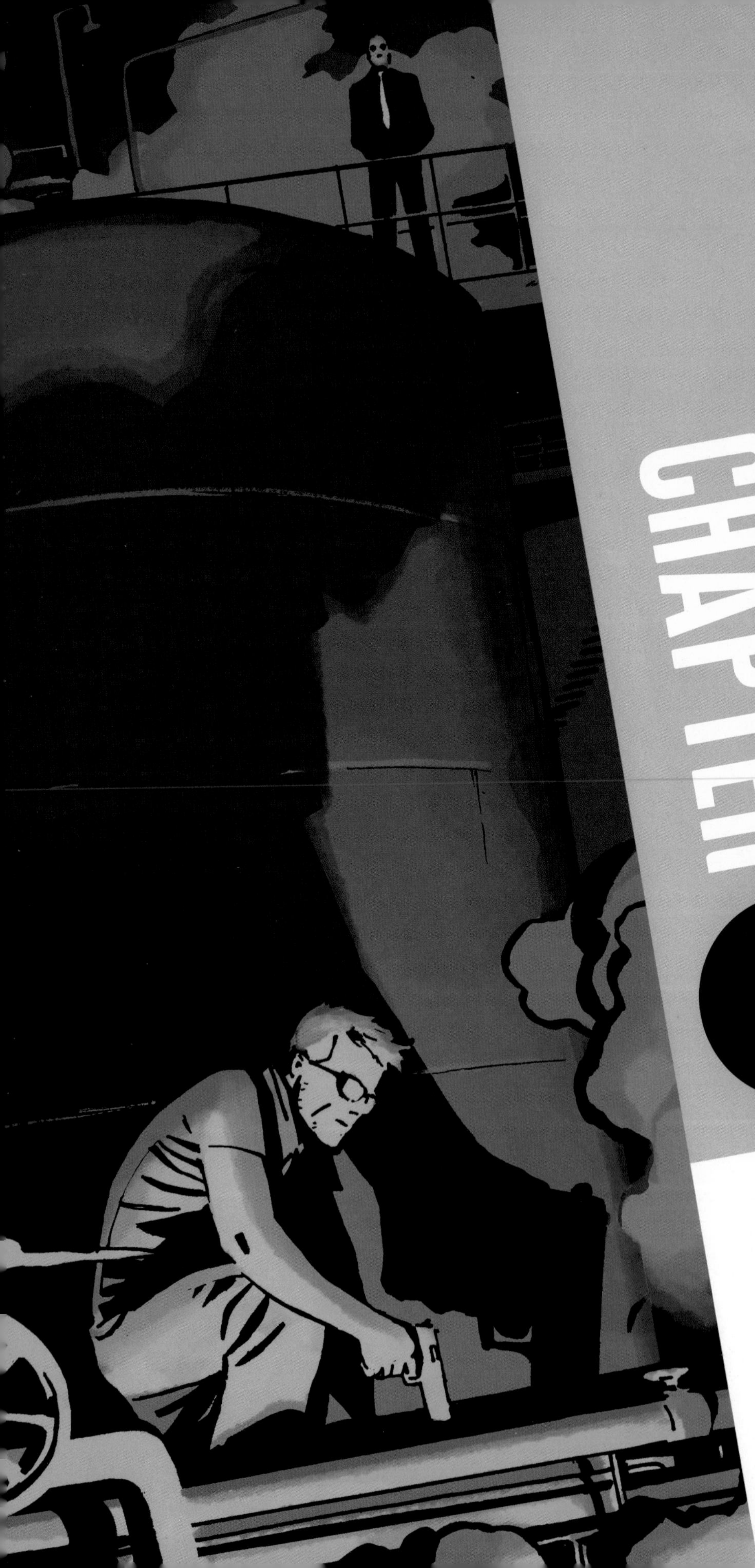

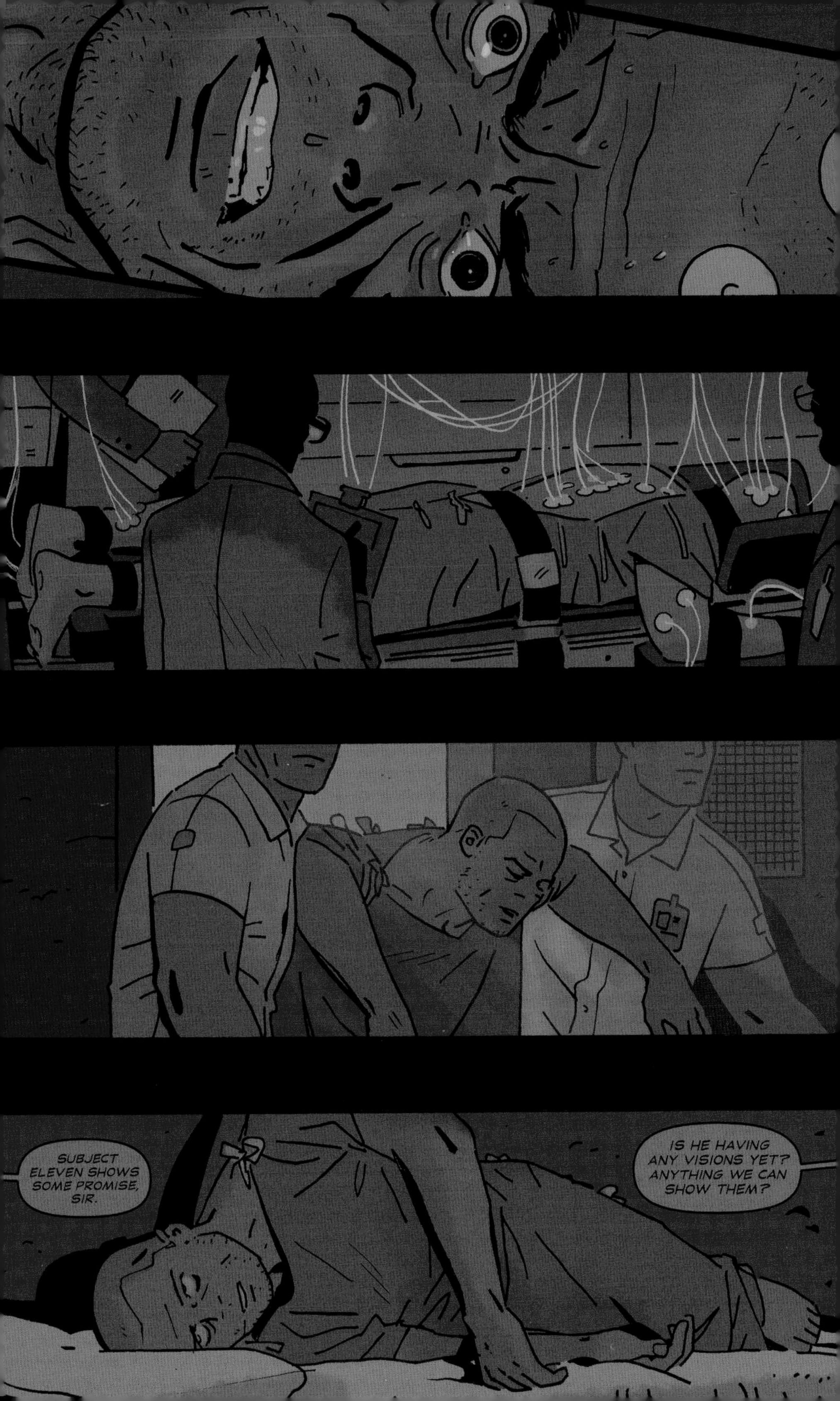
SUBJECT ELEVEN SHOWS SOME PROMISE, SIR.
IS HE HAVING ANY VISIONS YET? ANYTHING WE CAN SHOW THEM?

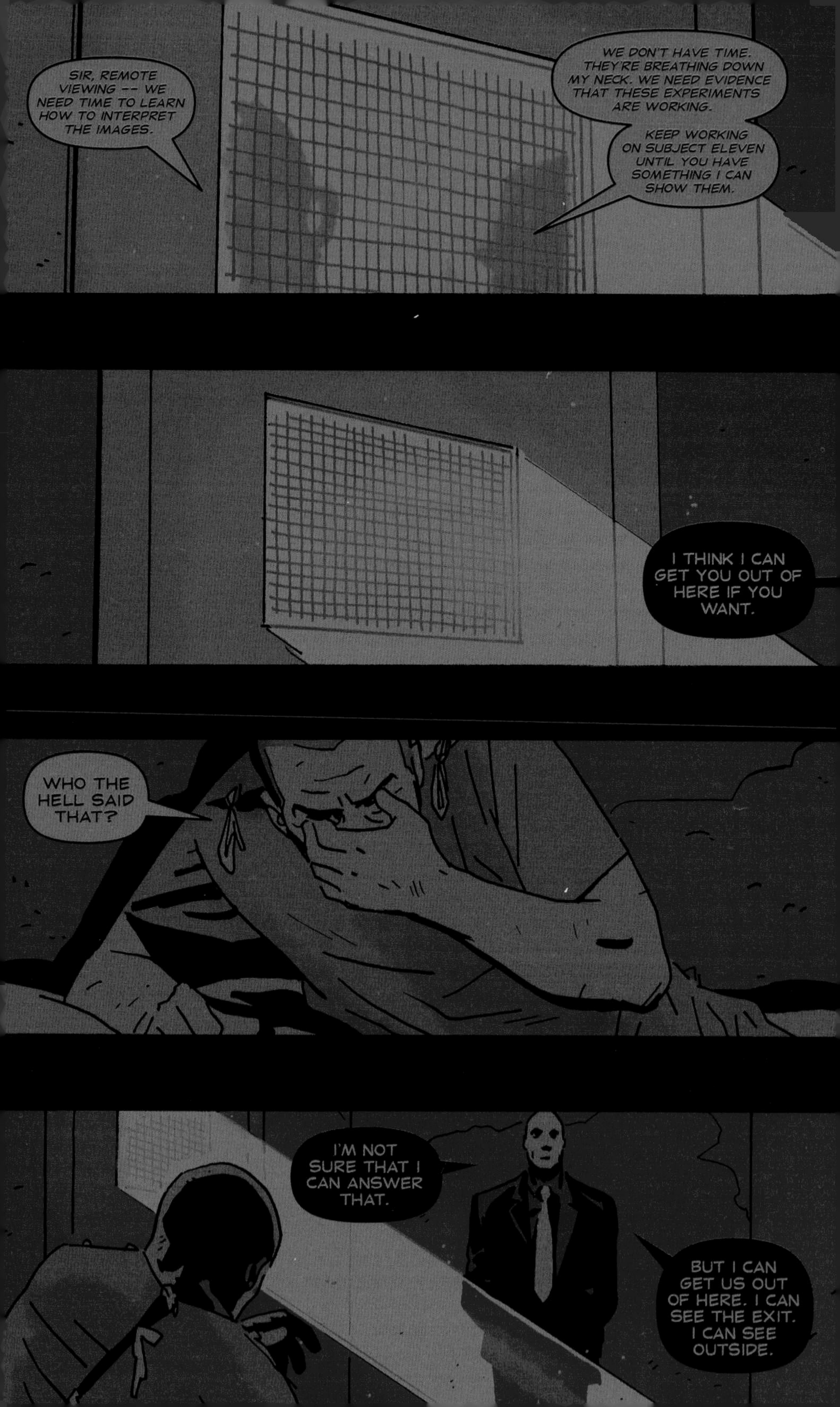
SIR, REMOTE VIEWING -- WE NEED TIME TO LEARN HOW TO INTERPRET THE IMAGES.
WE DON'T HAVE TIME. THEY'RE BREATHING DOWN MY NECK. WE NEED EVIDENCE THAT THESE EXPERIMENTS ARE WORKING.
KEEP WORKING ON SUBJECT ELEVEN UNTIL YOU HAVE SOMETHING I CAN SHOW THEM.
I THINK I CAN GET YOU OUT OF HERE IF YOU WANT.
WHO THE HELL SAID THAT?
I'M NOT SURE THAT I CAN ANSWER THAT.
BUT I CAN GET US OUT OF HERE. I CAN SEE THE EXIT. I CAN SEE OUTSIDE.

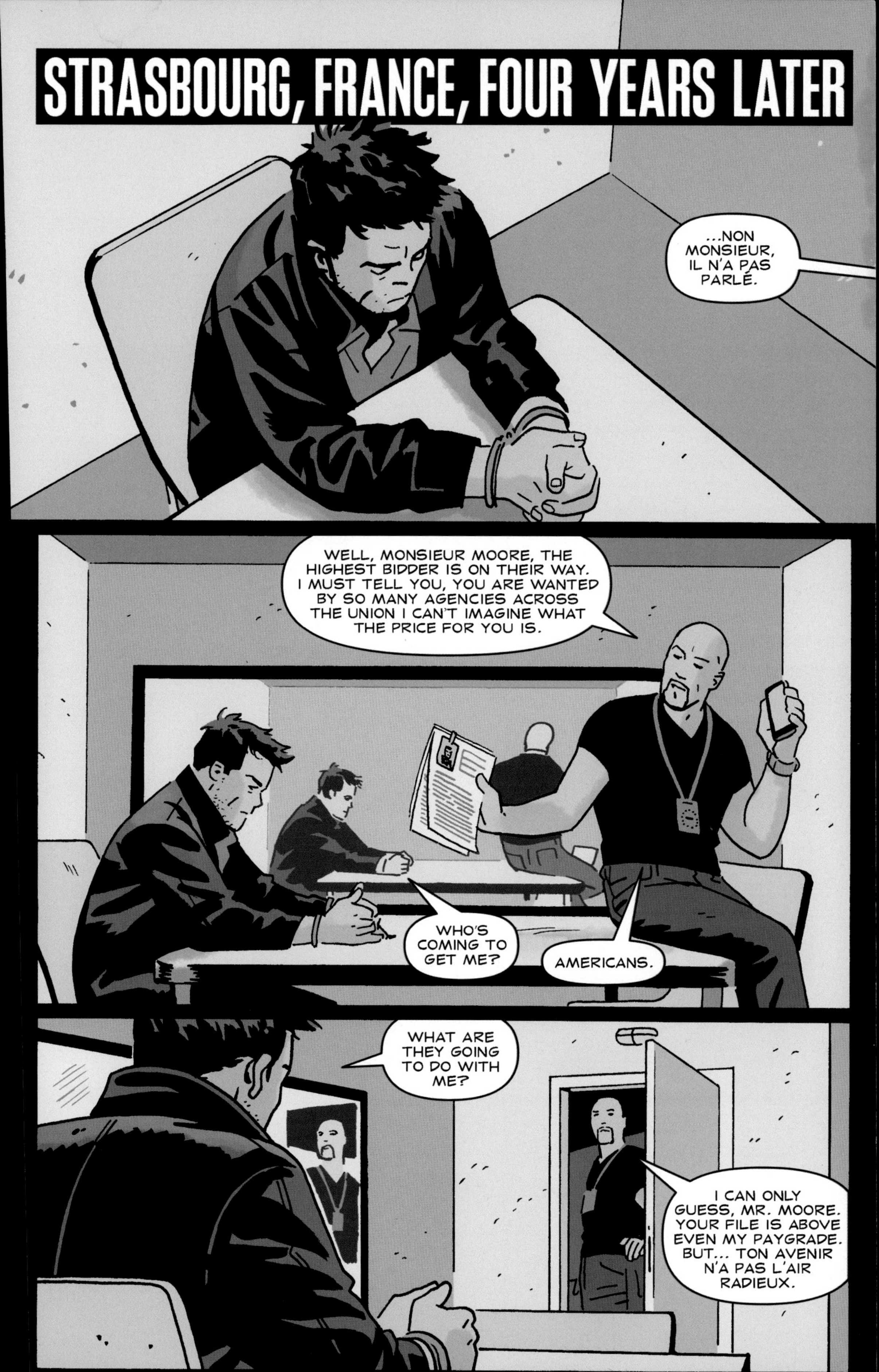
STRASBOURG, FRANCE, FOUR YEARS LATER
...NON MONSIEUR, IL N'A PAS PARLÉ.
WELL, MONSIEUR MOORE, THE HIGHEST BIDDER IS ON THEIR WAY. I MUST TELL YOU, YOU ARE WANTED BY SO MANY AGENCIES ACROSS THE UNION I CAN'T IMAGINE WHAT THE PRICE FOR YOU IS.
WHO'S COMING TO GET ME?
AMERICANS.
WHAT ARE THEY GOING TO DO WITH ME?
I CAN ONLY GUESS, MR. MOORE. YOUR FILE IS ABOVE EVEN MY PAYGRADE. BUT... TON AVENIR N'A PAS L'AIR RADIEUX.

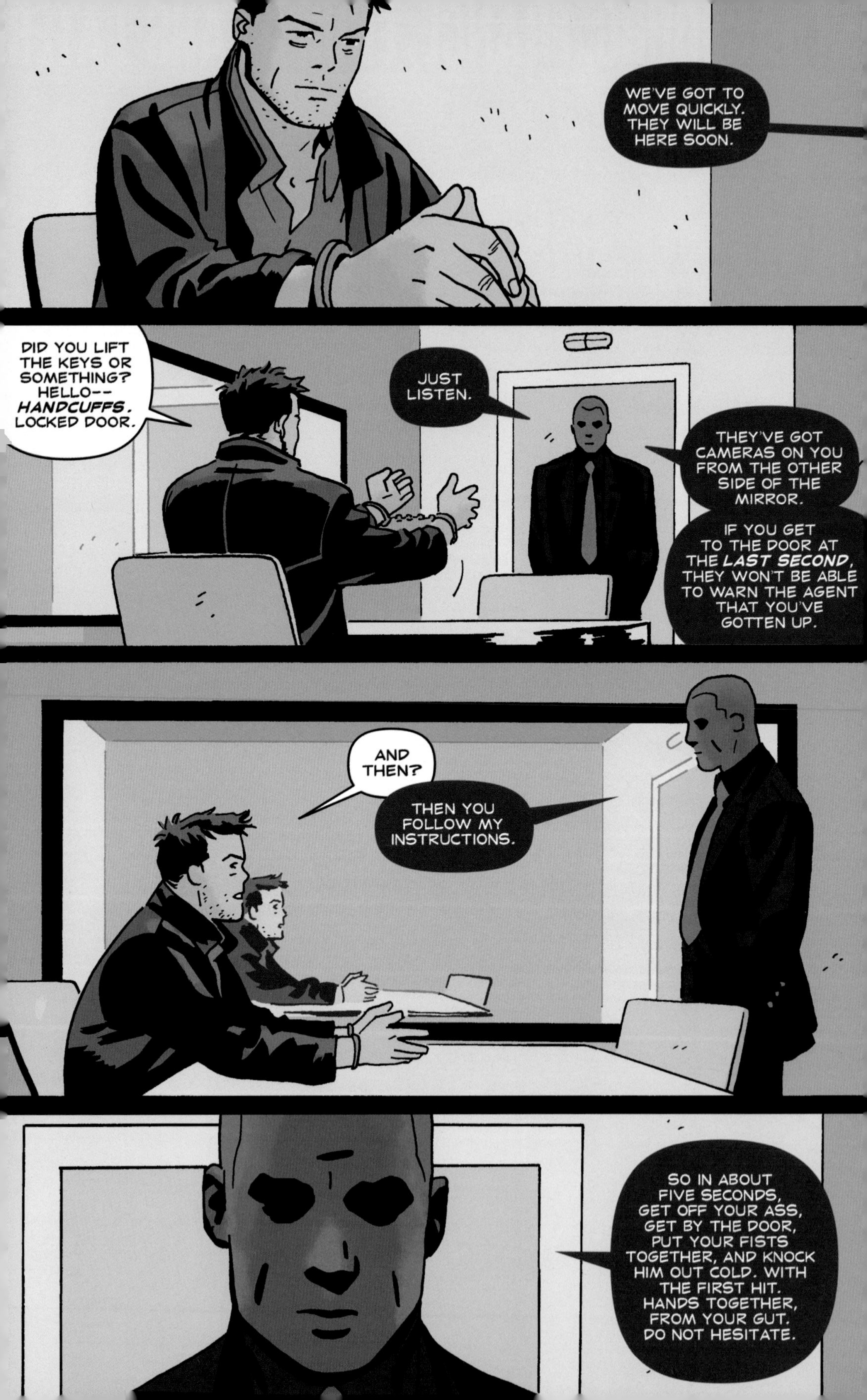
WE'VE GOT TO MOVE QUICKLY. THEY WILL BE HERE SOON.
DID YOU LIFT THE KEYS OR SOMETHING? HELLO-- HANDCUFFS. LOCKED DOOR.
JUST LISTEN.
THEY'VE GOT CAMERAS ON YOU FROM THE OTHER SIDE OF THE MIRROR.
IF YOU GET TO THE DOOR AT THE LAST SECOND, THEY WON'T BE ABLE TO WARN THE AGENT THAT YOU'VE GOTTEN UP.
AND THEN?
THEN YOU FOLLOW MY INSTRUCTIONS.
SO IN ABOUT FIVE SECONDS, GET OFF YOUR ASS, GET BY THE DOOR, PUT YOUR FISTS TOGETHER, AND KNOCK HIM OUT COLD. WITH THE FIRST HIT. HANDS TOGETHER, FROM YOUR GUT. DO NOT HESITATE.

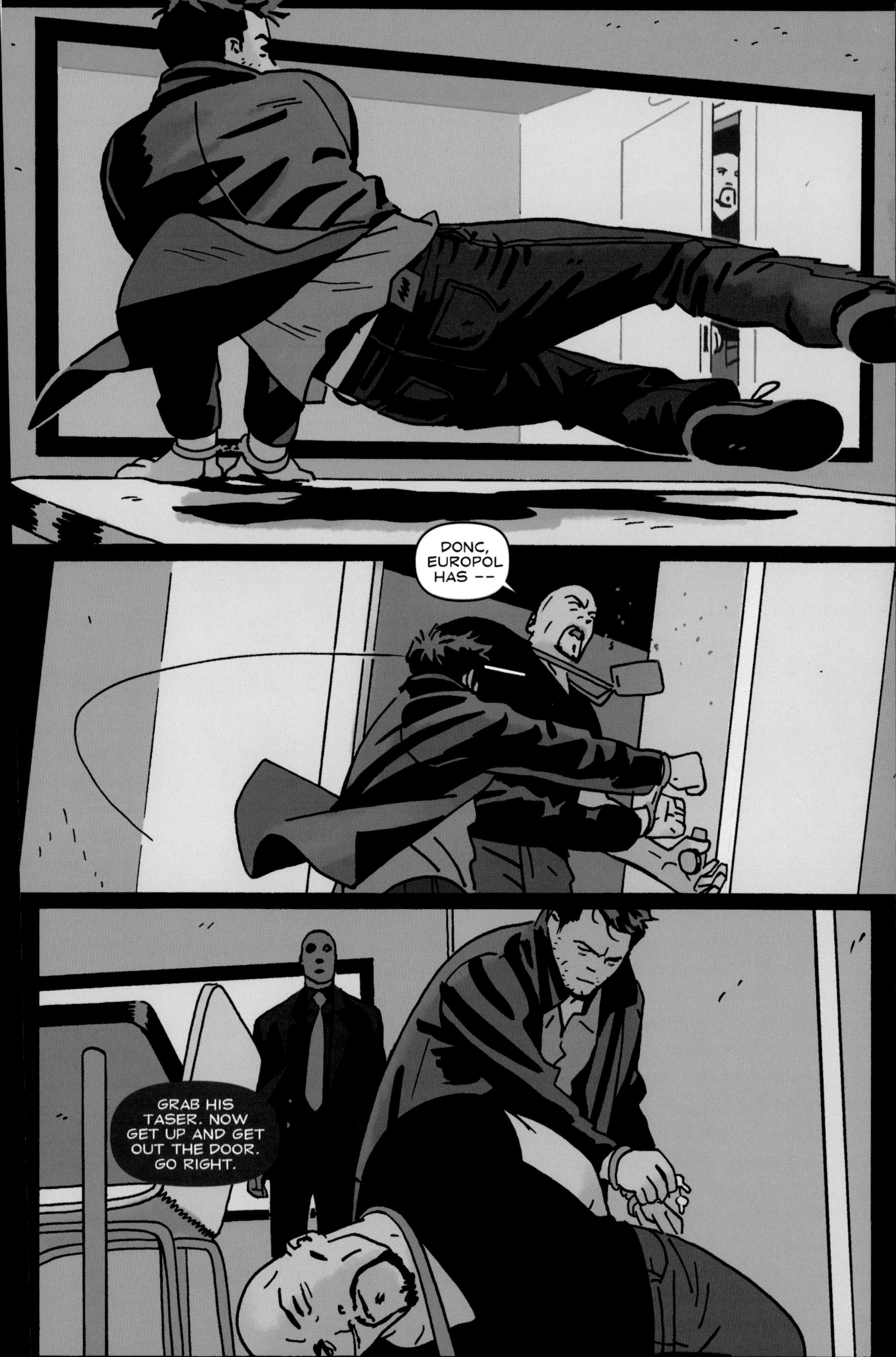
DONC, EUROPOL HAS --
GRAB HIS TASER. NOW GET UP AND GET OUT THE DOOR. GO RIGHT.

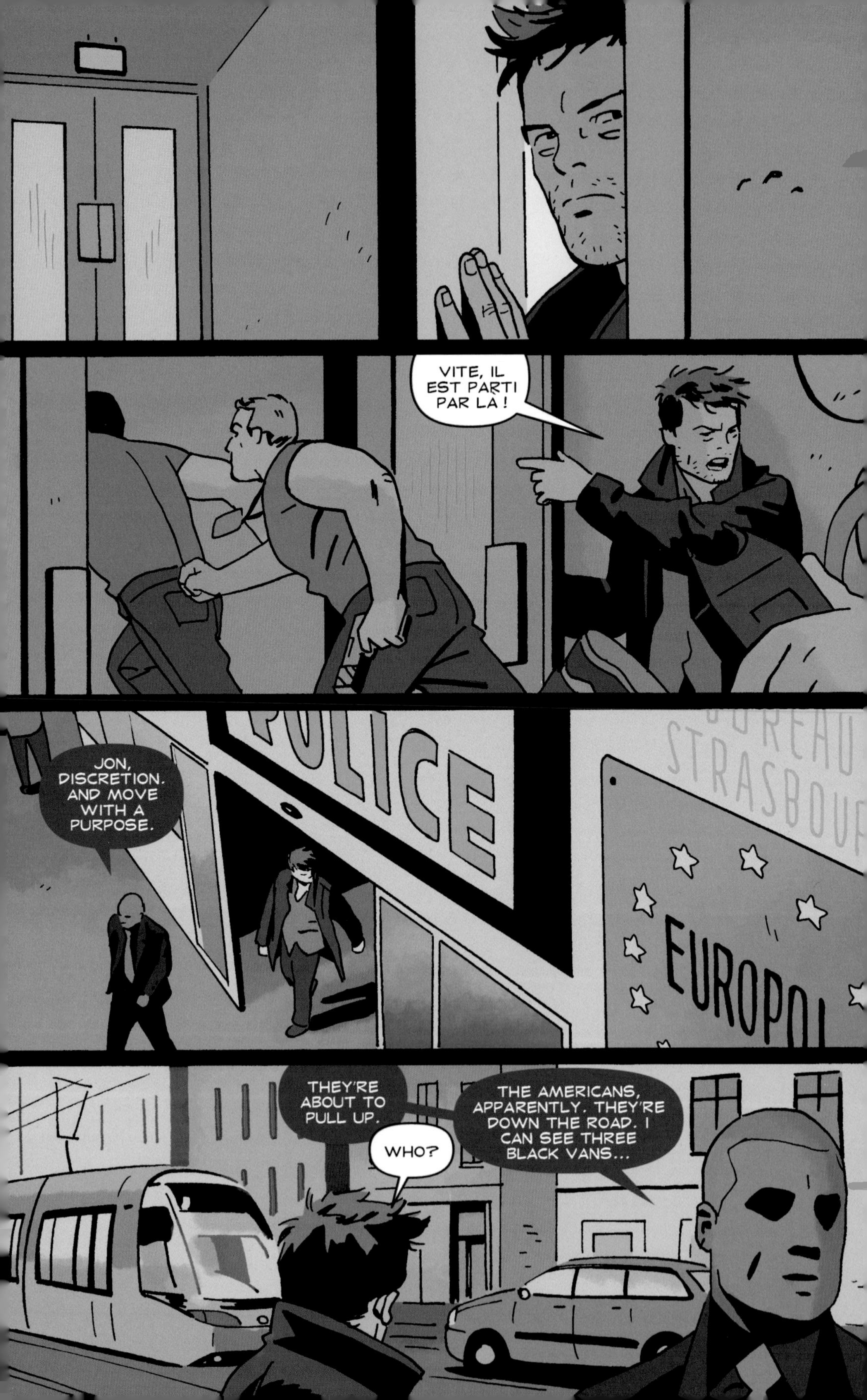
VITE, IL EST PARTI PAR LA !
JON, DISCRETION. AND MOVE WITH A PURPOSE.
POLICE
STRASBOUR
EUROPOL
THEY'RE ABOUT TO PULL UP.
WHO?
THE AMERICANS, APPARENTLY. THEY'RE DOWN THE ROAD. I CAN SEE THREE BLACK VANS...

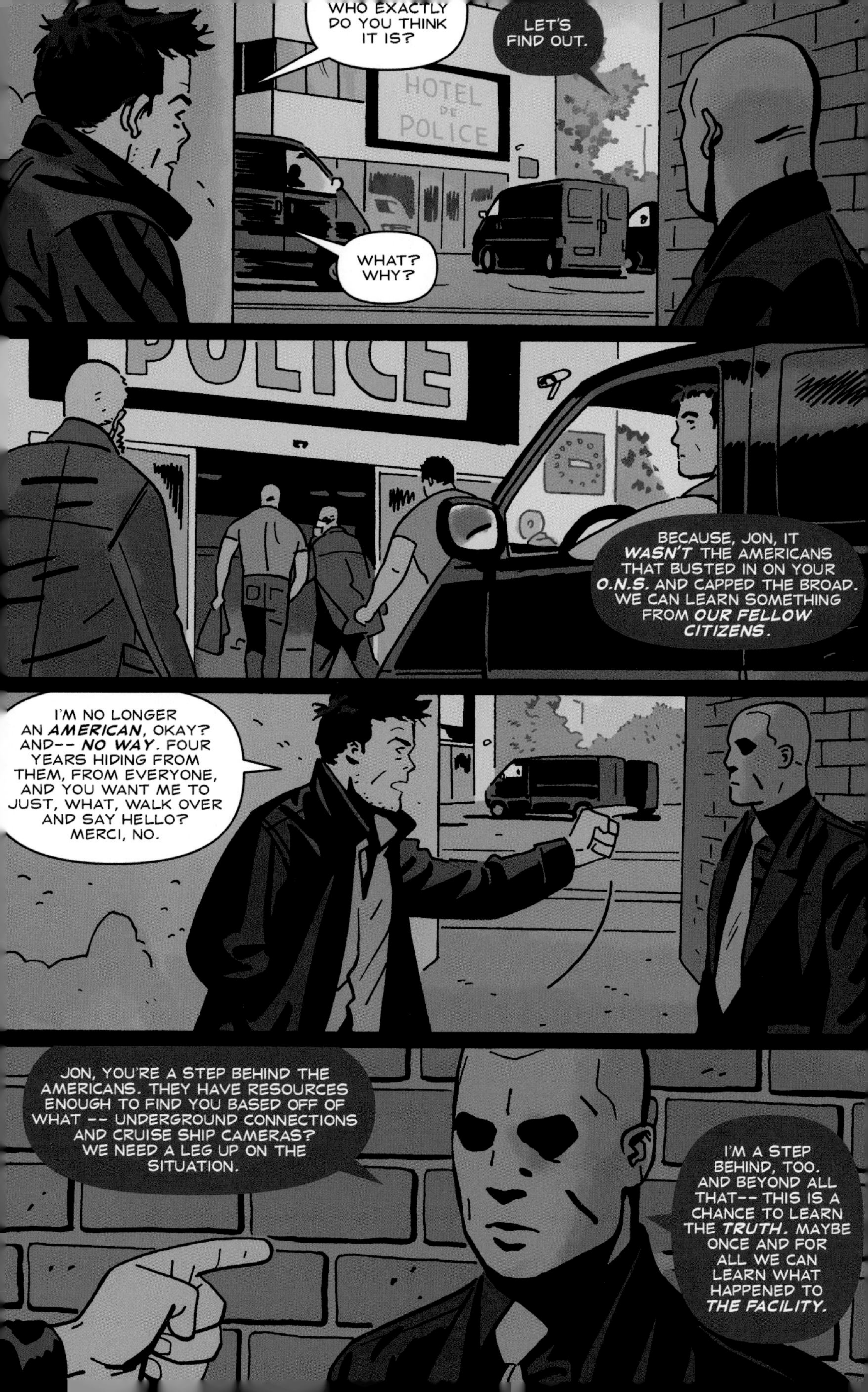
WHO EXACTLY DO YOU THINK IT IS?
LET'S FIND OUT.
HOTEL DE POLICE
WHAT? WHY?
POLICE
BECAUSE, JON, IT WASN'T THE AMERICANS THAT BUSTED IN ON YOUR O.N.S. AND CAPPED THE BROAD. WE CAN LEARN SOMETHING FROM OUR FELLOW CITIZENS.
I'M NO LONGER AN AMERICAN, OKAY? AND-- NO WAY. FOUR YEARS HIDING FROM THEM, FROM EVERYONE, AND YOU WANT ME TO JUST, WHAT, WALK OVER AND SAY HELLO? MERCI, NO.
JON, YOU'RE A STEP BEHIND THE AMERICANS. THEY HAVE RESOURCES ENOUGH TO FIND YOU BASED OFF OF WHAT -- UNDERGROUND CONNECTIONS AND CRUISE SHIP CAMERAS? WE NEED A LEG UP ON THE SITUATION.
I'M A STEP BEHIND, TOO. AND BEYOND ALL THAT-- THIS IS A CHANCE TO LEARN THE TRUTH. MAYBE ONCE AND FOR ALL WE CAN LEARN WHAT HAPPENED TO THE FACILITY.

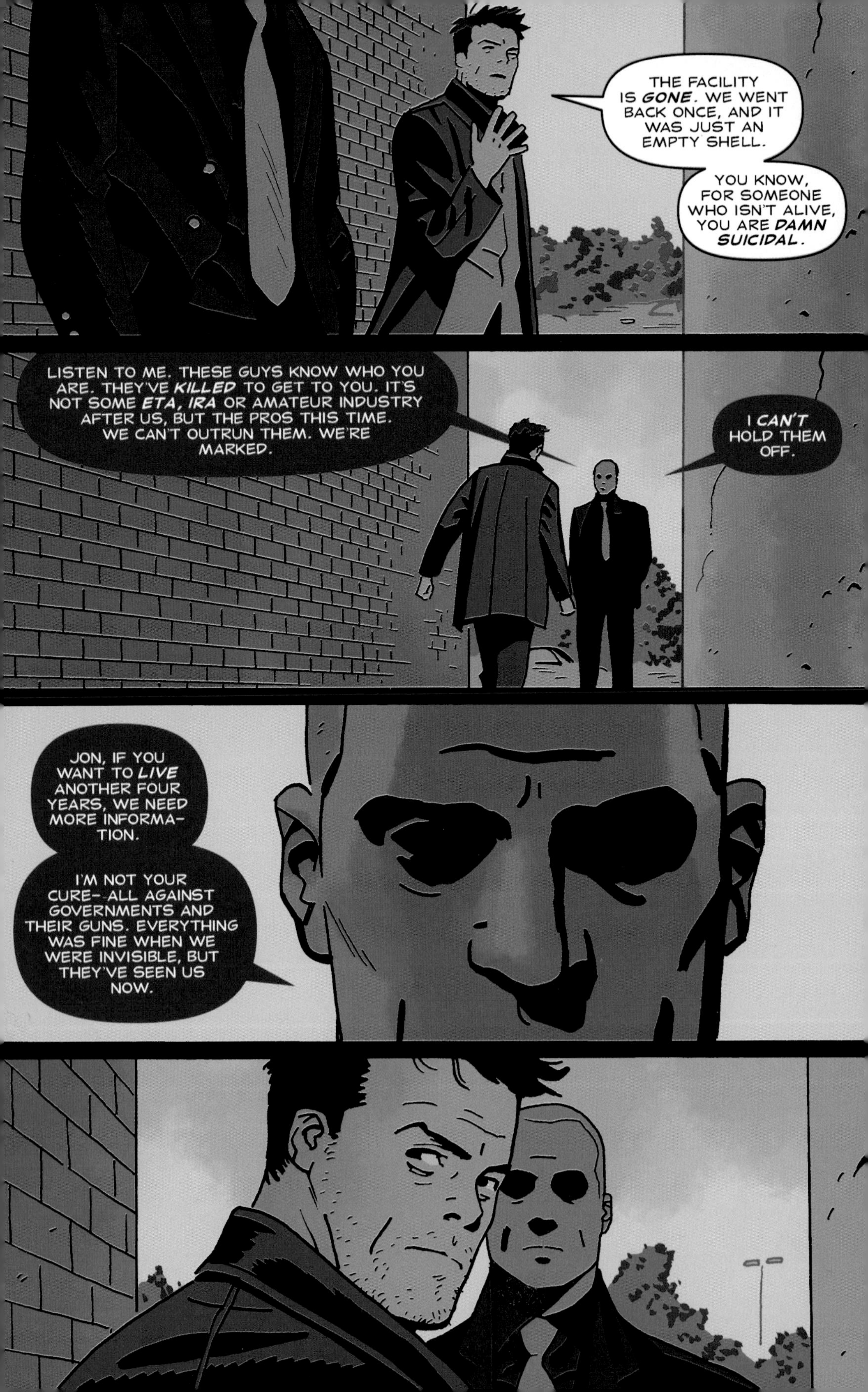
THE FACILITY IS GONE. WE WENT BACK ONCE, AND IT WAS JUST AN EMPTY SHELL.
YOU KNOW, FOR SOMEONE WHO ISN'T ALIVE, YOU ARE DAMN SUICIDAL.
LISTEN TO ME. THESE GUYS KNOW WHO YOU ARE. THEY'VE KILLED TO GET TO YOU. IT'S NOT SOME ETA, IRA OR AMATEUR INDUSTRY AFTER US, BUT THE PROS THIS TIME. WE CAN'T OUTRUN THEM. WE'RE MARKED.
I CAN'T HOLD THEM OFF.
JON, IF YOU WANT TO LIVE ANOTHER FOUR YEARS, WE NEED MORE INFORMA-TION.
I'M NOT YOUR CURE-ALL AGAINST GOVERNMENTS AND THEIR GUNS. EVERYTHING WAS FINE WHEN WE WERE INVISIBLE, BUT THEY'VE SEEN US NOW.

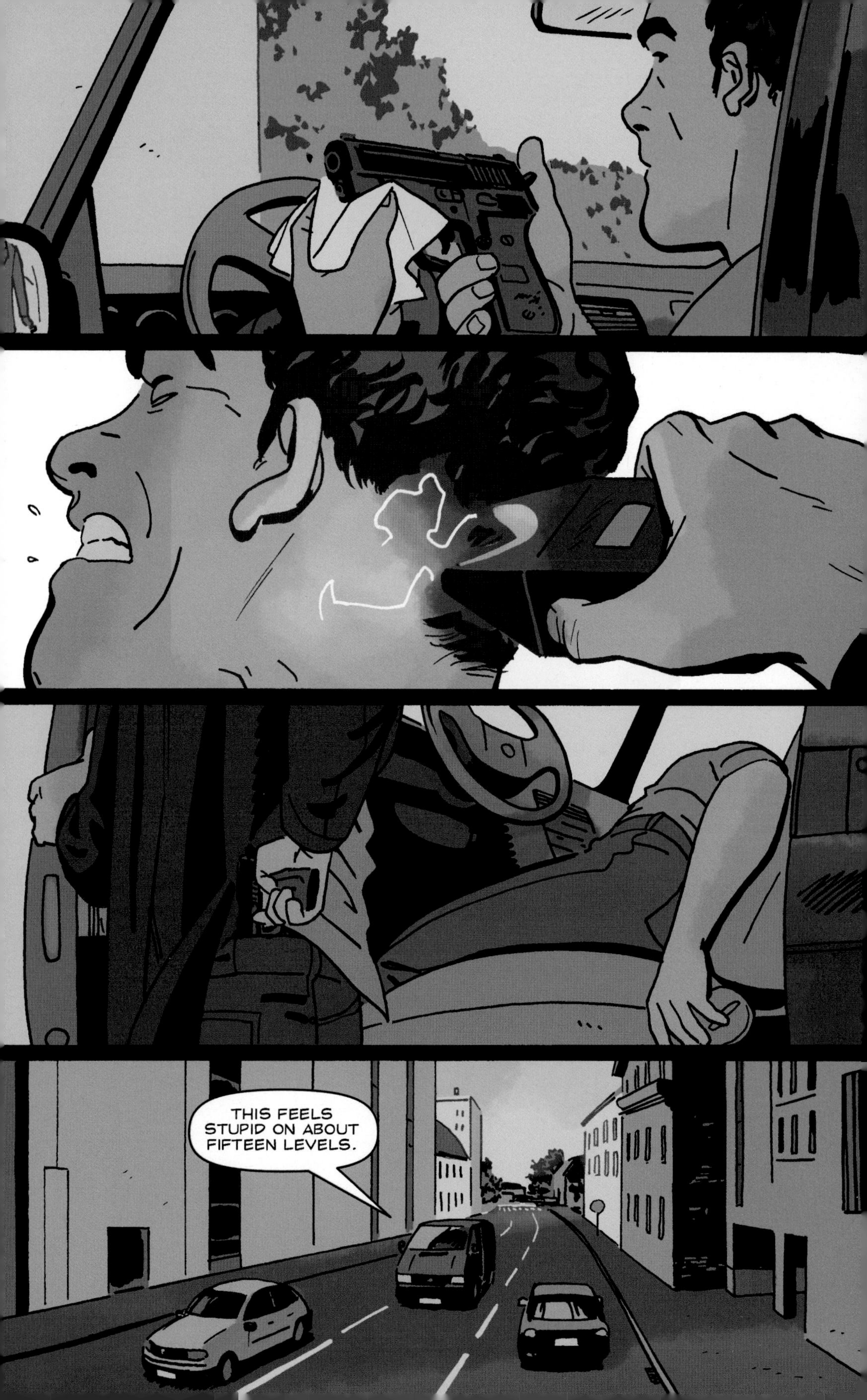
THIS FEELS STUPID ON ABOUT FIFTEEN LEVELS.

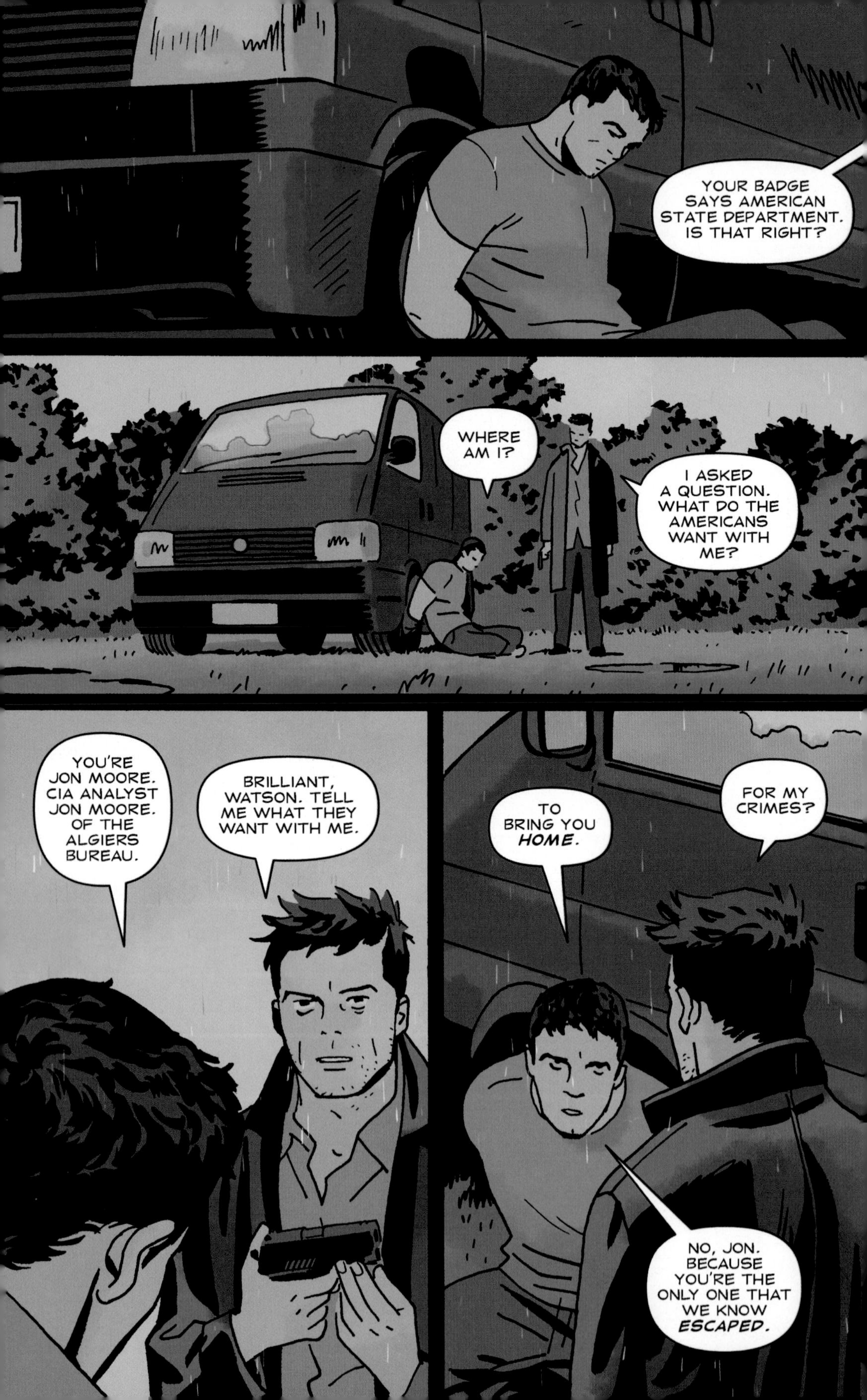
YOUR BADGE SAYS AMERICAN STATE DEPARTMENT. IS THAT RIGHT?
WHERE AM I?
I ASKED A QUESTION. WHAT DO THE AMERICANS WANT WITH ME?
YOU'RE JON MOORE. CIA ANALYST JON MOORE. OF THE ALGIERS BUREAU.
BRILLIANT, WATSON. TELL ME WHAT THEY WANT WITH ME.
TO BRING YOU HOME.
FOR MY CRIMES?
NO, JON. BECAUSE YOU'RE THE ONLY ONE THAT WE KNOW ESCAPED.

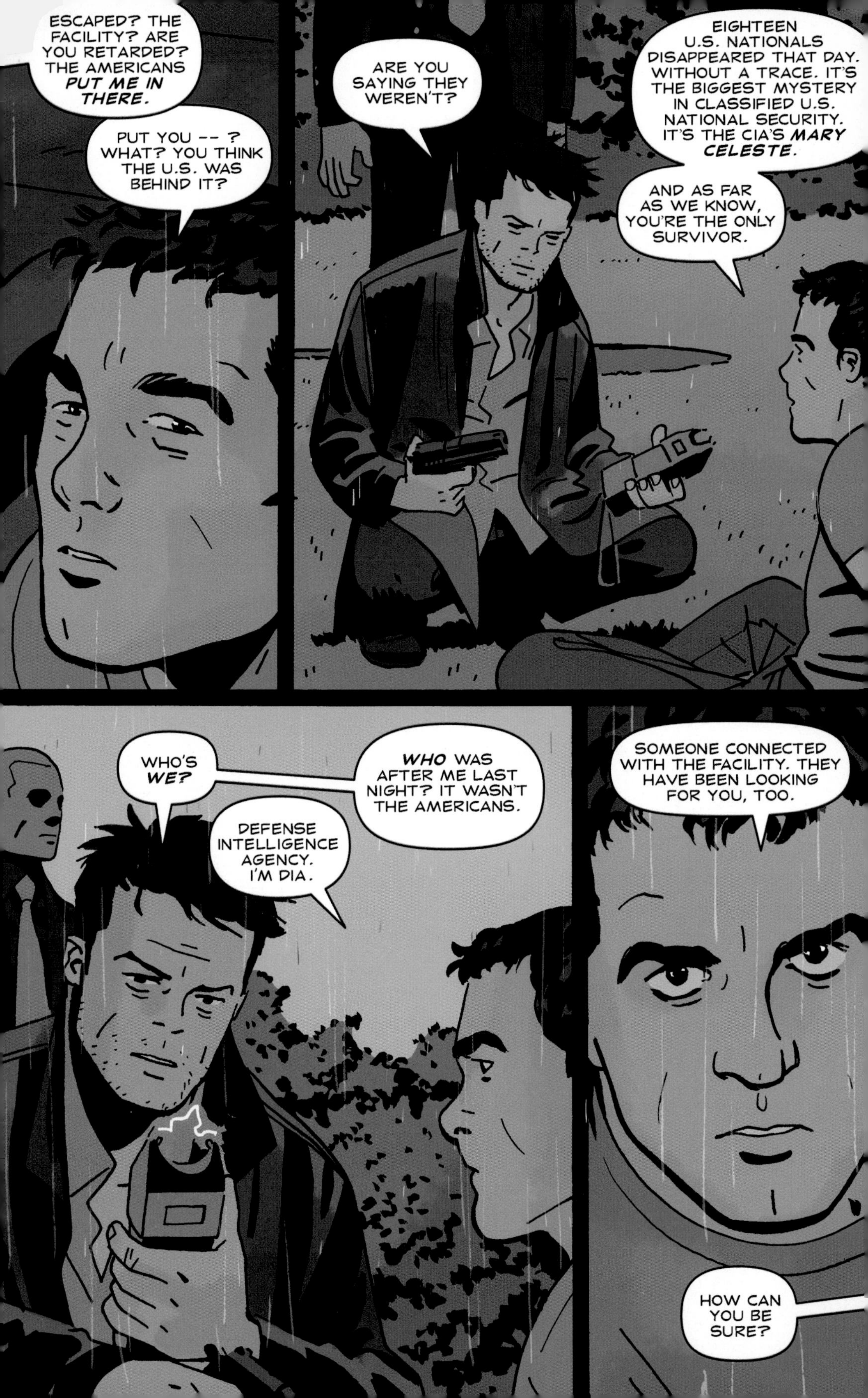
ESCAPED? THE FACILITY? ARE YOU RETARDED? THE AMERICANS *PUT ME IN THERE.*
PUT YOU -- ? WHAT? YOU THINK THE U.S. WAS BEHIND IT?
ARE YOU SAYING THEY WEREN'T?
EIGHTEEN U.S. NATIONALS DISAPPEARED THAT DAY. WITHOUT A TRACE. IT'S THE BIGGEST MYSTERY IN CLASSIFIED U.S. NATIONAL SECURITY. IT'S THE CIA'S *MARY CELESTE*.
AND AS FAR AS WE KNOW, YOU'RE THE ONLY SURVIVOR.
WHO'S *WE?*
DEFENSE INTELLIGENCE AGENCY. I'M DIA.
WHO WAS AFTER ME LAST NIGHT? IT WASN'T THE AMERICANS.
SOMEONE CONNECTED WITH THE FACILITY. THEY HAVE BEEN LOOKING FOR YOU, TOO.
HOW CAN YOU BE SURE?

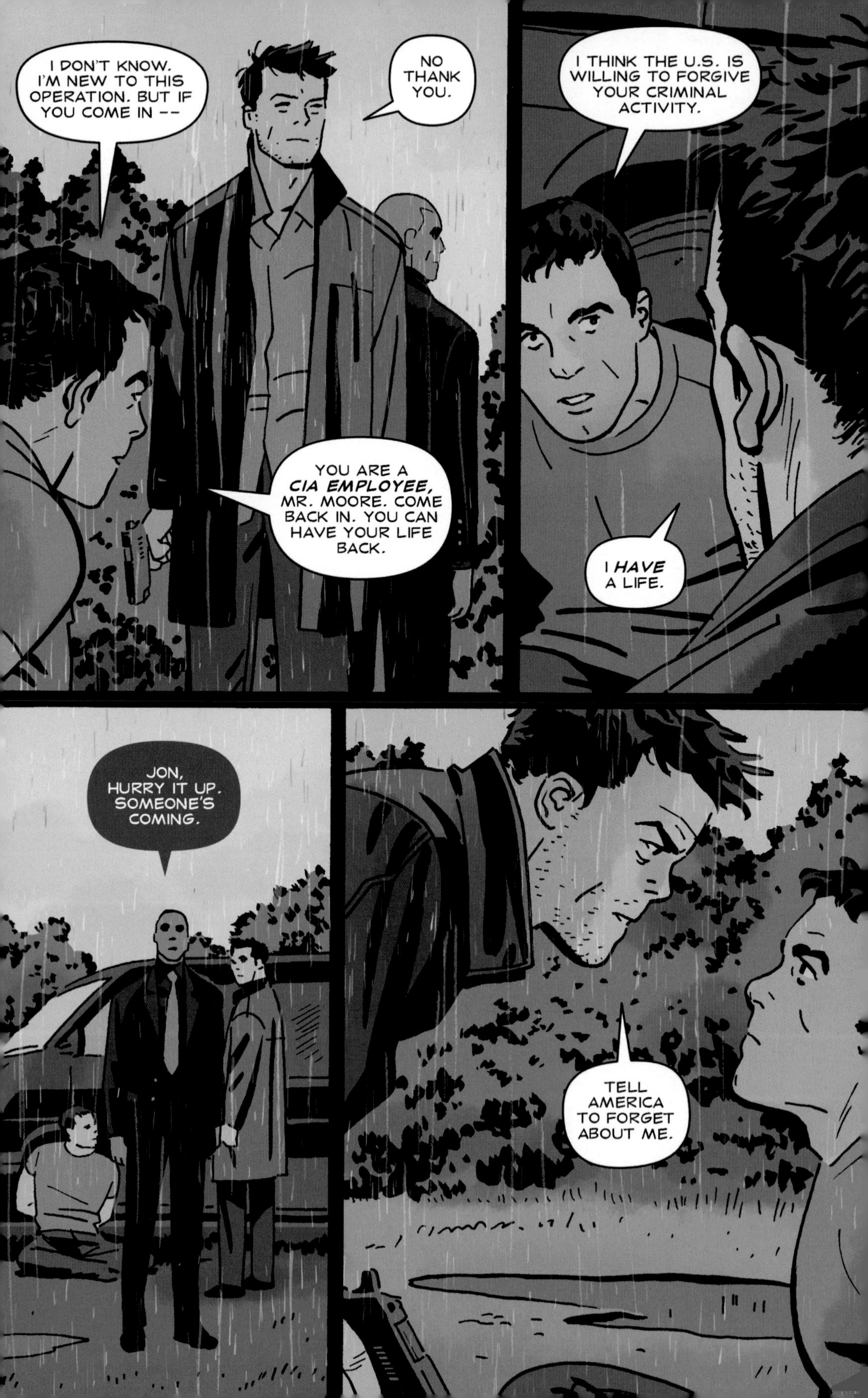
I DON'T KNOW. I'M NEW TO THIS OPERATION. BUT IF YOU COME IN --
NO THANK YOU.
YOU ARE A *CIA EMPLOYEE,* MR. MOORE. COME BACK IN. YOU CAN HAVE YOUR LIFE BACK.
I THINK THE U.S. IS WILLING TO FORGIVE YOUR CRIMINAL ACTIVITY.
I *HAVE* A LIFE.
JON, HURRY IT UP. SOMEONE'S COMING.
TELL AMERICA TO FORGET ABOUT ME.

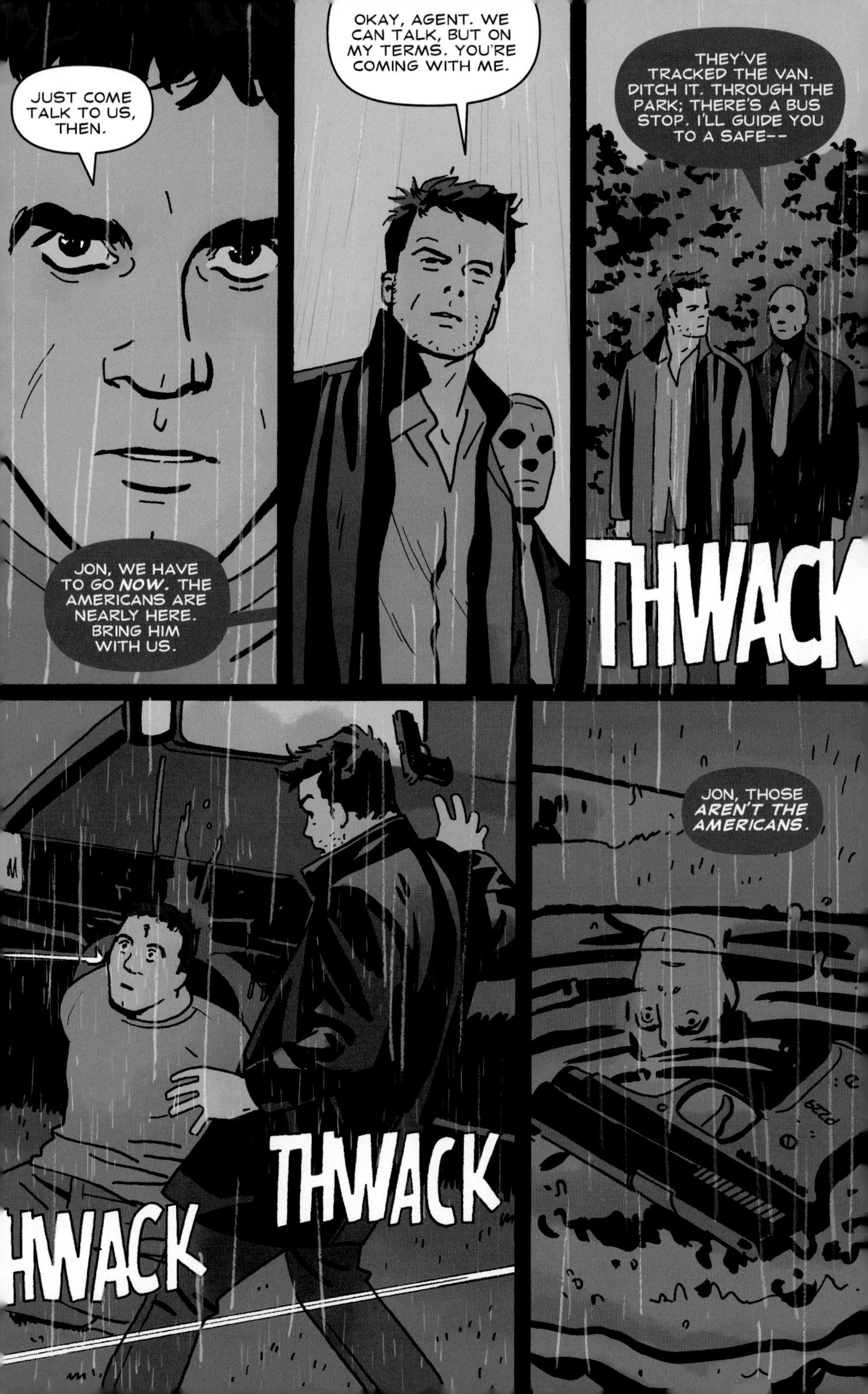
JUST COME TALK TO US, THEN.
JON, WE HAVE TO GO *NOW.* THE AMERICANS ARE NEARLY HERE. BRING HIM WITH US.
OKAY, AGENT. WE CAN TALK, BUT ON MY TERMS. YOU'RE COMING WITH ME.
THEY'VE TRACKED THE VAN. DITCH IT. THROUGH THE PARK; THERE'S A BUS STOP. I'LL GUIDE YOU TO A SAFE--
THWACK
THWACK
HWACK
JON, THOSE *AREN'T THE AMERICANS*.

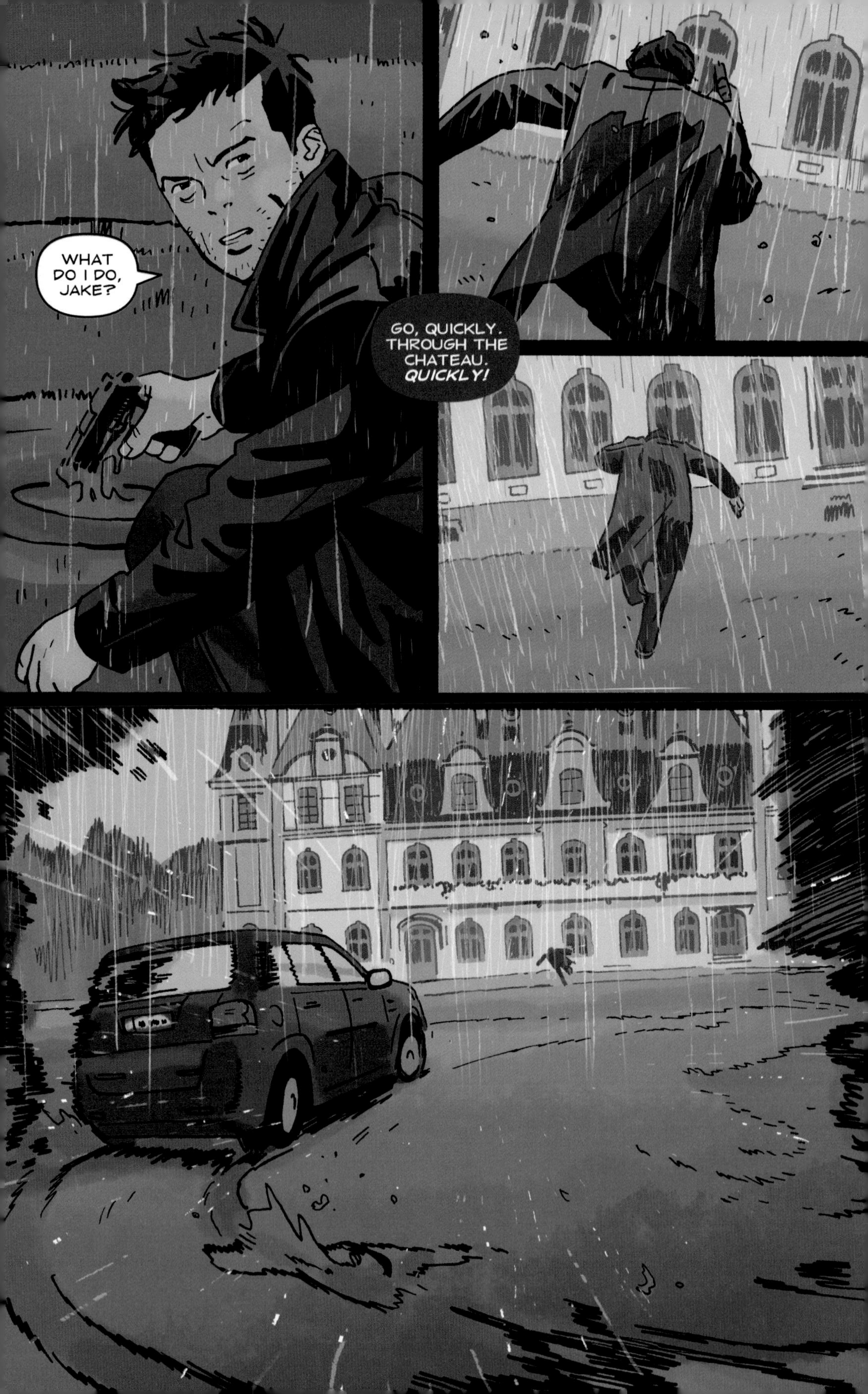
WHAT DO I DO, JAKE?
GO, QUICKLY. THROUGH THE CHATEAU. *QUICKLY!*

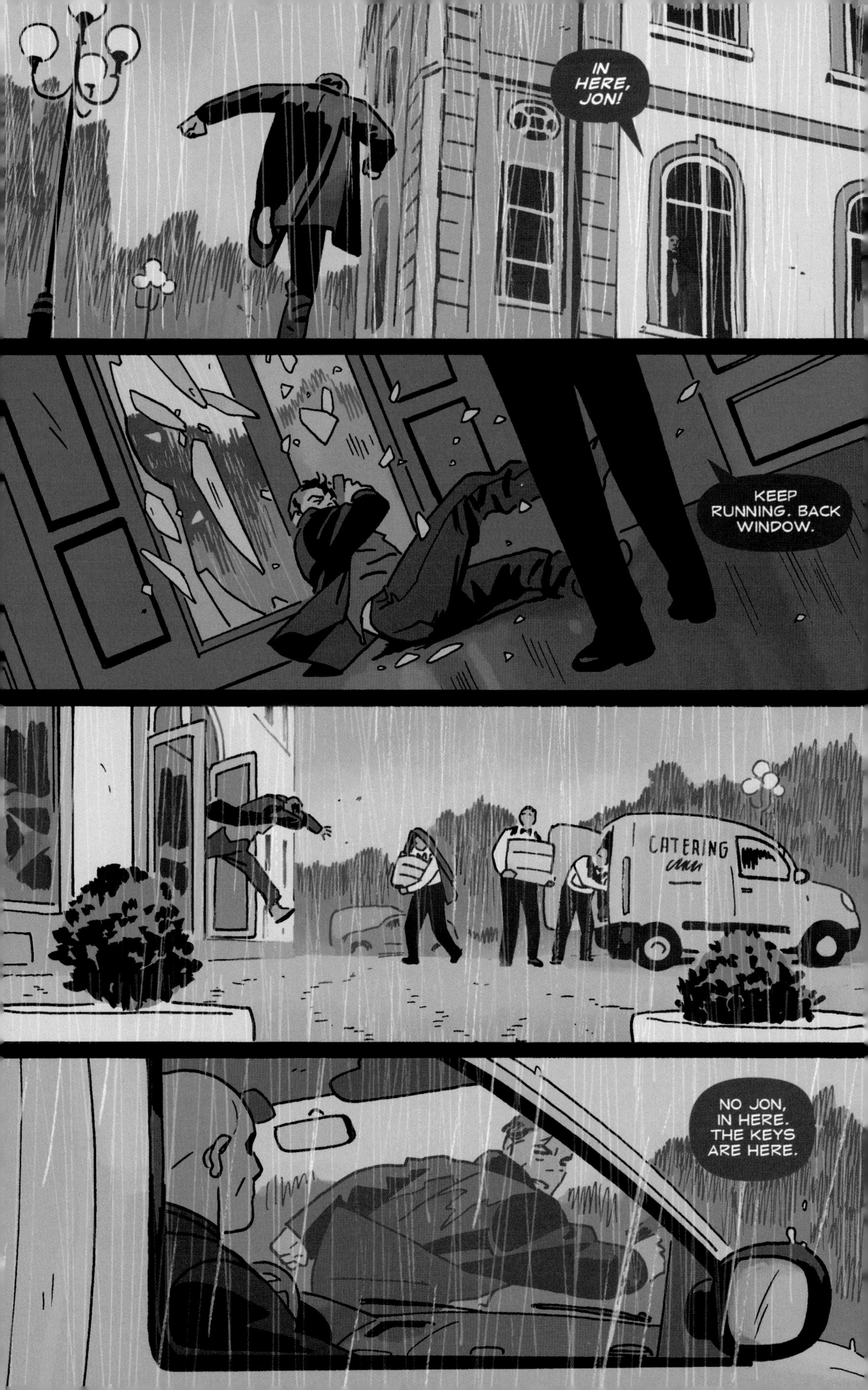
IN HERE, JON!
KEEP RUNNING. BACK WINDOW.
CATERING
NO JON, IN HERE. THE KEYS ARE HERE.

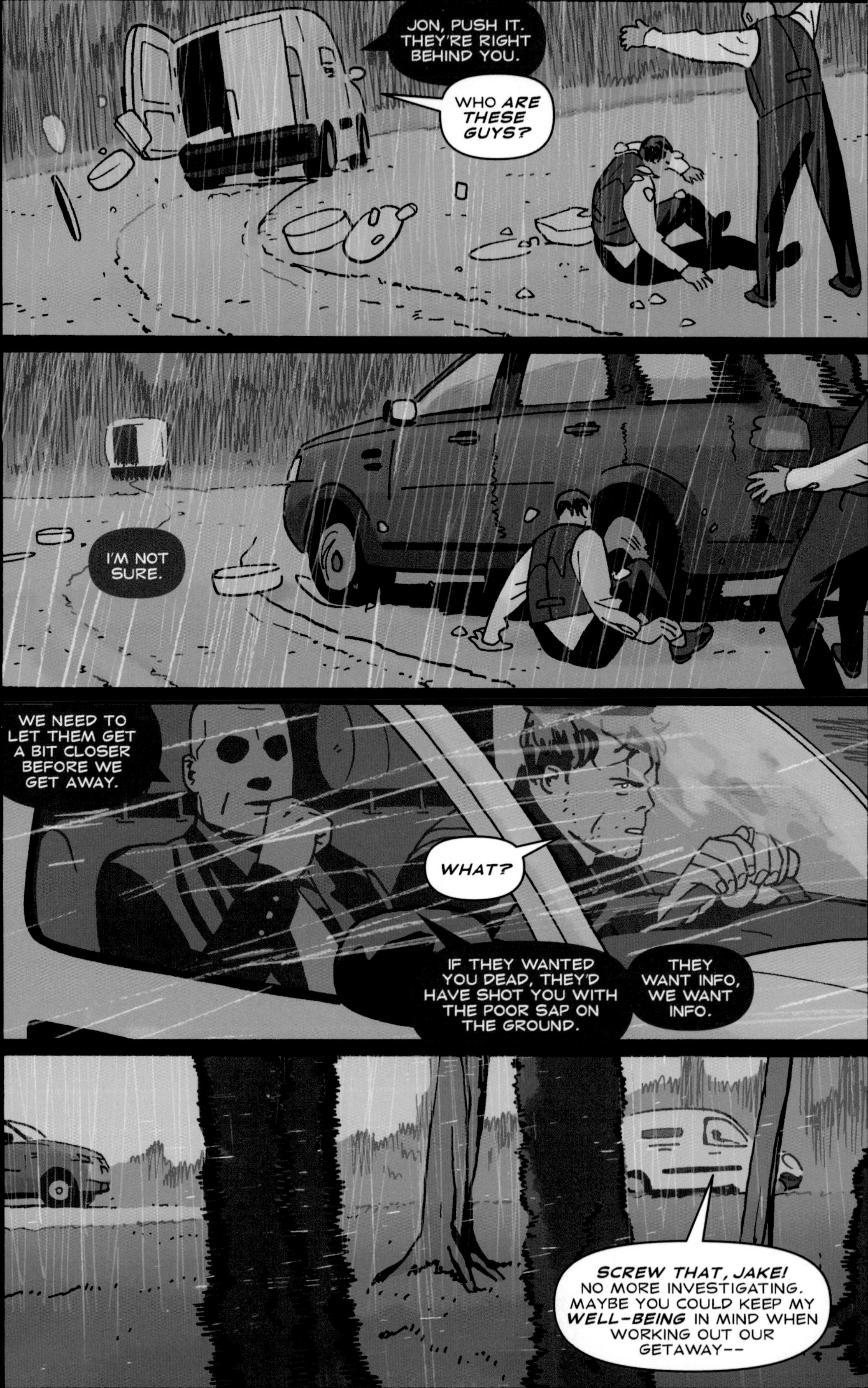
JON, PUSH IT. THEY'RE RIGHT BEHIND YOU.
WHO *ARE THESE GUYS?*
I'M NOT SURE.
WE NEED TO LET THEM GET A BIT CLOSER BEFORE WE GET AWAY.
WHAT?
IF THEY WANTED YOU DEAD, THEY'D HAVE SHOT YOU WITH THE POOR SAP ON THE GROUND.
THEY WANT INFO, WE WANT INFO.
SCREW THAT, JAKE! NO MORE INVESTIGATING. MAYBE YOU COULD KEEP MY *WELL-BEING* IN MIND WHEN WORKING OUT OUR GETAWAY--

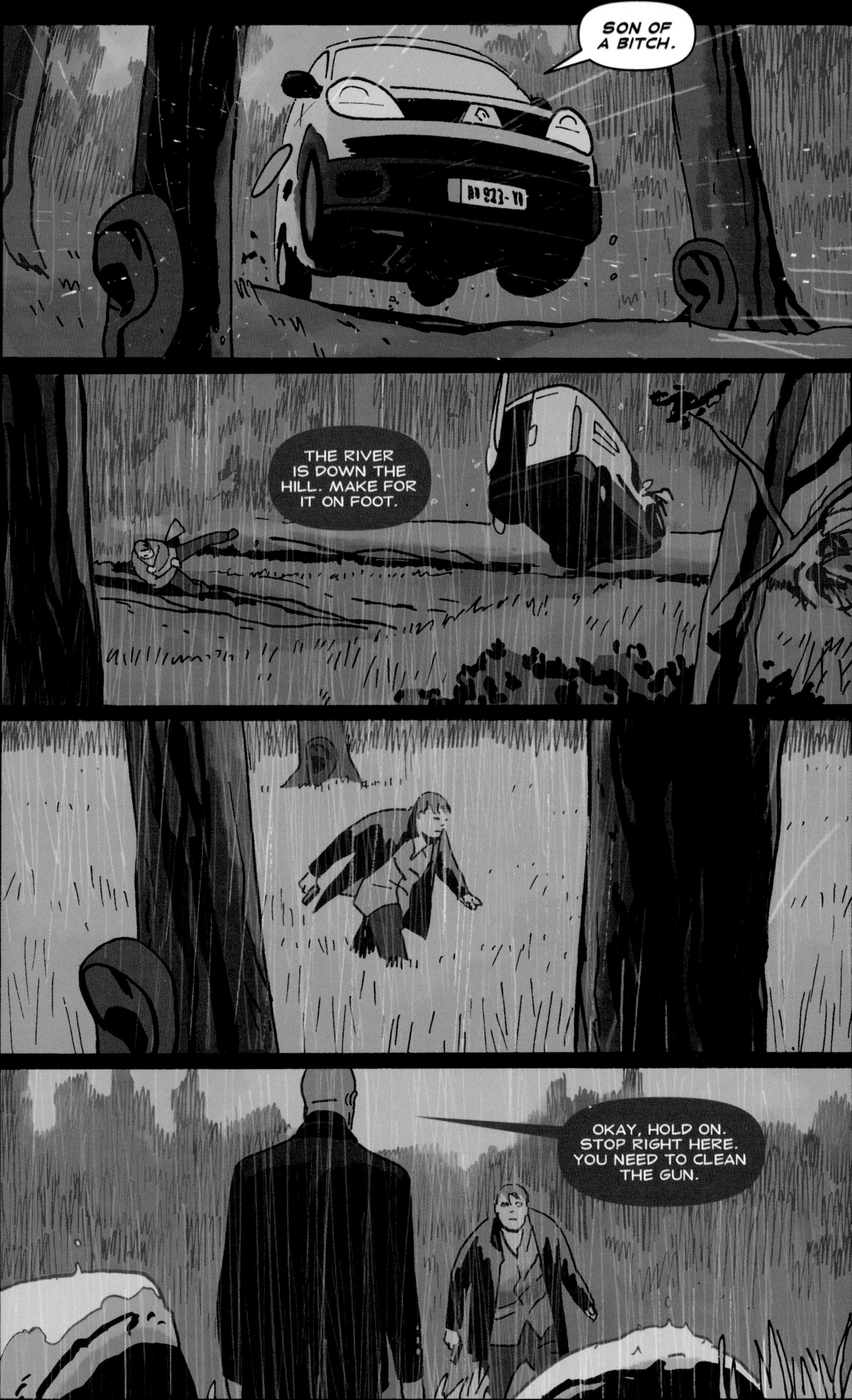
SON OF A BITCH.
THE RIVER IS DOWN THE HILL. MAKE FOR IT ON FOOT.
OKAY, HOLD ON. STOP RIGHT HERE. YOU NEED TO CLEAN THE GUN.

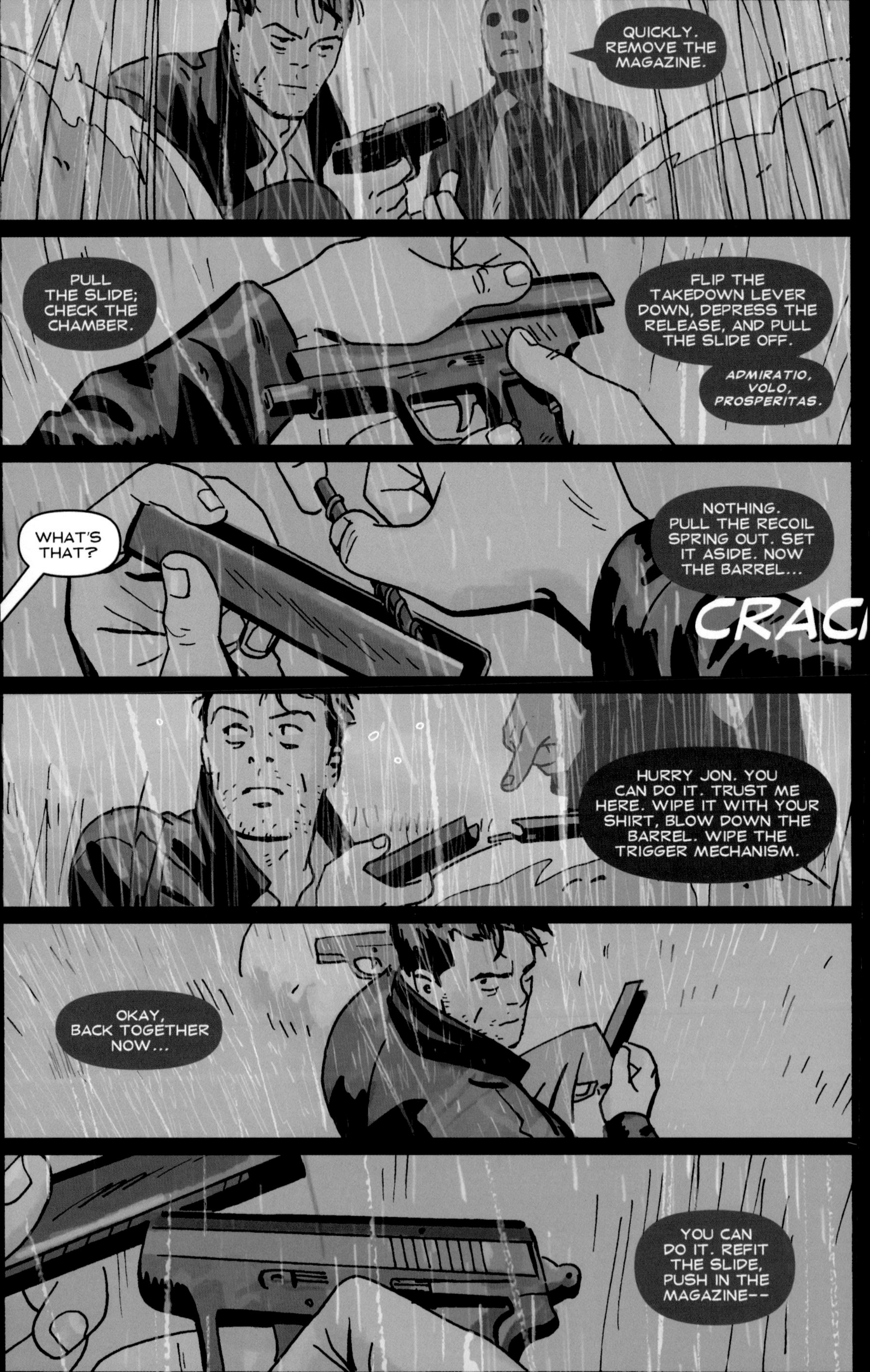
QUICKLY. REMOVE THE MAGAZINE.
PULL THE SLIDE; CHECK THE CHAMBER.
FLIP THE TAKEDOWN LEVER DOWN, DEPRESS THE RELEASE, AND PULL THE SLIDE OFF.
ADMIRATIO, VOLO, PROSPERITAS.
WHAT'S THAT?
NOTHING. PULL THE RECOIL SPRING OUT. SET IT ASIDE. NOW THE BARREL...
CRAC
HURRY JON. YOU CAN DO IT. TRUST ME HERE. WIPE IT WITH YOUR SHIRT, BLOW DOWN THE BARREL. WIPE THE TRIGGER MECHANISM.
OKAY, BACK TOGETHER NOW...
YOU CAN DO IT. REFIT THE SLIDE, PUSH IN THE MAGAZINE--

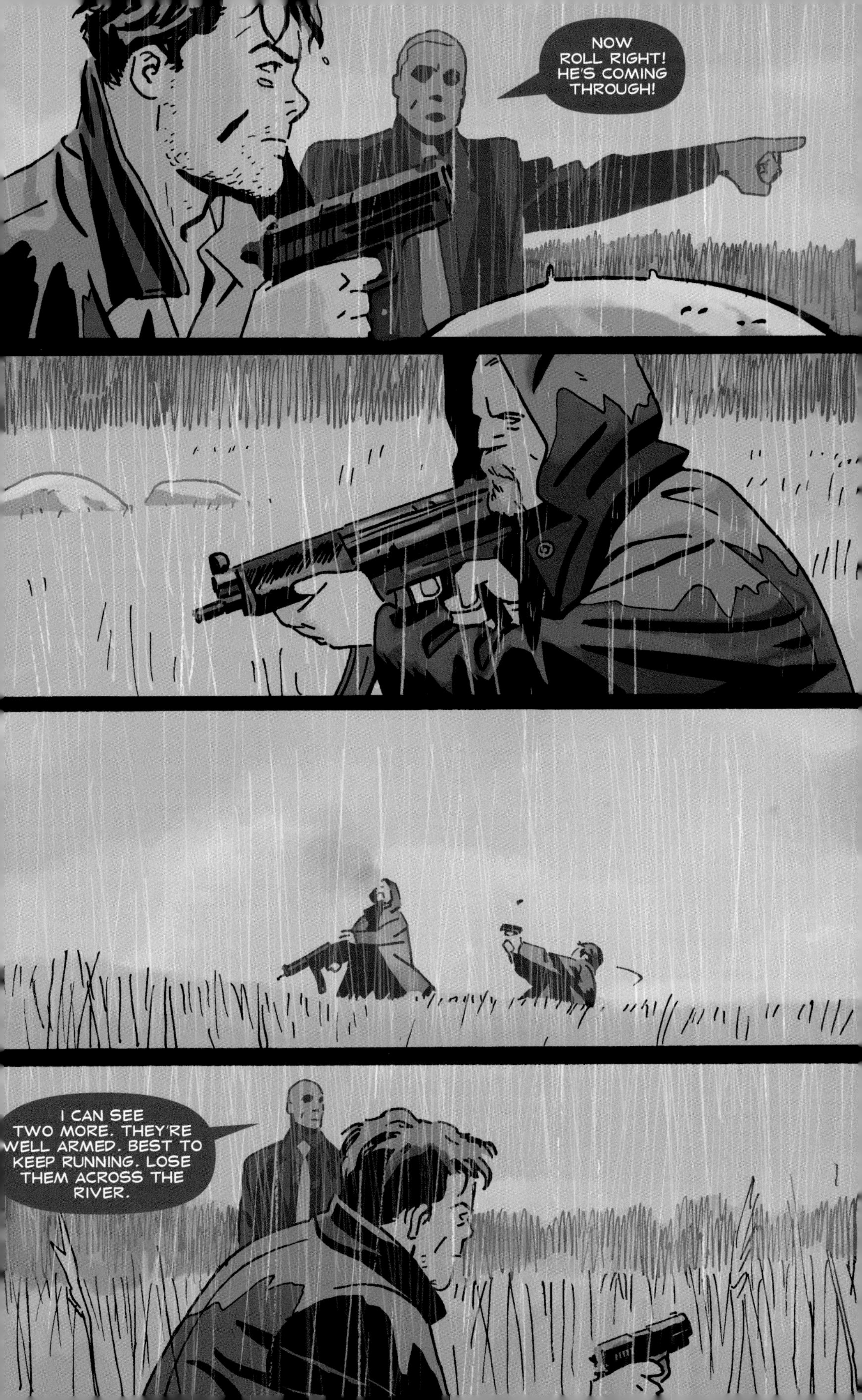
NOW ROLL RIGHT! HE'S COMING THROUGH!
I CAN SEE TWO MORE. THEY'RE WELL ARMED. BEST TO KEEP RUNNING. LOSE THEM ACROSS THE RIVER.

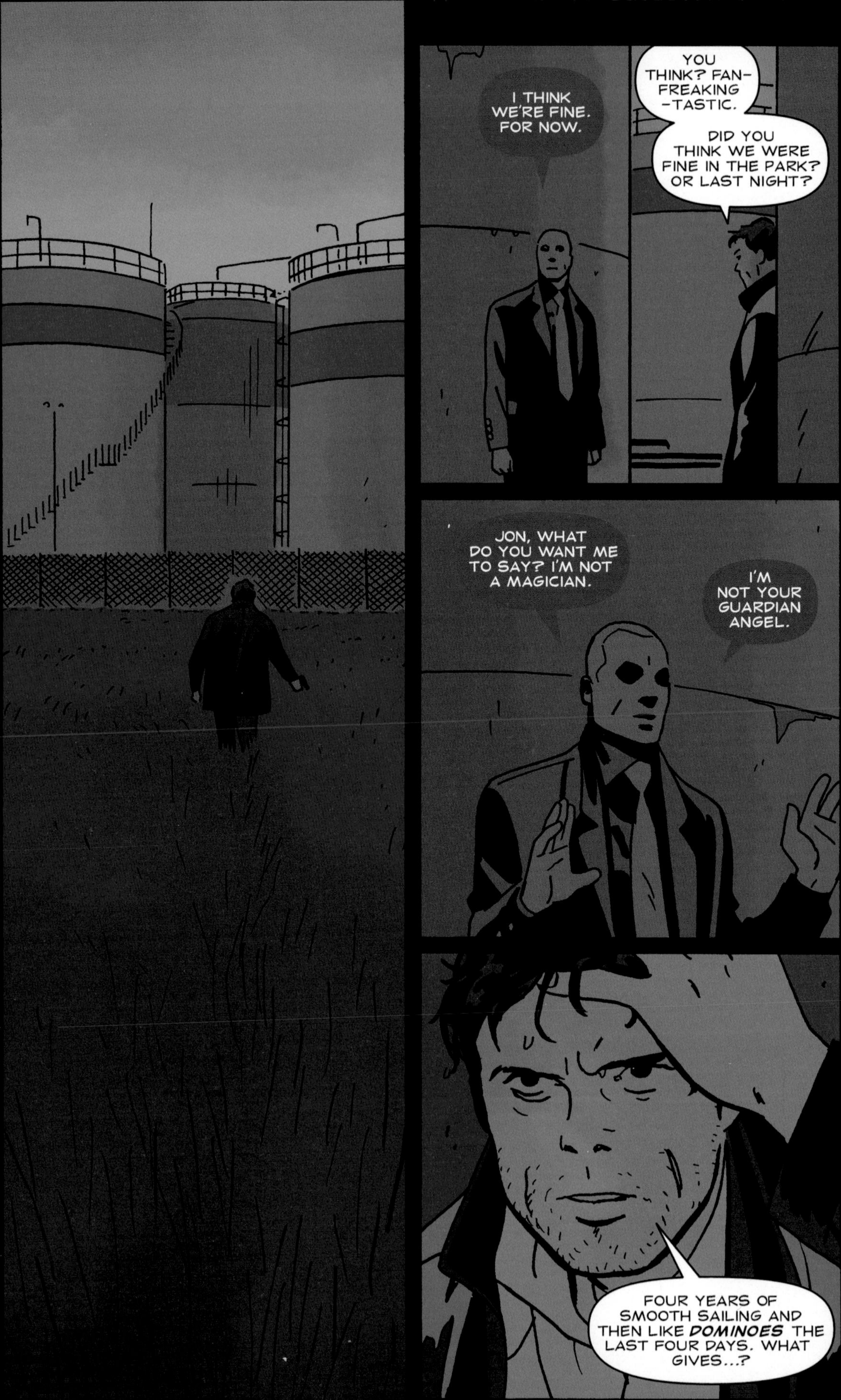
I THINK WE'RE FINE. FOR NOW.
YOU THINK? FAN-FREAKING-TASTIC.
DID YOU THINK WE WERE FINE IN THE PARK? OR LAST NIGHT?
JON, WHAT DO YOU WANT ME TO SAY? I'M NOT A MAGICIAN.
I'M NOT YOUR GUARDIAN ANGEL.
FOUR YEARS OF SMOOTH SAILING AND THEN LIKE *DOMINOES* THE LAST FOUR DAYS. WHAT GIVES...?

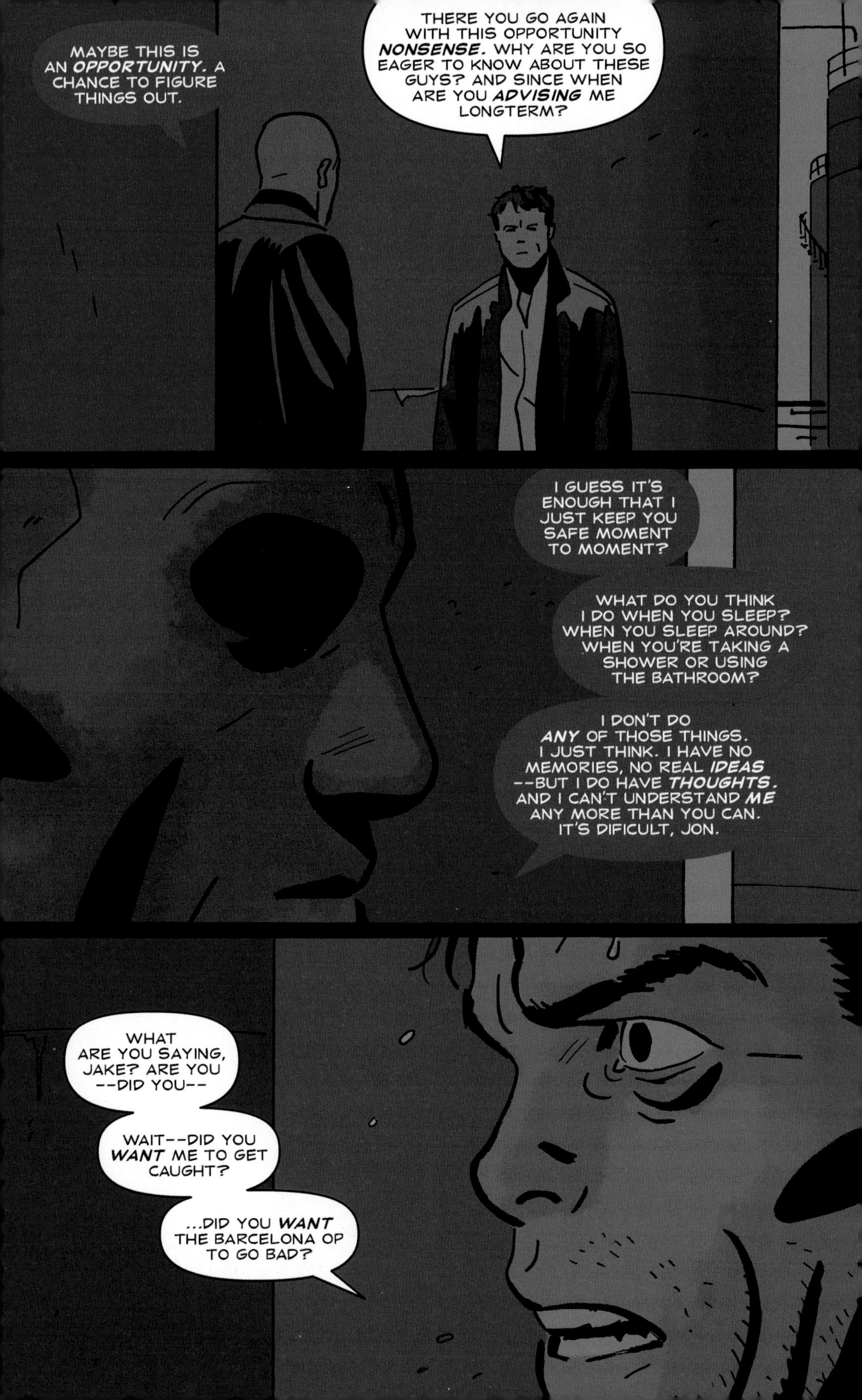
MAYBE THIS IS AN OPPORTUNITY. A CHANCE TO FIGURE THINGS OUT.
THERE YOU GO AGAIN WITH THIS OPPORTUNITY NONSENSE. WHY ARE YOU SO EAGER TO KNOW ABOUT THESE GUYS? AND SINCE WHEN ARE YOU ADVISING ME LONGTERM?
I GUESS IT'S ENOUGH THAT I JUST KEEP YOU SAFE MOMENT TO MOMENT?
WHAT DO YOU THINK I DO WHEN YOU SLEEP? WHEN YOU SLEEP AROUND? WHEN YOU'RE TAKING A SHOWER OR USING THE BATHROOM?
I DON'T DO ANY OF THOSE THINGS. I JUST THINK. I HAVE NO MEMORIES, NO REAL IDEAS --BUT I DO HAVE THOUGHTS. AND I CAN'T UNDERSTAND ME ANY MORE THAN YOU CAN. IT'S DIFICULT, JON.
WHAT ARE YOU SAYING, JAKE? ARE YOU --DID YOU--
WAIT--DID YOU WANT ME TO GET CAUGHT?
...DID YOU WANT THE BARCELONA OP TO GO BAD?

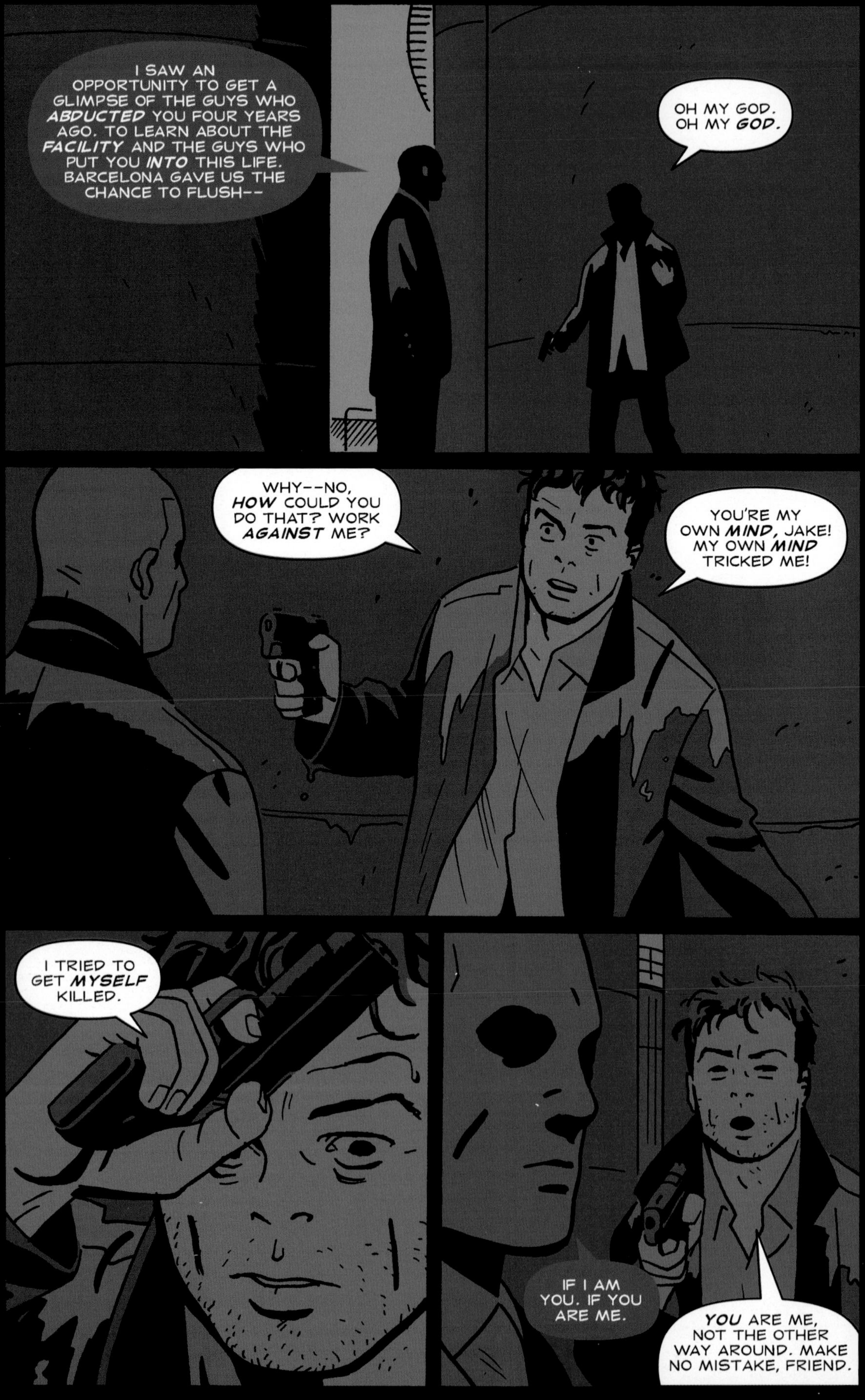
I SAW AN OPPORTUNITY TO GET A GLIMPSE OF THE GUYS WHO ABDUCTED YOU FOUR YEARS AGO. TO LEARN ABOUT THE FACILITY AND THE GUYS WHO PUT YOU INTO THIS LIFE. BARCELONA GAVE US THE CHANCE TO FLUSH--
OH MY GOD. OH MY GOD.
WHY--NO, HOW COULD YOU DO THAT? WORK AGAINST ME?
YOU'RE MY OWN MIND, JAKE! MY OWN MIND TRICKED ME!
I TRIED TO GET MYSELF KILLED.
IF I AM YOU. IF YOU ARE ME.
YOU ARE ME, NOT THE OTHER WAY AROUND. MAKE NO MISTAKE, FRIEND.

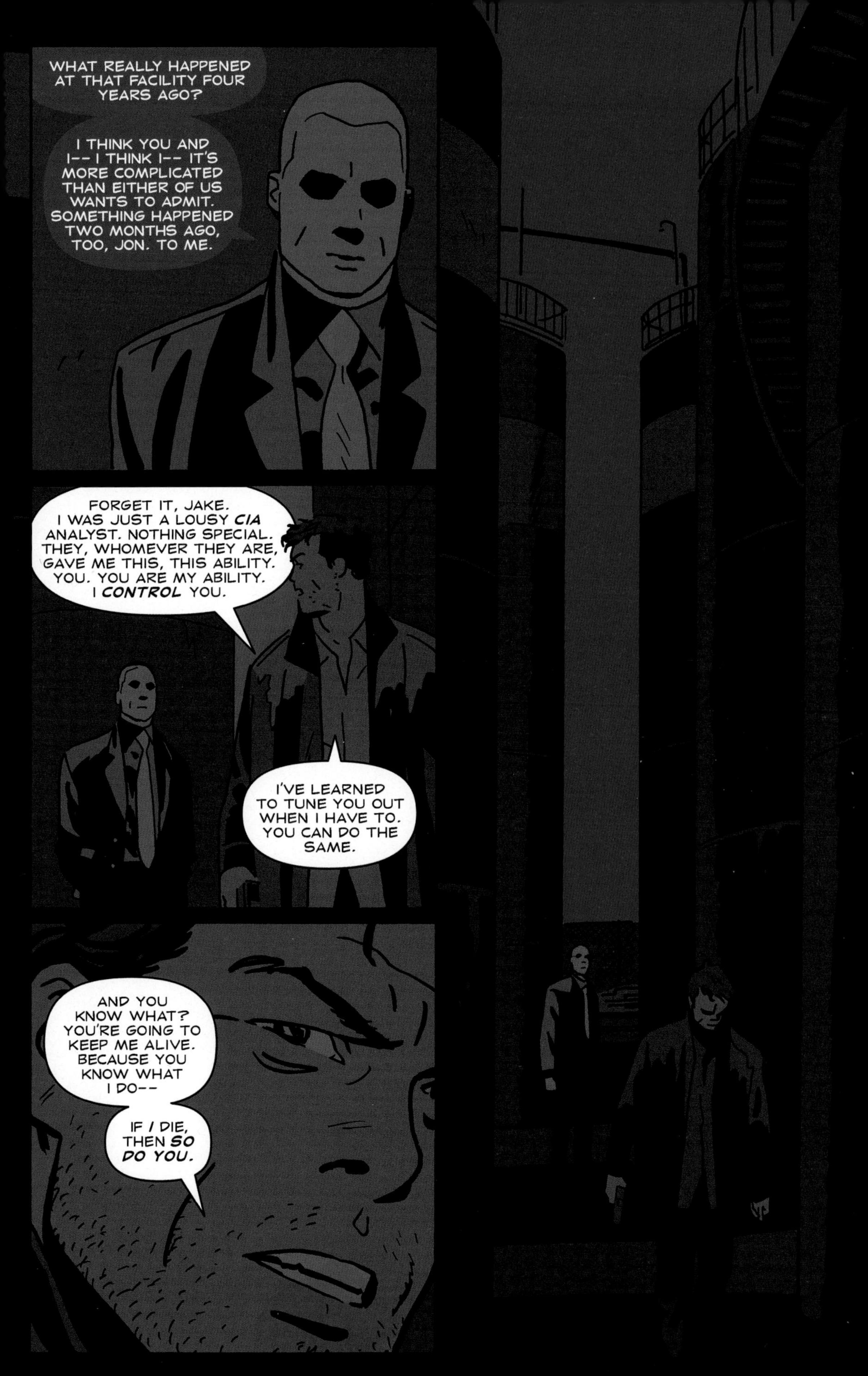
WHAT REALLY HAPPENED AT THAT FACILITY FOUR YEARS AGO?
I THINK YOU AND I-- I THINK I-- IT'S MORE COMPLICATED THAN EITHER OF US WANTS TO ADMIT. SOMETHING HAPPENED TWO MONTHS AGO, TOO, JON. TO ME.
FORGET IT, JAKE. I WAS JUST A LOUSY *CIA* ANALYST. NOTHING SPECIAL. THEY, WHOMEVER THEY ARE, GAVE ME THIS, THIS ABILITY. YOU. YOU ARE MY ABILITY. I ***CONTROL*** YOU.
I'VE LEARNED TO TUNE YOU OUT WHEN I HAVE TO. YOU CAN DO THE SAME.
AND YOU KNOW WHAT? YOU'RE GOING TO KEEP ME ALIVE. BECAUSE YOU KNOW WHAT I DO--
IF *I* DIE, THEN ***SO DO YOU.***

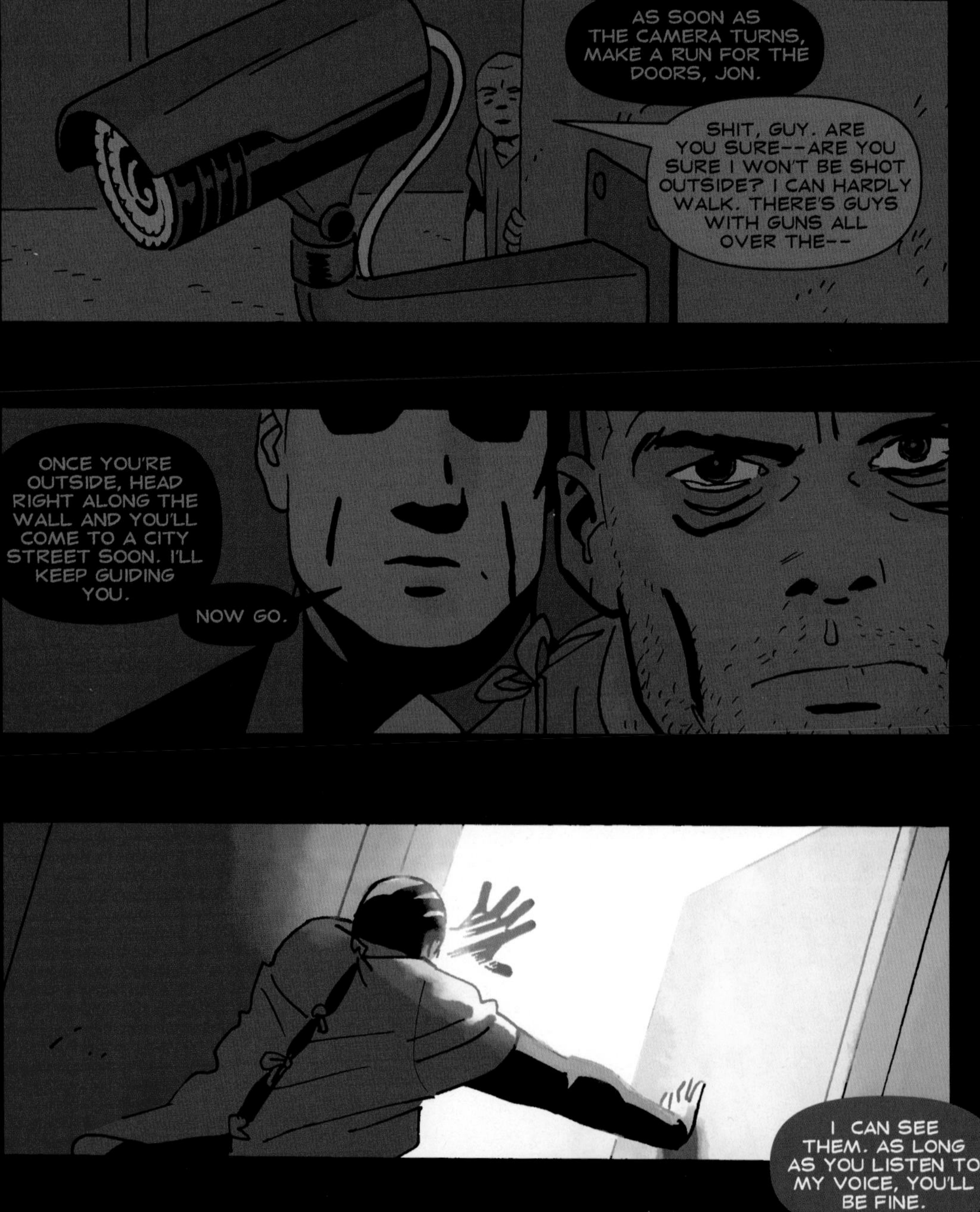
AS SOON AS THE CAMERA TURNS, MAKE A RUN FOR THE DOORS, JON.
SHIT, GUY. ARE YOU SURE--ARE YOU SURE I WON'T BE SHOT OUTSIDE? I CAN HARDLY WALK. THERE'S GUYS WITH GUNS ALL OVER THE--
ONCE YOU'RE OUTSIDE, HEAD RIGHT ALONG THE WALL AND YOU'LL COME TO A CITY STREET SOON. I'LL KEEP GUIDING YOU.
NOW GO.
I CAN SEE THEM. AS LONG AS YOU LISTEN TO MY VOICE, YOU'LL BE FINE.

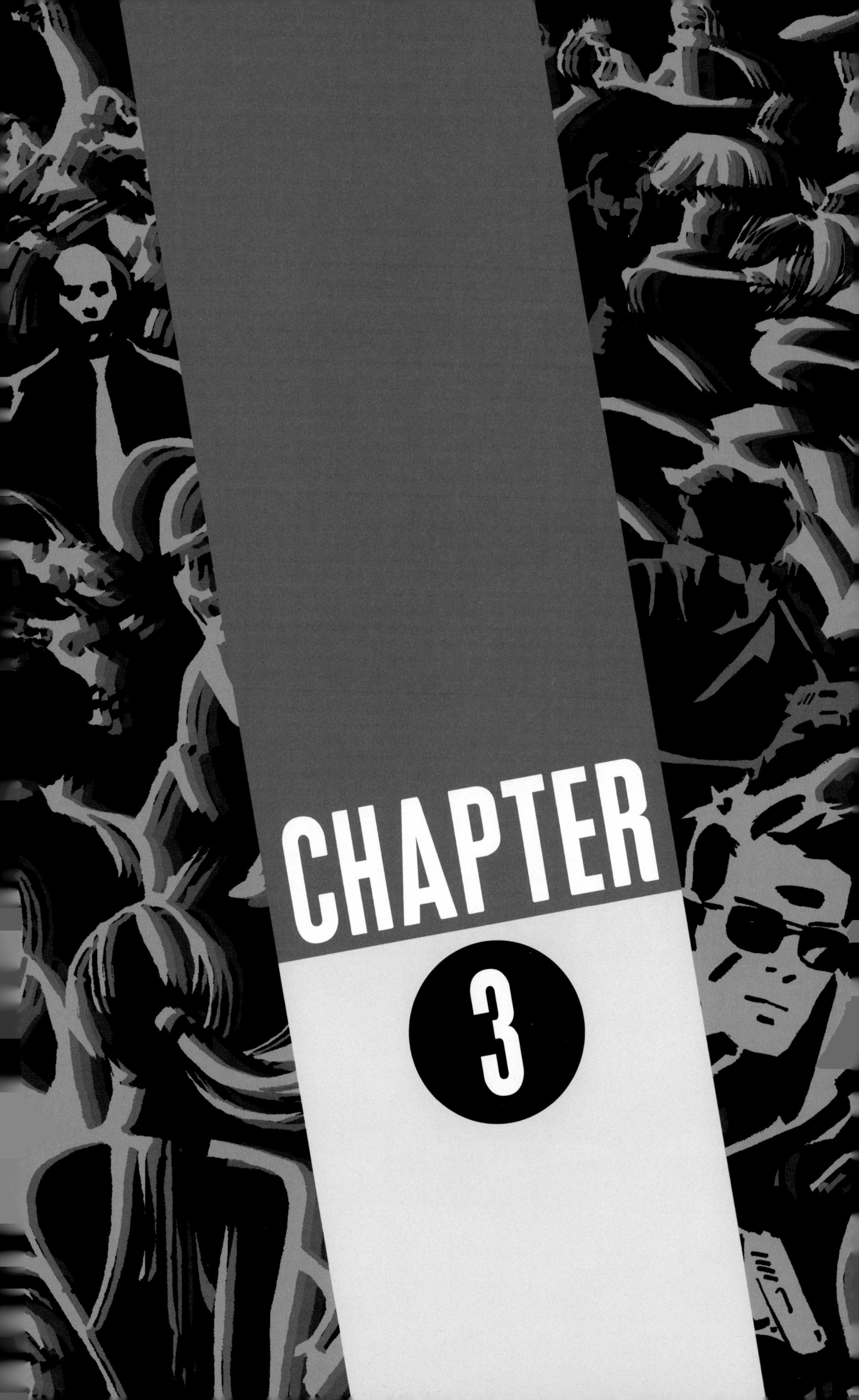
CHAPTER
3

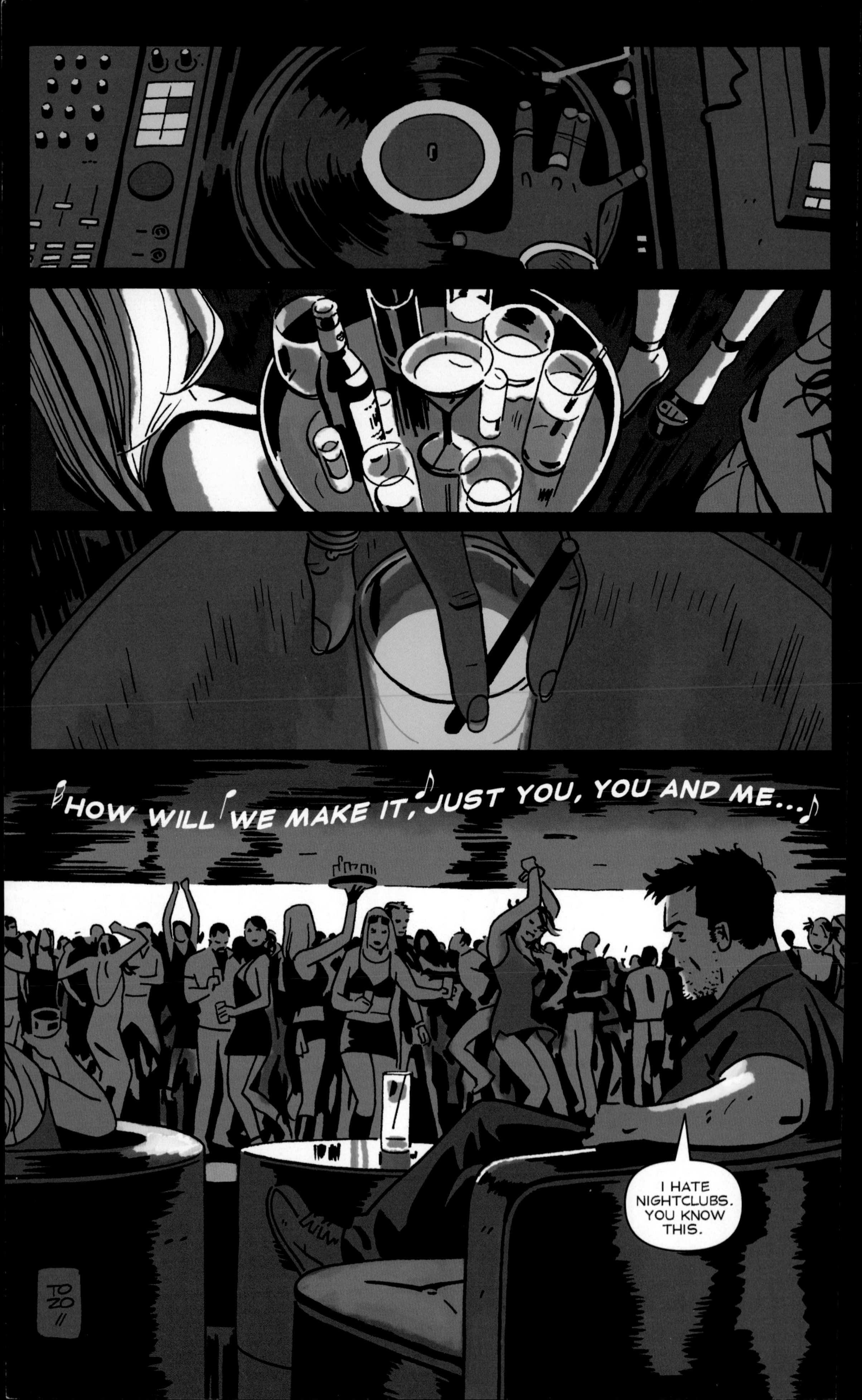
HOW WILL WE MAKE IT, JUST YOU, YOU AND ME...
I HATE NIGHTCLUBS. YOU KNOW THIS.
TOZO 11

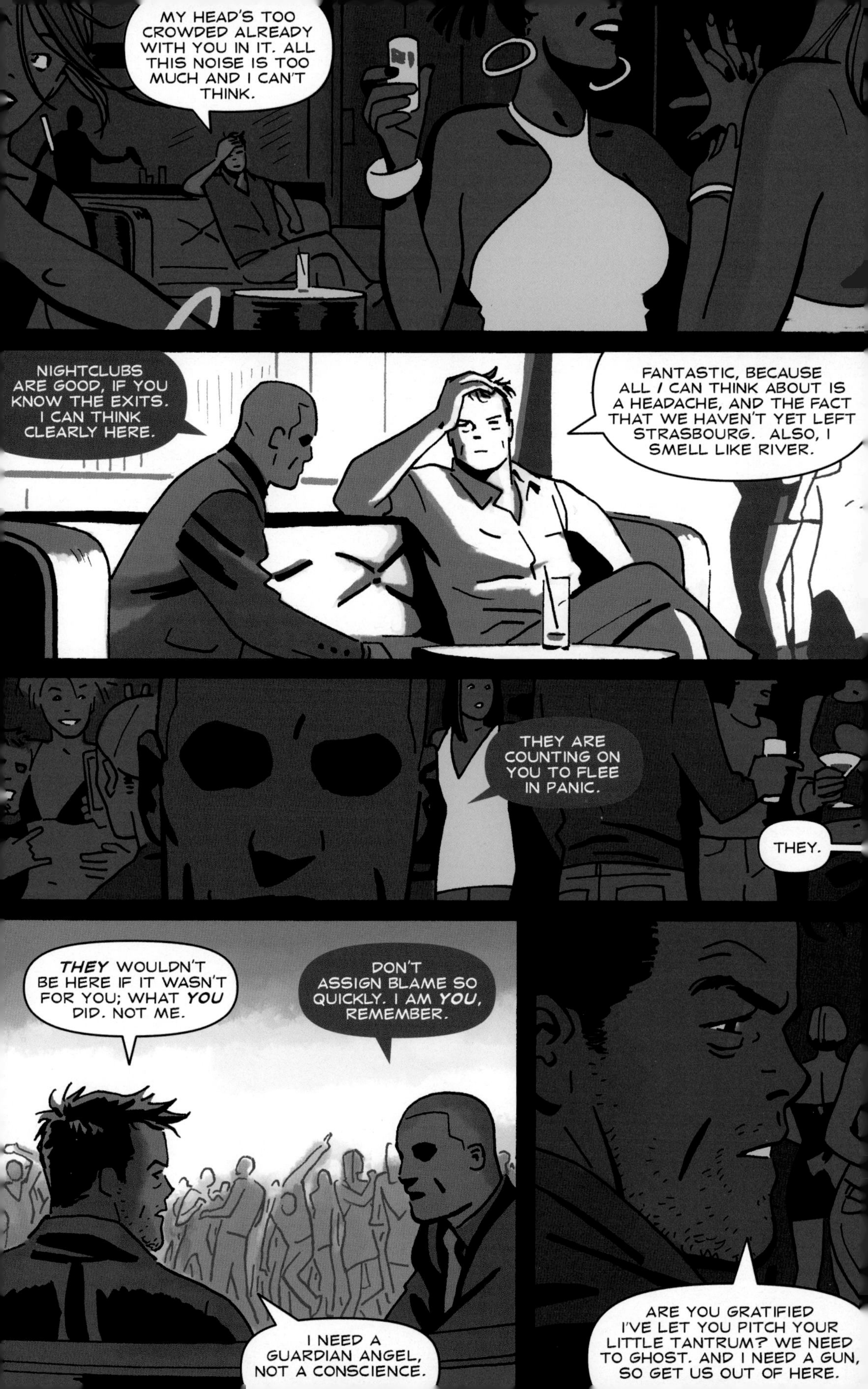

MY HEAD'S TOO CROWDED ALREADY WITH YOU IN IT. ALL THIS NOISE IS TOO MUCH AND I CAN'T THINK.
NIGHTCLUBS ARE GOOD, IF YOU KNOW THE EXITS. I CAN THINK CLEARLY HERE.
FANTASTIC, BECAUSE ALL *I* CAN THINK ABOUT IS A HEADACHE, AND THE FACT THAT WE HAVEN'T YET LEFT STRASBOURG. ALSO, I SMELL LIKE RIVER.
THEY ARE COUNTING ON YOU TO FLEE IN PANIC.
THEY.
THEY WOULDN'T BE HERE IF IT WASN'T FOR YOU; WHAT *YOU* DID. NOT ME.
DON'T ASSIGN BLAME SO QUICKLY. I AM *YOU*, REMEMBER.
I NEED A GUARDIAN ANGEL, NOT A CONSCIENCE.
ARE YOU GRATIFIED I'VE LET YOU PITCH YOUR LITTLE TANTRUM? WE NEED TO GHOST. AND I NEED A GUN, SO GET US OUT OF HERE.

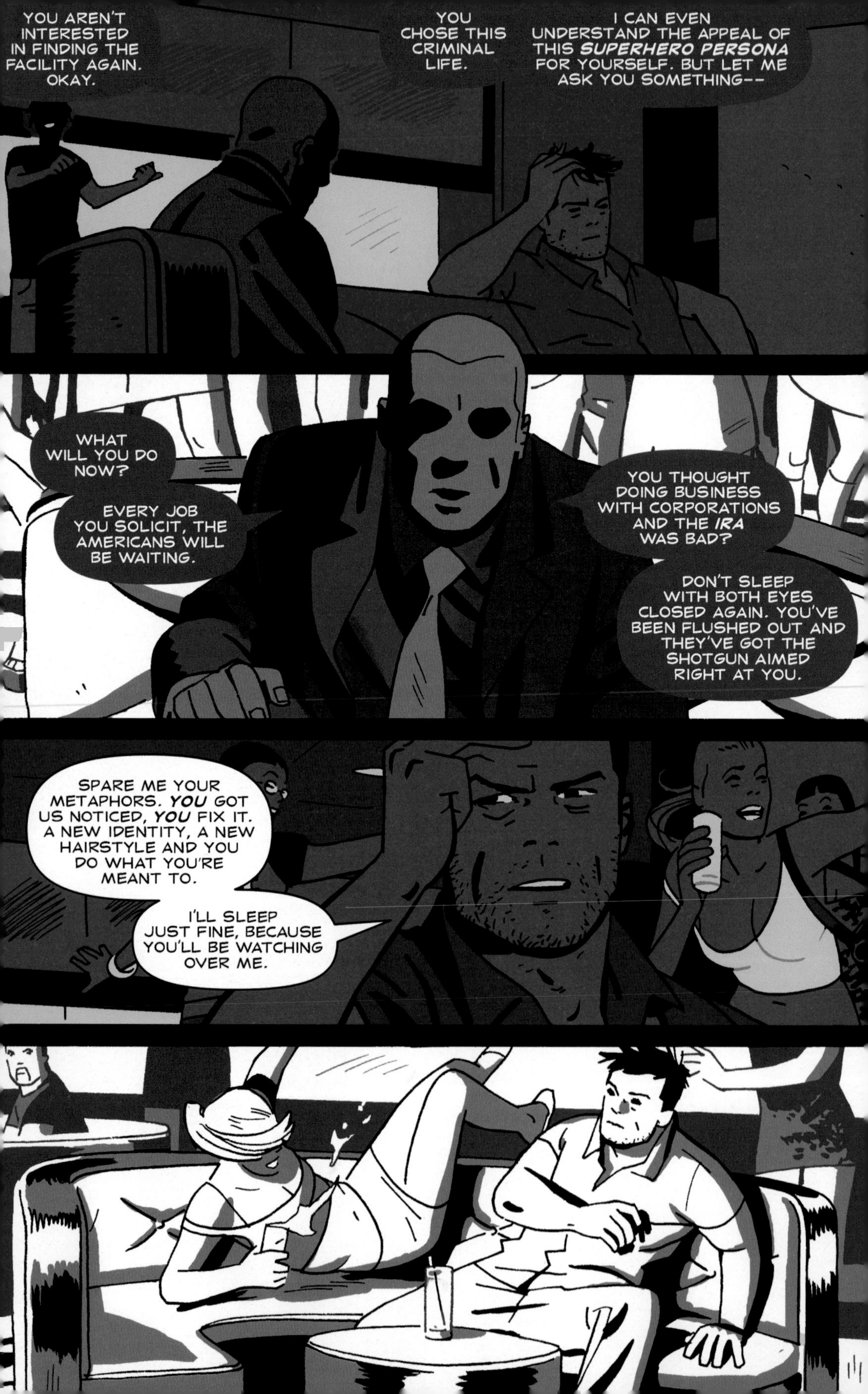
YOU AREN'T INTERESTED IN FINDING THE FACILITY AGAIN. OKAY.
YOU CHOSE THIS CRIMINAL LIFE.
I CAN EVEN UNDERSTAND THE APPEAL OF THIS *SUPERHERO PERSONA* FOR YOURSELF. BUT LET ME ASK YOU SOMETHING--
WHAT WILL YOU DO NOW?
EVERY JOB YOU SOLICIT, THE AMERICANS WILL BE WAITING.
YOU THOUGHT DOING BUSINESS WITH CORPORATIONS AND THE *IRA* WAS BAD?
DON'T SLEEP WITH BOTH EYES CLOSED AGAIN. YOU'VE BEEN FLUSHED OUT AND THEY'VE GOT THE SHOTGUN AIMED RIGHT AT YOU.
SPARE ME YOUR METAPHORS. ***YOU*** GOT US NOTICED, ***YOU*** FIX IT. A NEW IDENTITY, A NEW HAIRSTYLE AND YOU DO WHAT YOU'RE MEANT TO.
I'LL SLEEP JUST FINE, BECAUSE YOU'LL BE WATCHING OVER ME.

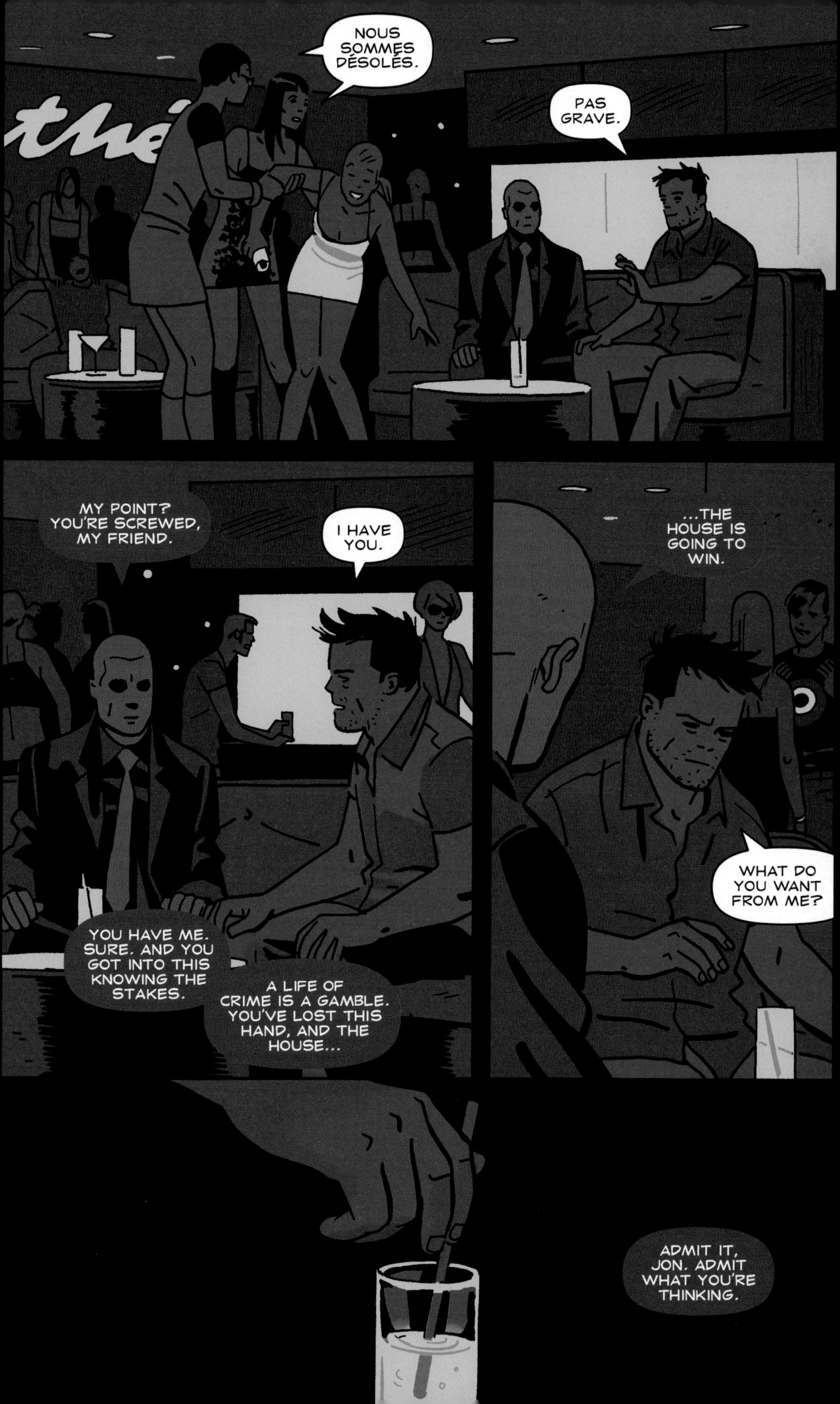

NOUS SOMMES DÉSOLÉS.
PAS GRAVE.
MY POINT? YOU'RE SCREWED, MY FRIEND.
I HAVE YOU.
YOU HAVE ME. SURE. AND YOU GOT INTO THIS KNOWING THE STAKES.
A LIFE OF CRIME IS A GAMBLE. YOU'VE LOST THIS HAND, AND THE HOUSE...
...THE HOUSE IS GOING TO WIN.
WHAT DO YOU WANT FROM ME?
ADMIT IT, JON. ADMIT WHAT YOU'RE THINKING.

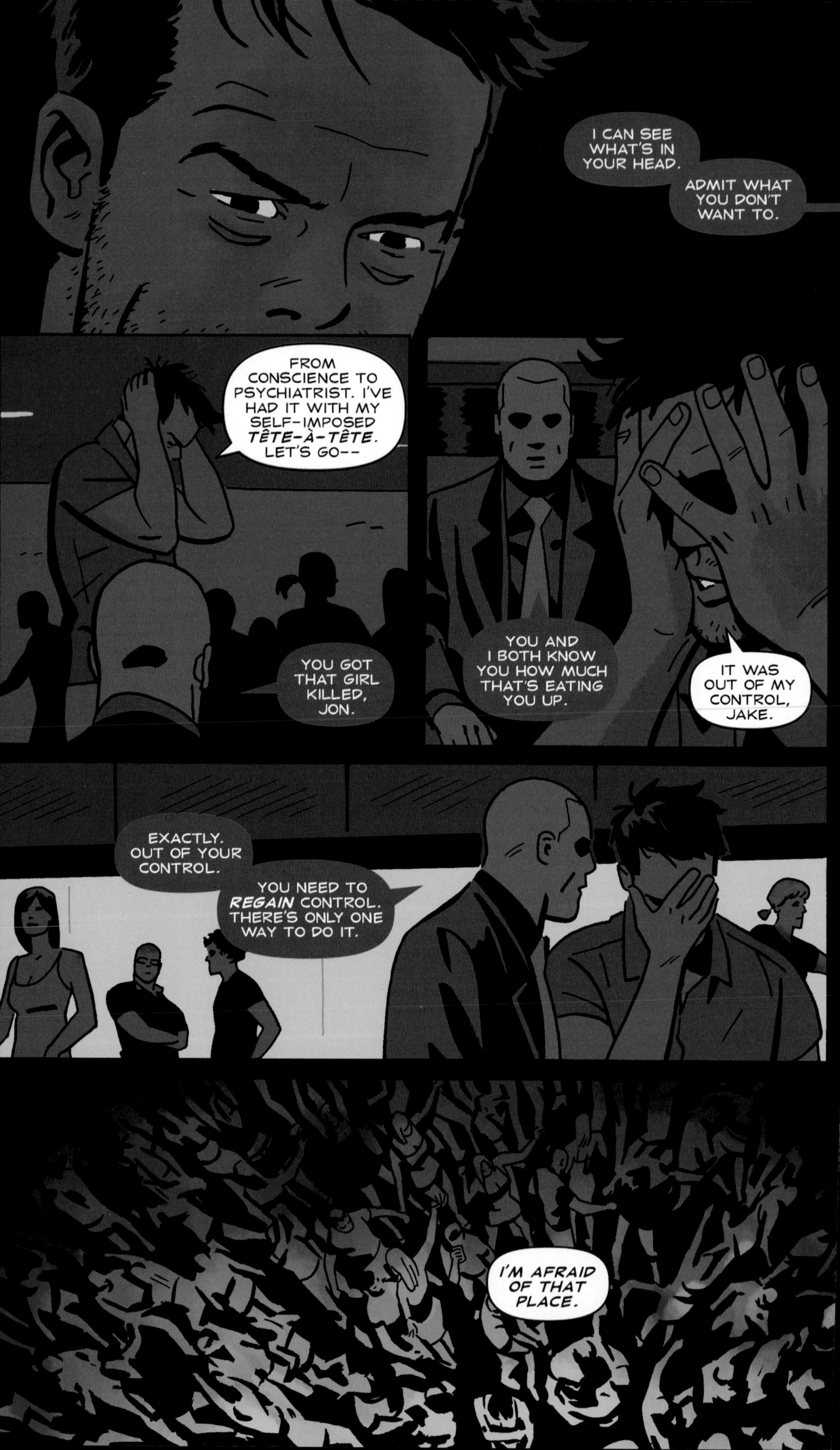
I CAN SEE WHAT'S IN YOUR HEAD.
ADMIT WHAT YOU DON'T WANT TO.
FROM CONSCIENCE TO PSYCHIATRIST. I'VE HAD IT WITH MY SELF-IMPOSED *TÊTE-À-TÊTE*. LET'S GO--
YOU GOT THAT GIRL KILLED, JON.
YOU AND I BOTH KNOW YOU HOW MUCH THAT'S EATING YOU UP.
IT WAS OUT OF MY CONTROL, JAKE.
EXACTLY. OUT OF YOUR CONTROL.
YOU NEED TO *REGAIN* CONTROL. THERE'S ONLY ONE WAY TO DO IT.
I'M AFRAID OF THAT PLACE.

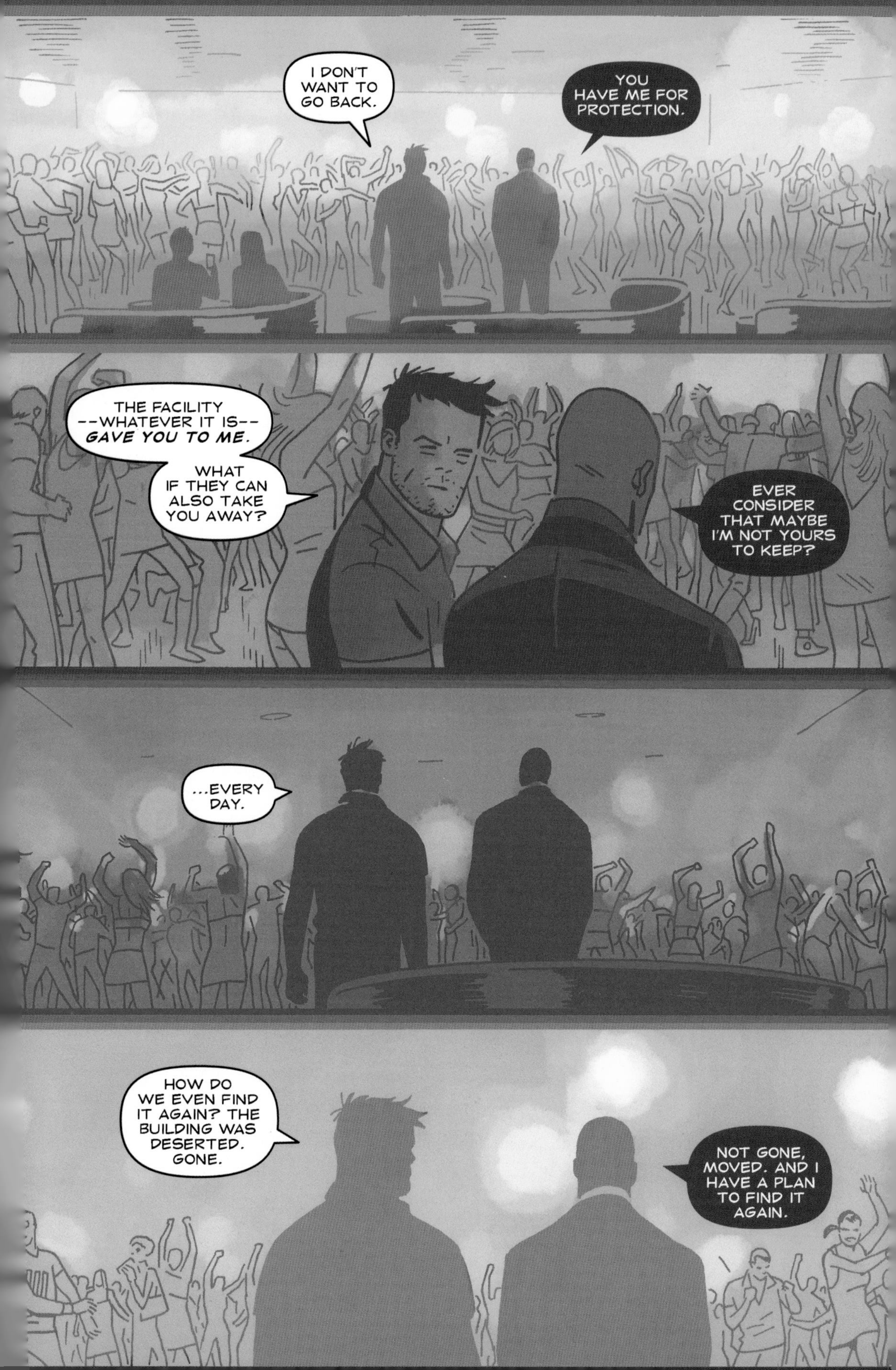
I DON'T WANT TO GO BACK.
YOU HAVE ME FOR PROTECTION.
THE FACILITY --WHATEVER IT IS-- GAVE YOU TO ME.
WHAT IF THEY CAN ALSO TAKE YOU AWAY?
EVER CONSIDER THAT MAYBE I'M NOT YOURS TO KEEP?
...EVERY DAY.
HOW DO WE EVEN FIND IT AGAIN? THE BUILDING WAS DESERTED. GONE.
NOT GONE, MOVED. AND I HAVE A PLAN TO FIND IT AGAIN.

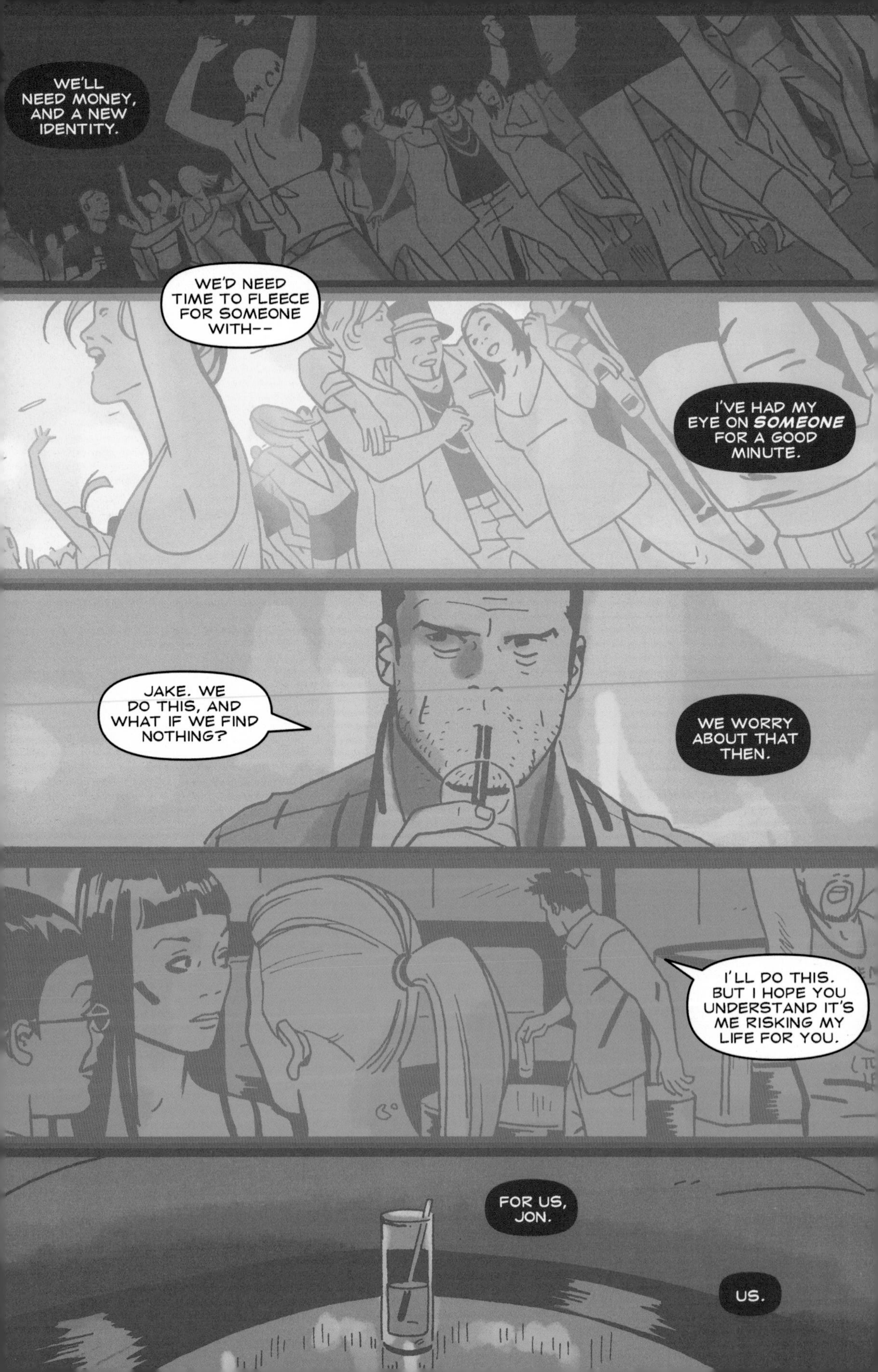
WE'LL NEED MONEY, AND A NEW IDENTITY.
WE'D NEED TIME TO FLEECE FOR SOMEONE WITH--
I'VE HAD MY EYE ON *SOMEONE* FOR A GOOD MINUTE.
JAKE. WE DO THIS, AND WHAT IF WE FIND NOTHING?
WE WORRY ABOUT THAT THEN.
I'LL DO THIS. BUT I HOPE YOU UNDERSTAND IT'S ME RISKING MY LIFE FOR YOU.
FOR US, JON.
US.

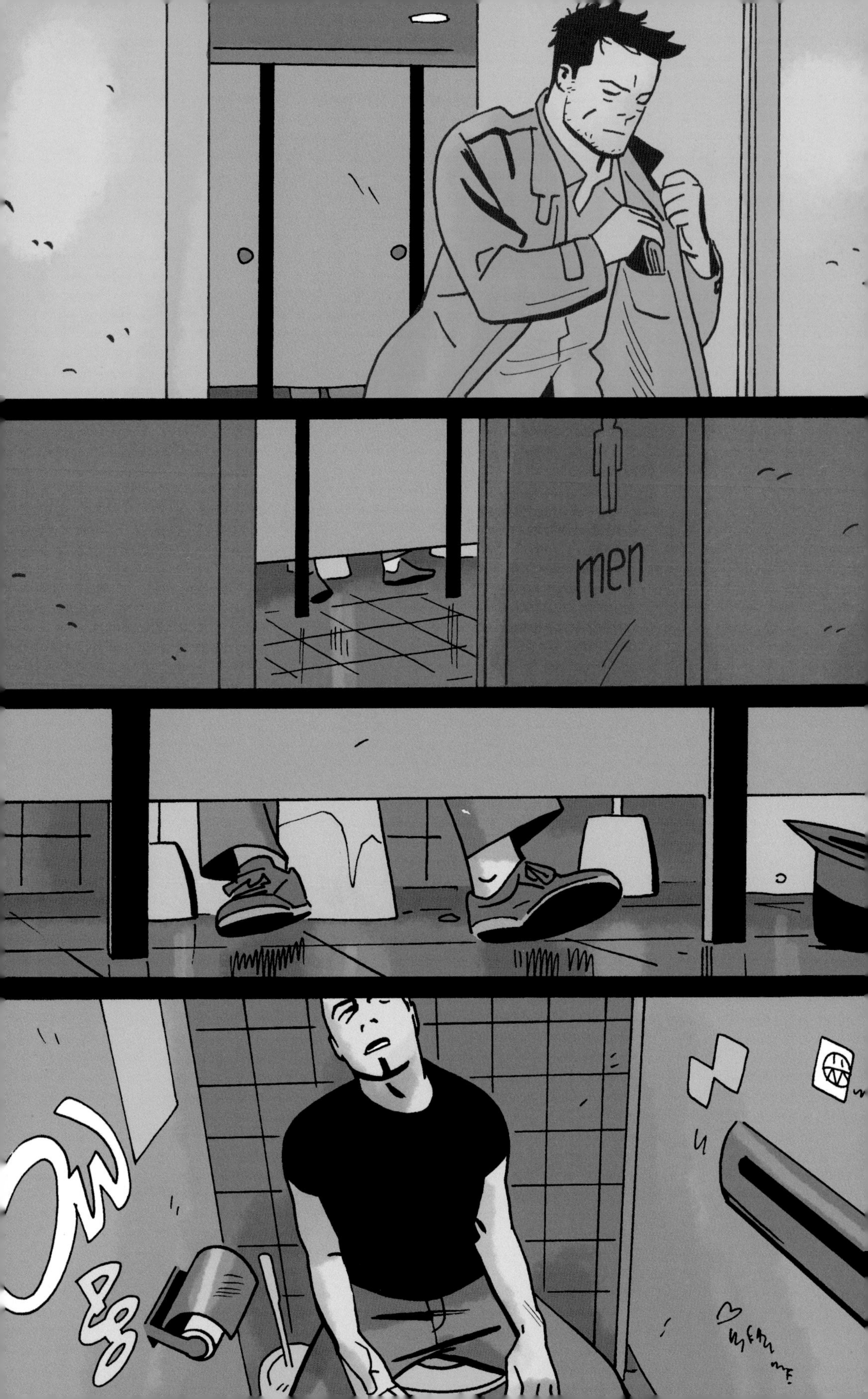
men
OW

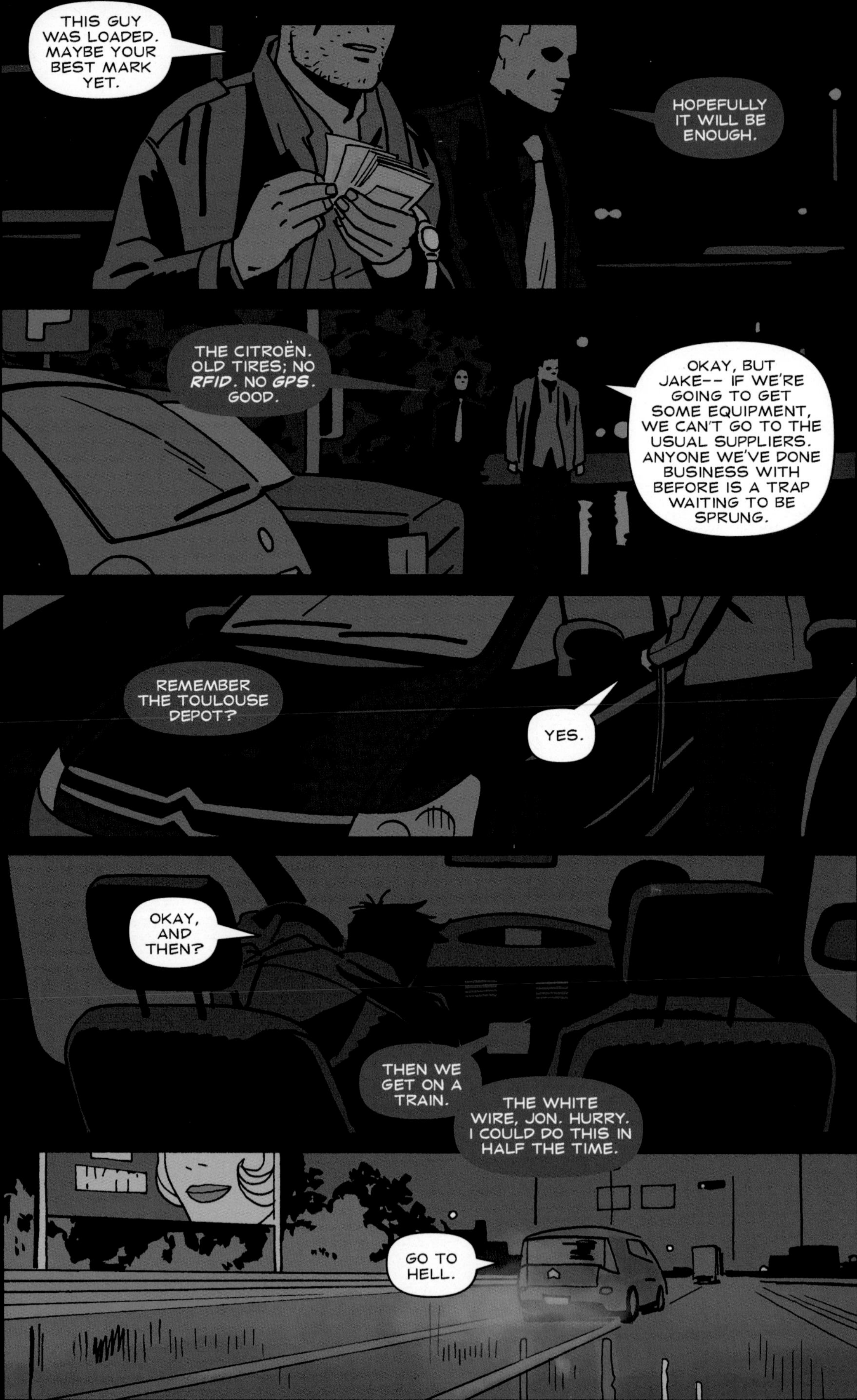
THIS GUY WAS LOADED. MAYBE YOUR BEST MARK YET.
HOPEFULLY IT WILL BE ENOUGH.
THE CITROËN. OLD TIRES; NO *RFID*. NO *GPS*. GOOD.
OKAY, BUT JAKE-- IF WE'RE GOING TO GET SOME EQUIPMENT, WE CAN'T GO TO THE USUAL SUPPLIERS. ANYONE WE'VE DONE BUSINESS WITH BEFORE IS A TRAP WAITING TO BE SPRUNG.
REMEMBER THE TOULOUSE DEPOT?
YES.
OKAY, AND THEN?
THEN WE GET ON A TRAIN.
THE WHITE WIRE, JON. HURRY. I COULD DO THIS IN HALF THE TIME.
GO TO HELL.

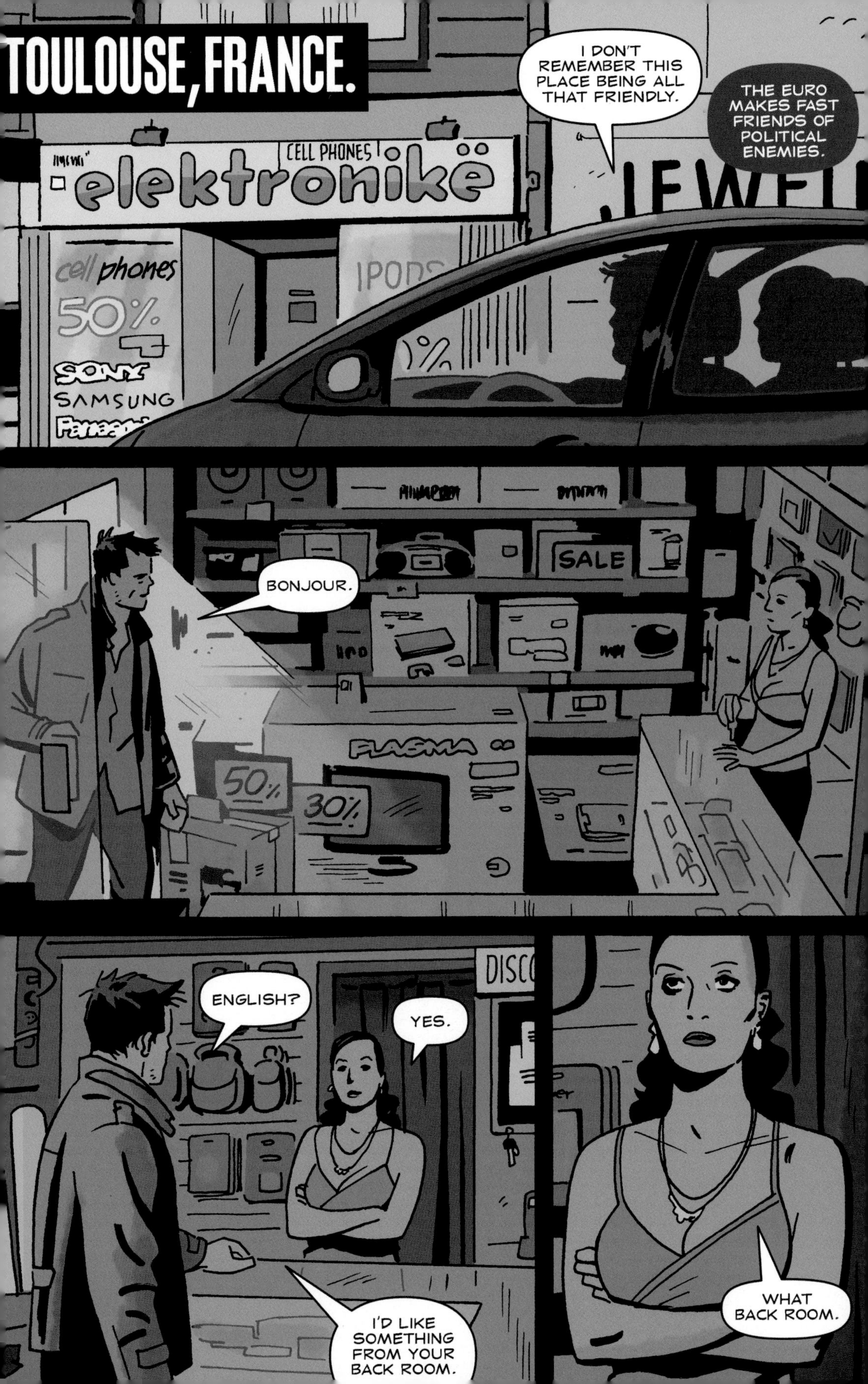
TOULOUSE, FRANCE.
CELL PHONES
elektronikë
cell phones
50%
SONY
SAMSUNG
I DON'T REMEMBER THIS PLACE BEING ALL THAT FRIENDLY.
THE EURO MAKES FAST FRIENDS OF POLITICAL ENEMIES.
SALE
BONJOUR.
PLASMA
50%
30%
ENGLISH?
YES.
I'D LIKE SOMETHING FROM YOUR BACK ROOM.
WHAT BACK ROOM.

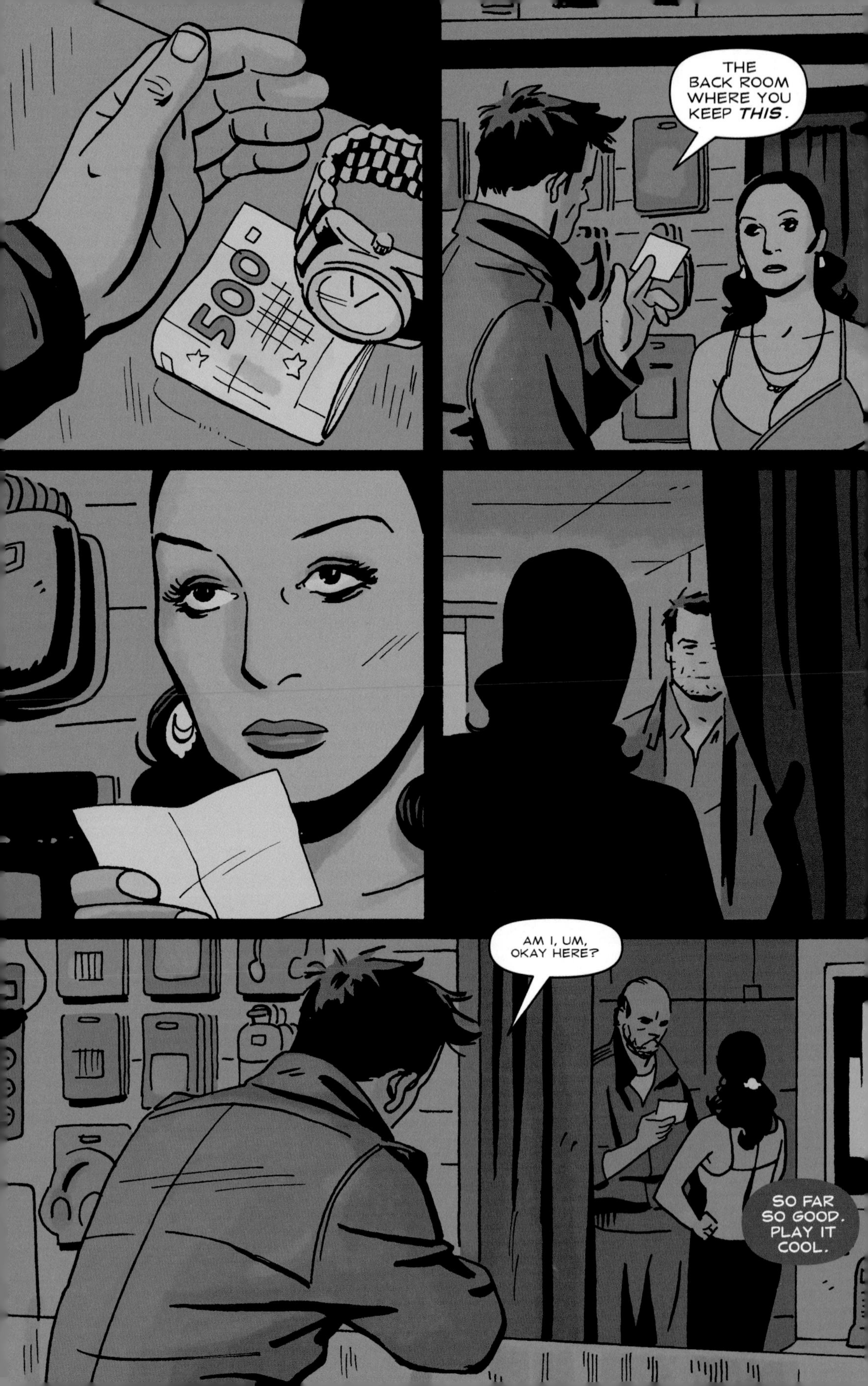
500
THE BACK ROOM WHERE YOU KEEP *THIS*.
AM I, UM, OKAY HERE?
SO FAR SO GOOD. PLAY IT COOL.

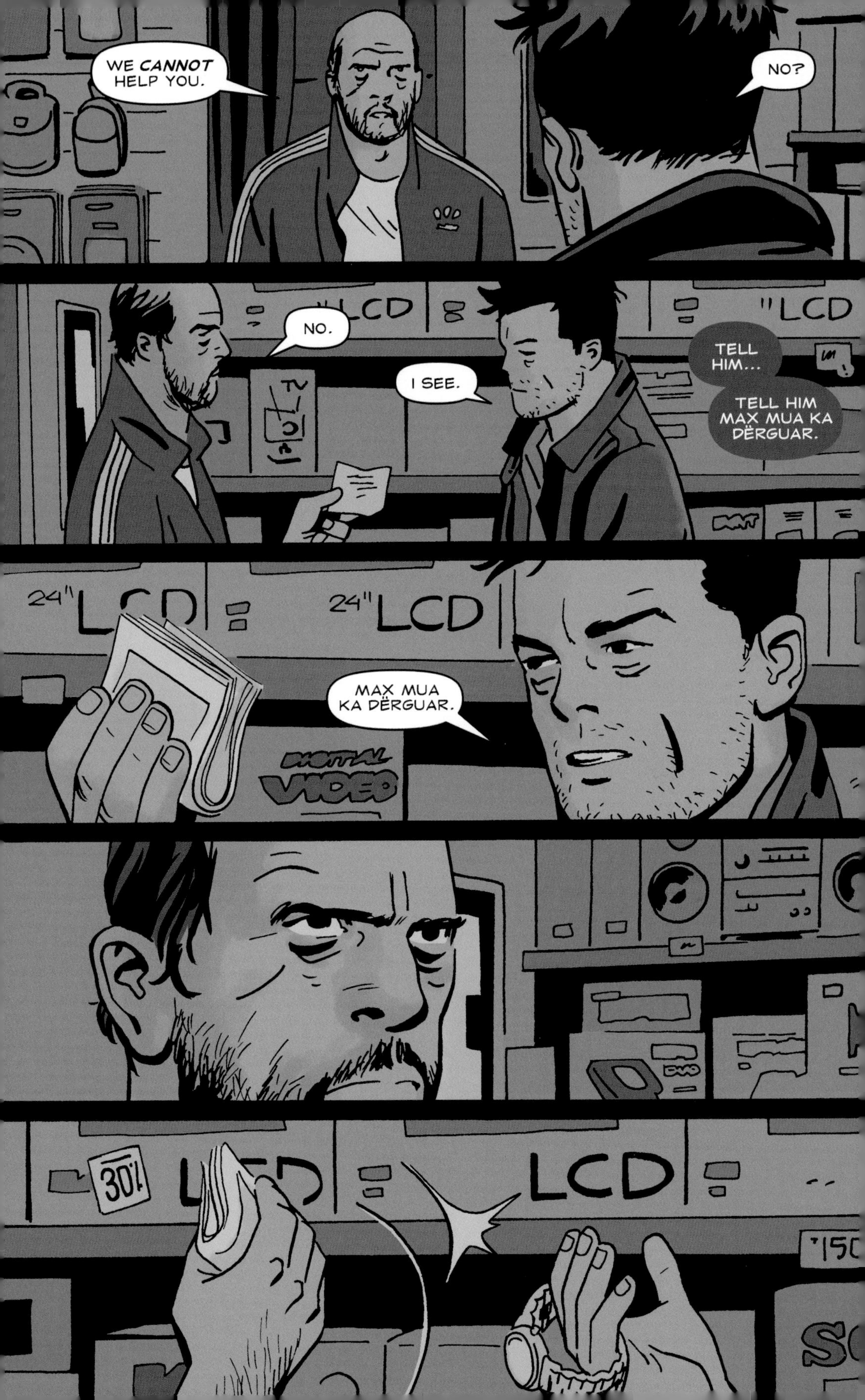
WE *CANNOT* HELP YOU.
NO?
"LCD
"LCD
NO.
I SEE.
TV
TELL HIM...
TELL HIM MAX MUA KA DËRGUAR.
24" LCD
24" LCD
MAX MUA KA DËRGUAR.
LCD

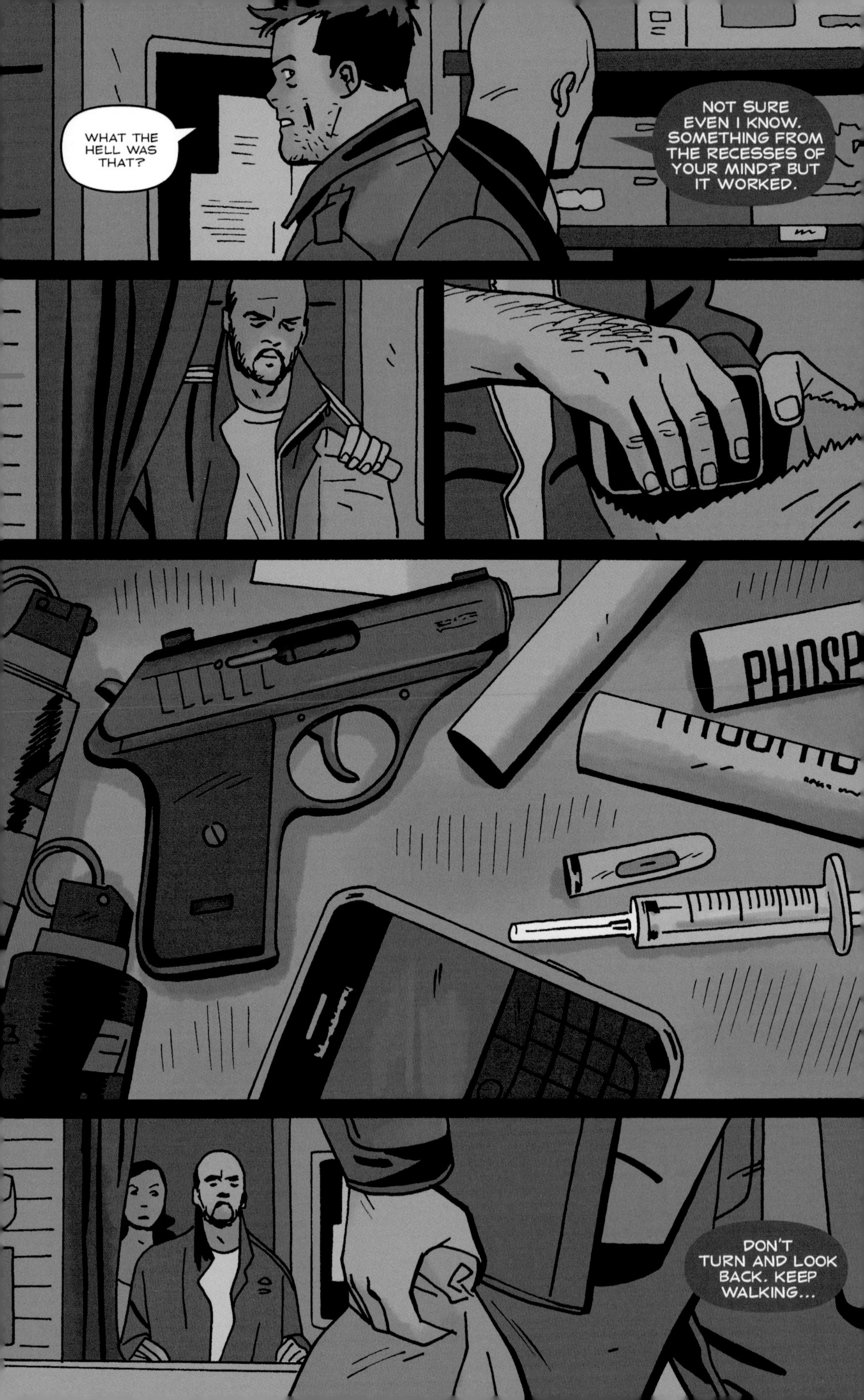
WHAT THE HELL WAS THAT?
NOT SURE EVEN I KNOW. SOMETHING FROM THE RECESSES OF YOUR MIND? BUT IT WORKED.
PHOSP
DON'T TURN AND LOOK BACK. KEEP WALKING...

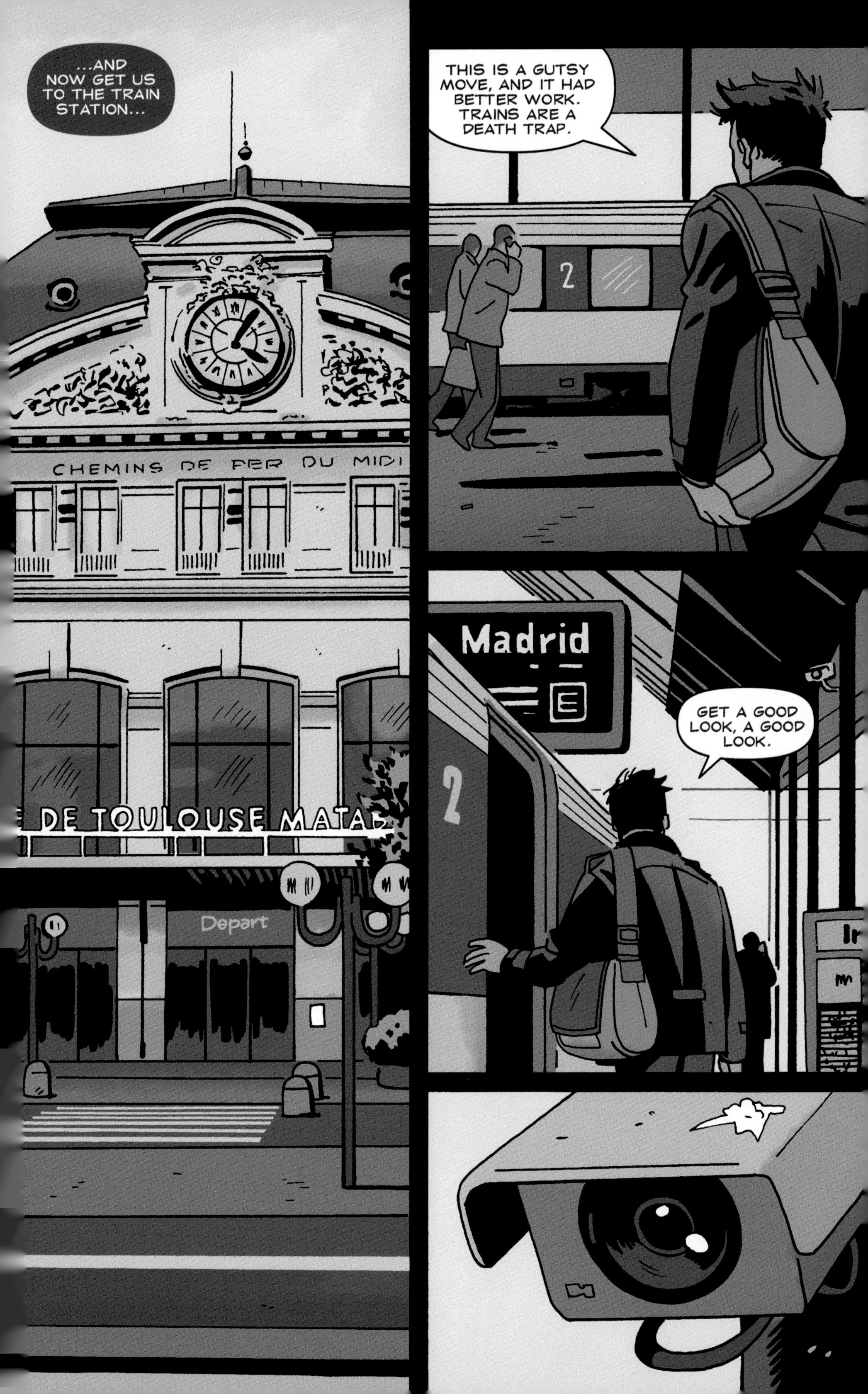
...AND NOW GET US TO THE TRAIN STATION...
CHEMINS DE FER DU MIDI
DE TOULOUSE MATAB
Depart
THIS IS A GUTSY MOVE, AND IT HAD BETTER WORK. TRAINS ARE A DEATH TRAP.
2
Madrid
2
GET A GOOD LOOK, A GOOD LOOK.

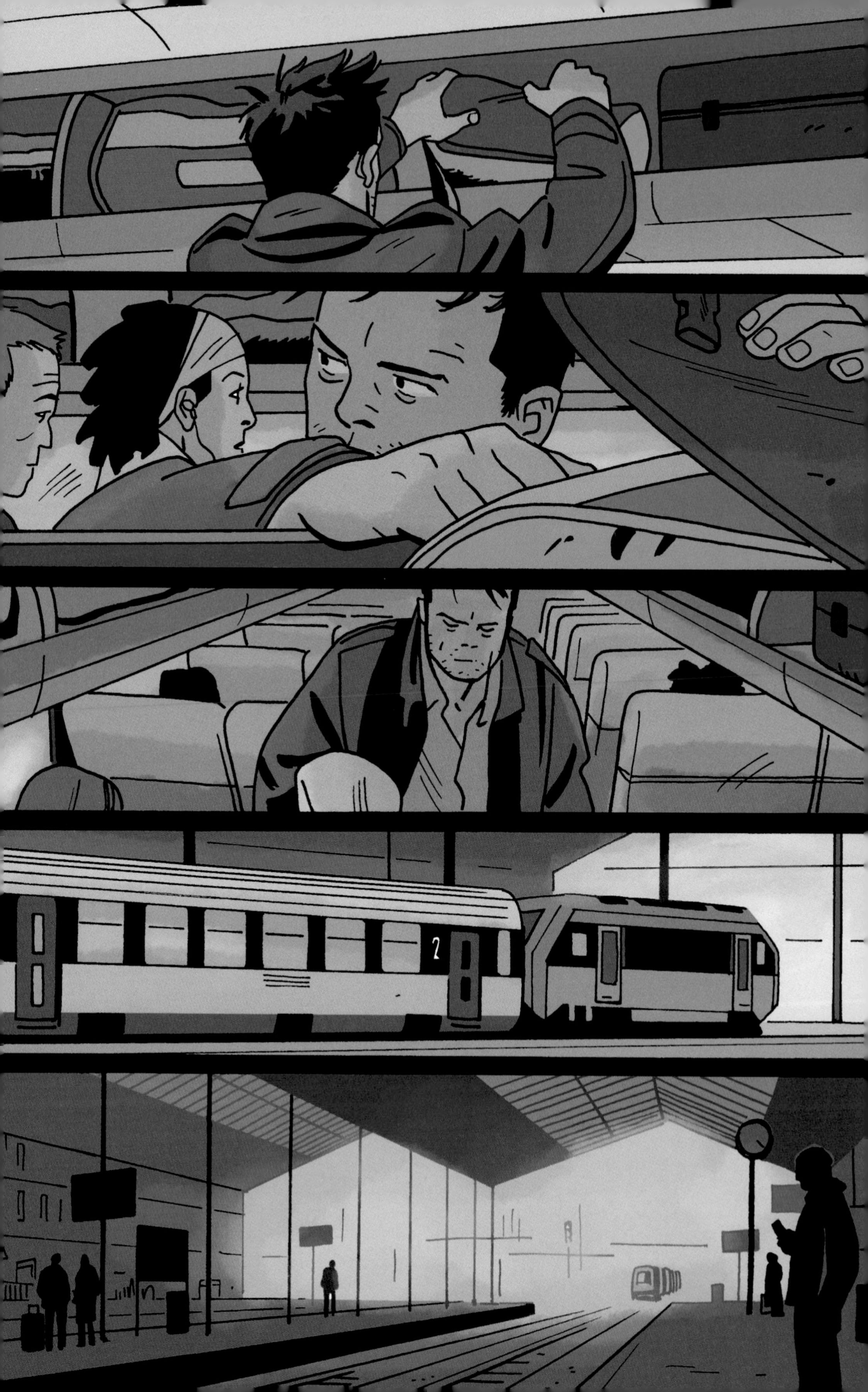
2

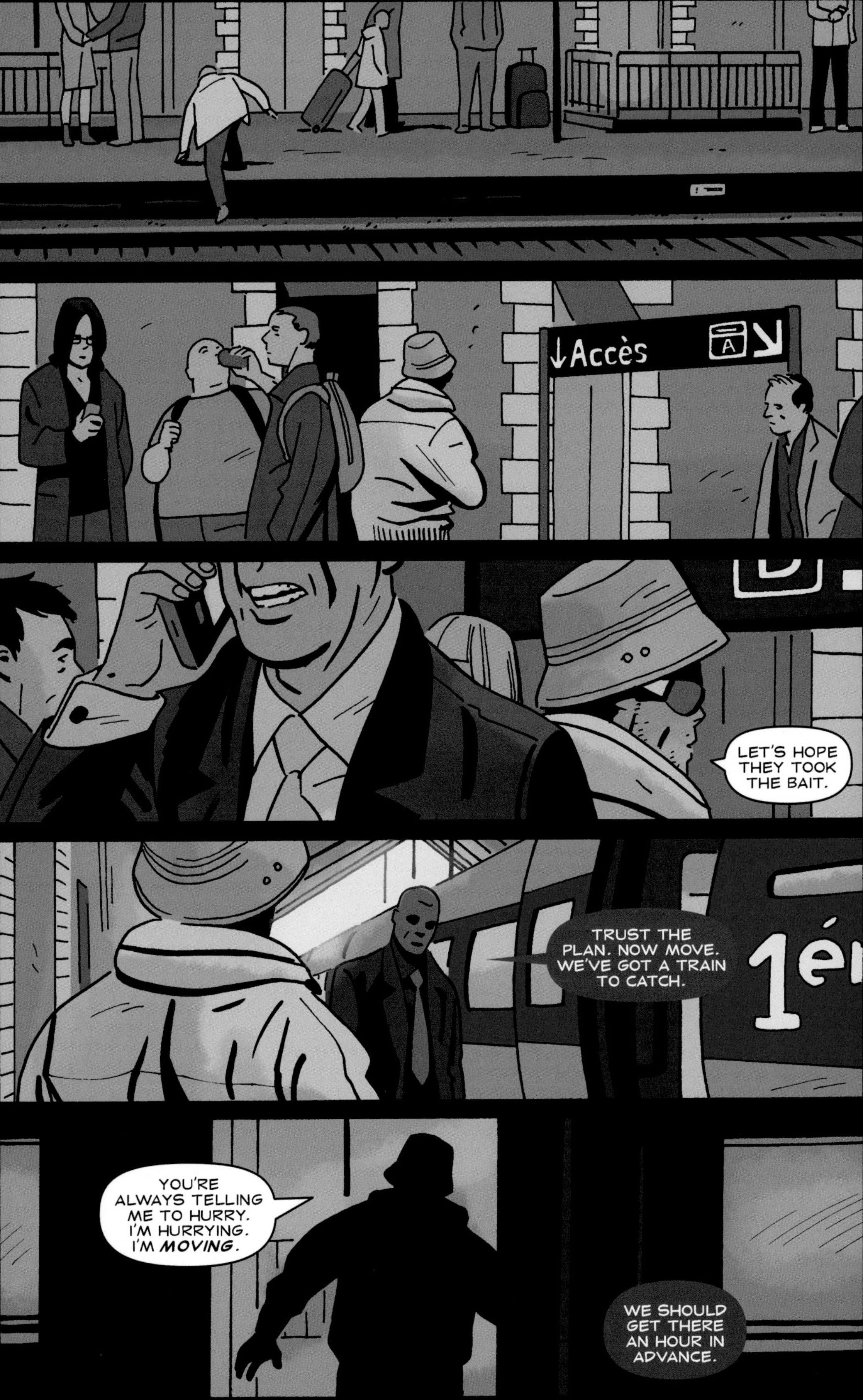

↓Accès
A
LET'S HOPE THEY TOOK THE BAIT.
TRUST THE PLAN. NOW MOVE. WE'VE GOT A TRAIN TO CATCH.
1ér
YOU'RE ALWAYS TELLING ME TO HURRY. I'M HURRYING. I'M *MOVING*.
WE SHOULD GET THERE AN HOUR IN ADVANCE.

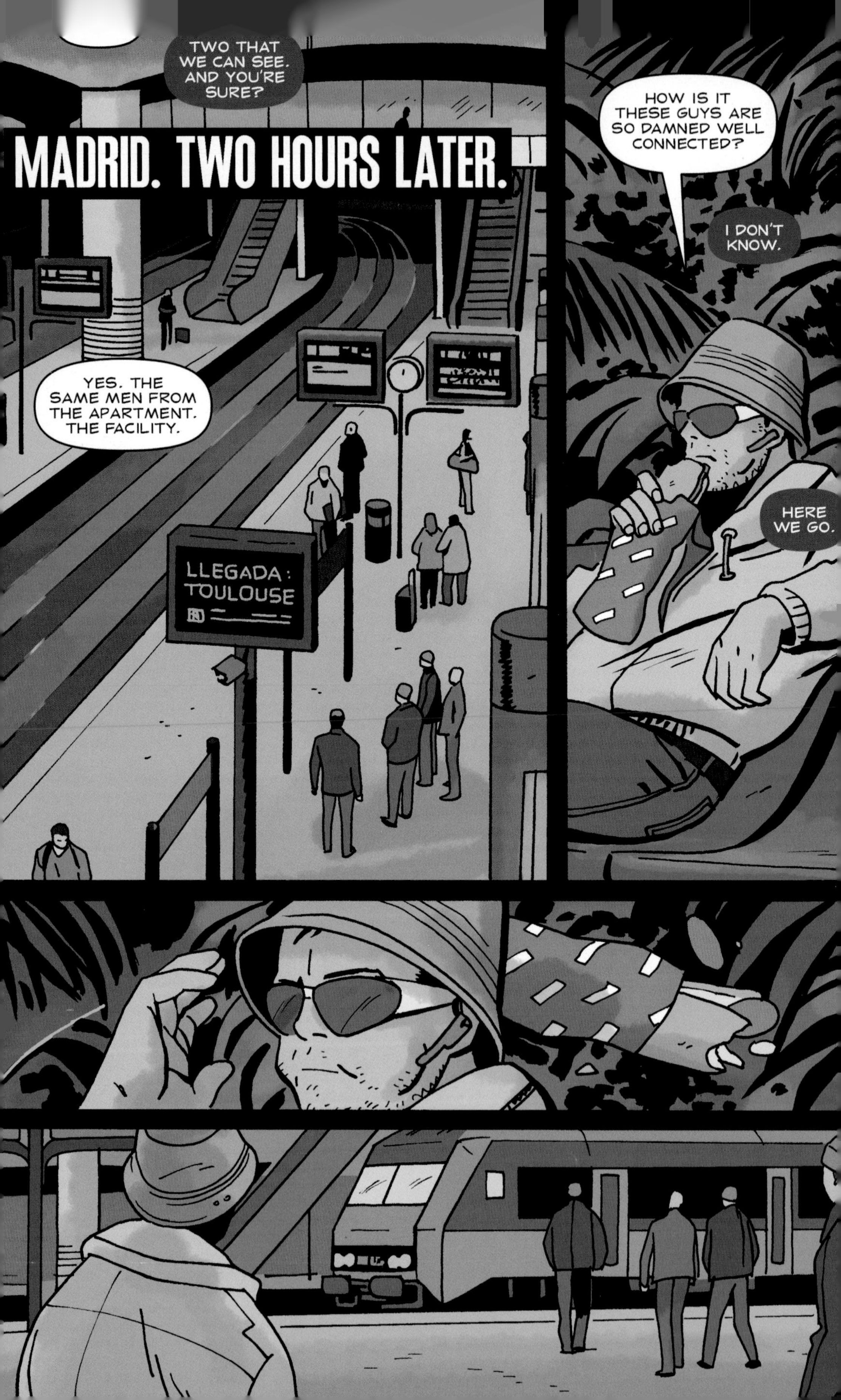
TWO THAT WE CAN SEE. AND YOU'RE SURE?
MADRID. TWO HOURS LATER.
YES. THE SAME MEN FROM THE APARTMENT. THE FACILITY.
LLEGADA: TOULOUSE
HOW IS IT THESE GUYS ARE SO DAMNED WELL CONNECTED?
I DON'T KNOW.
HERE WE GO.

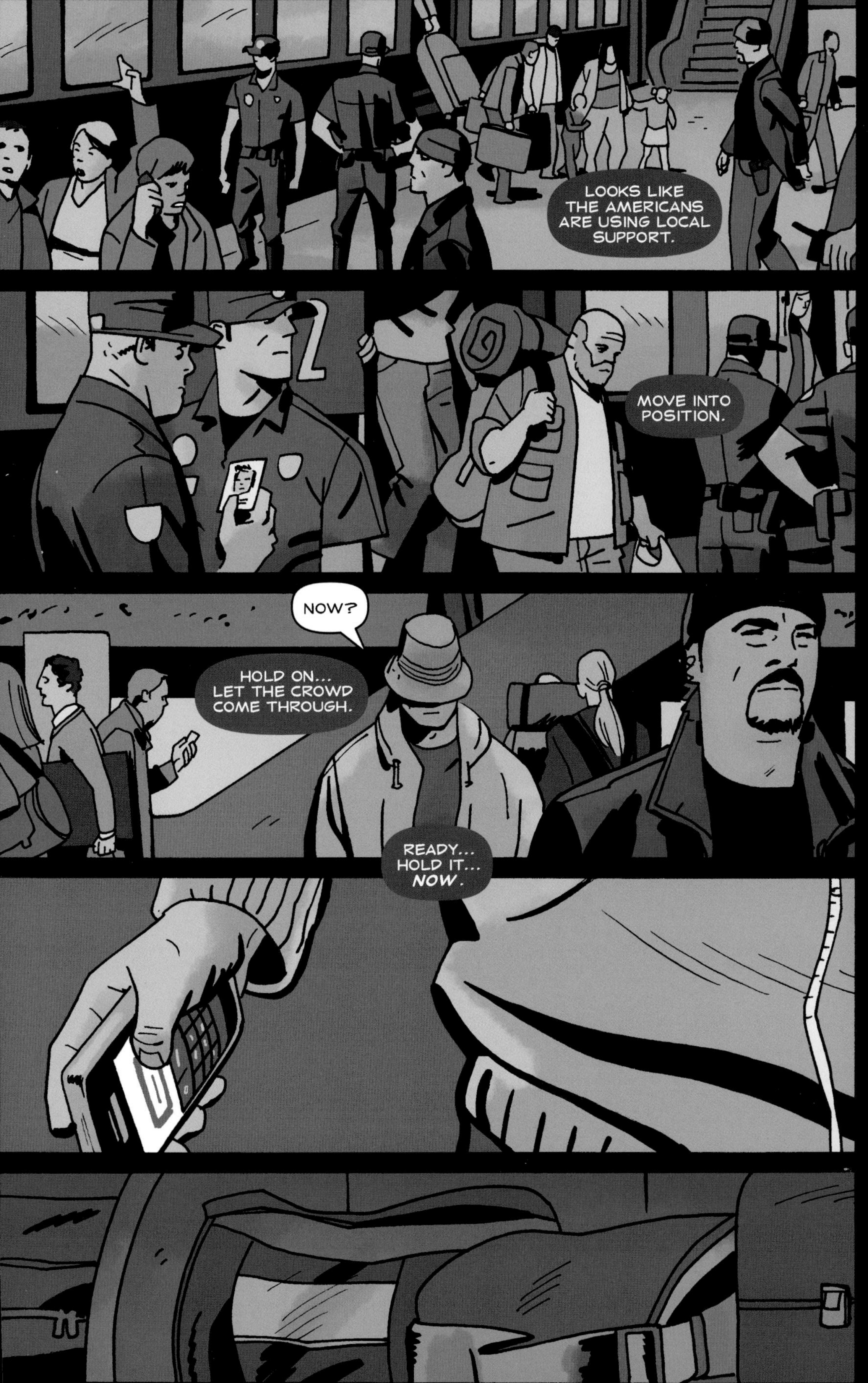
LOOKS LIKE THE AMERICANS ARE USING LOCAL SUPPORT.
MOVE INTO POSITION.
NOW?
HOLD ON... LET THE CROWD COME THROUGH.
READY... HOLD IT... NOW.

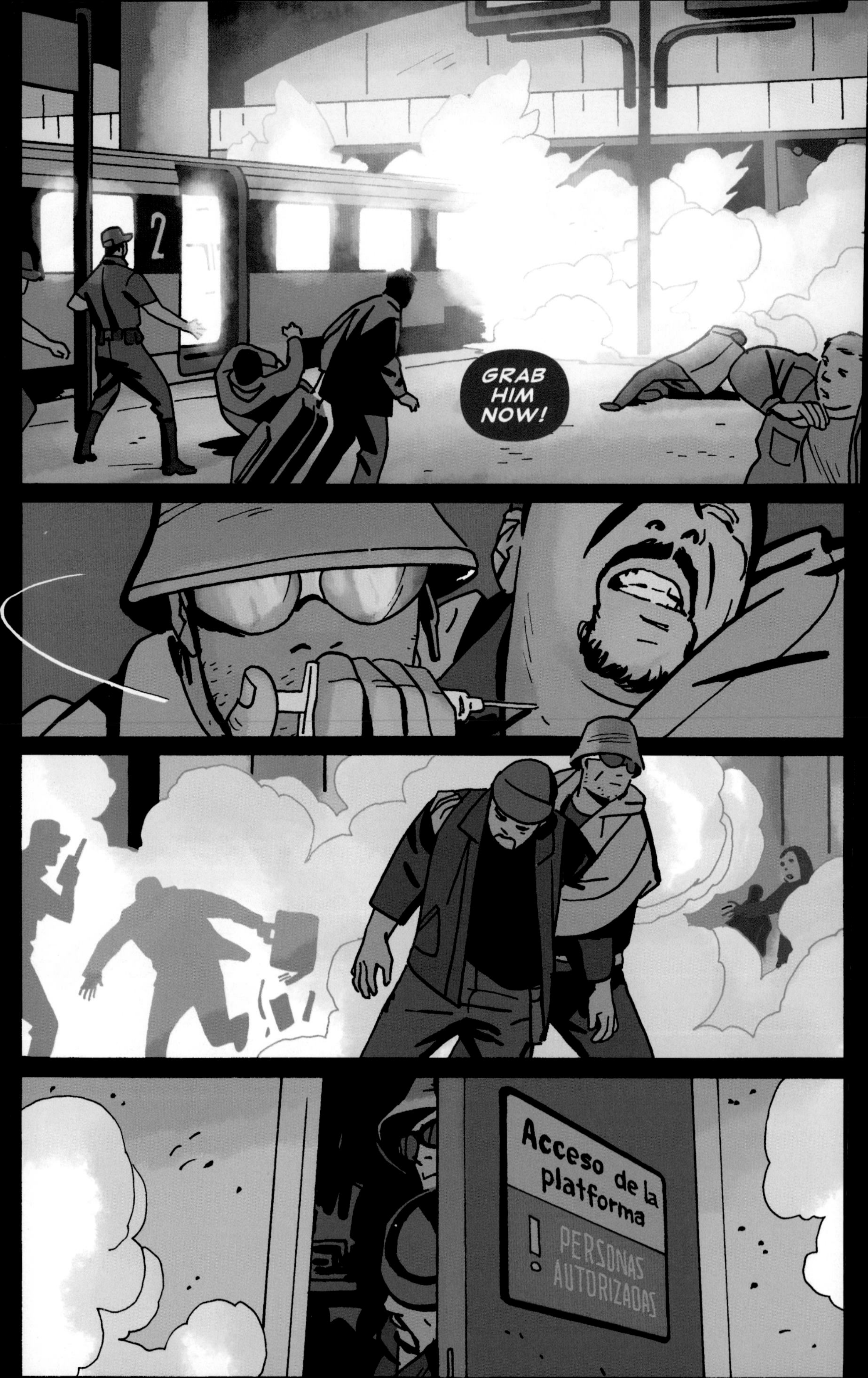

2
GRAB HIM NOW!
Acceso de la platforma
!
PERSONAS AUTORIZADAS

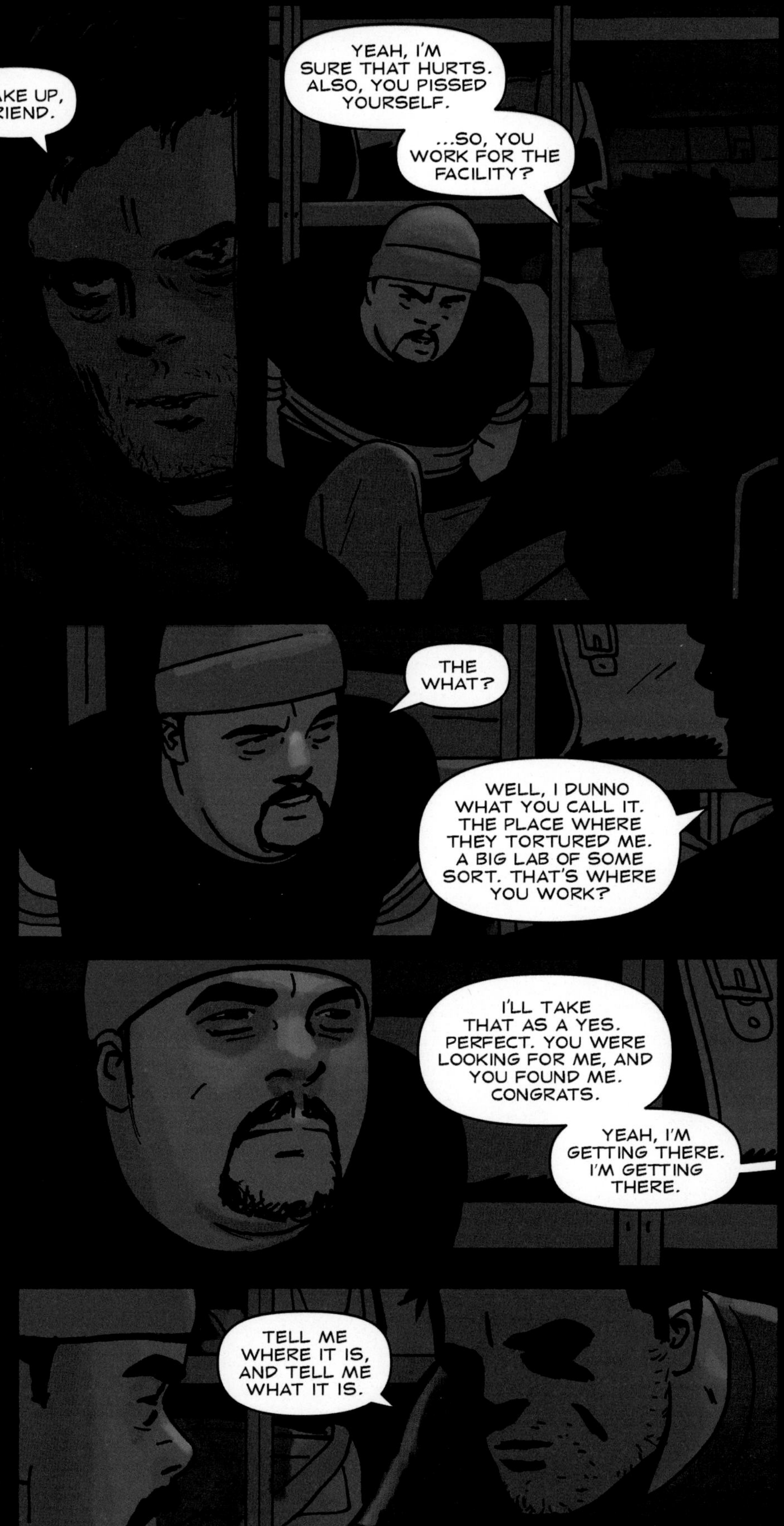
WAKE UP, FRIEND.
YEAH, I'M SURE THAT HURTS. ALSO, YOU PISSED YOURSELF.
...SO, YOU WORK FOR THE FACILITY?
THE WHAT?
WELL, I DUNNO WHAT YOU CALL IT. THE PLACE WHERE THEY TORTURED ME. A BIG LAB OF SOME SORT. THAT'S WHERE YOU WORK?
I'LL TAKE THAT AS A YES. PERFECT. YOU WERE LOOKING FOR ME, AND YOU FOUND ME. CONGRATS.
YEAH, I'M GETTING THERE. I'M GETTING THERE.
TELL ME WHERE IT IS, AND TELL ME WHAT IT IS.

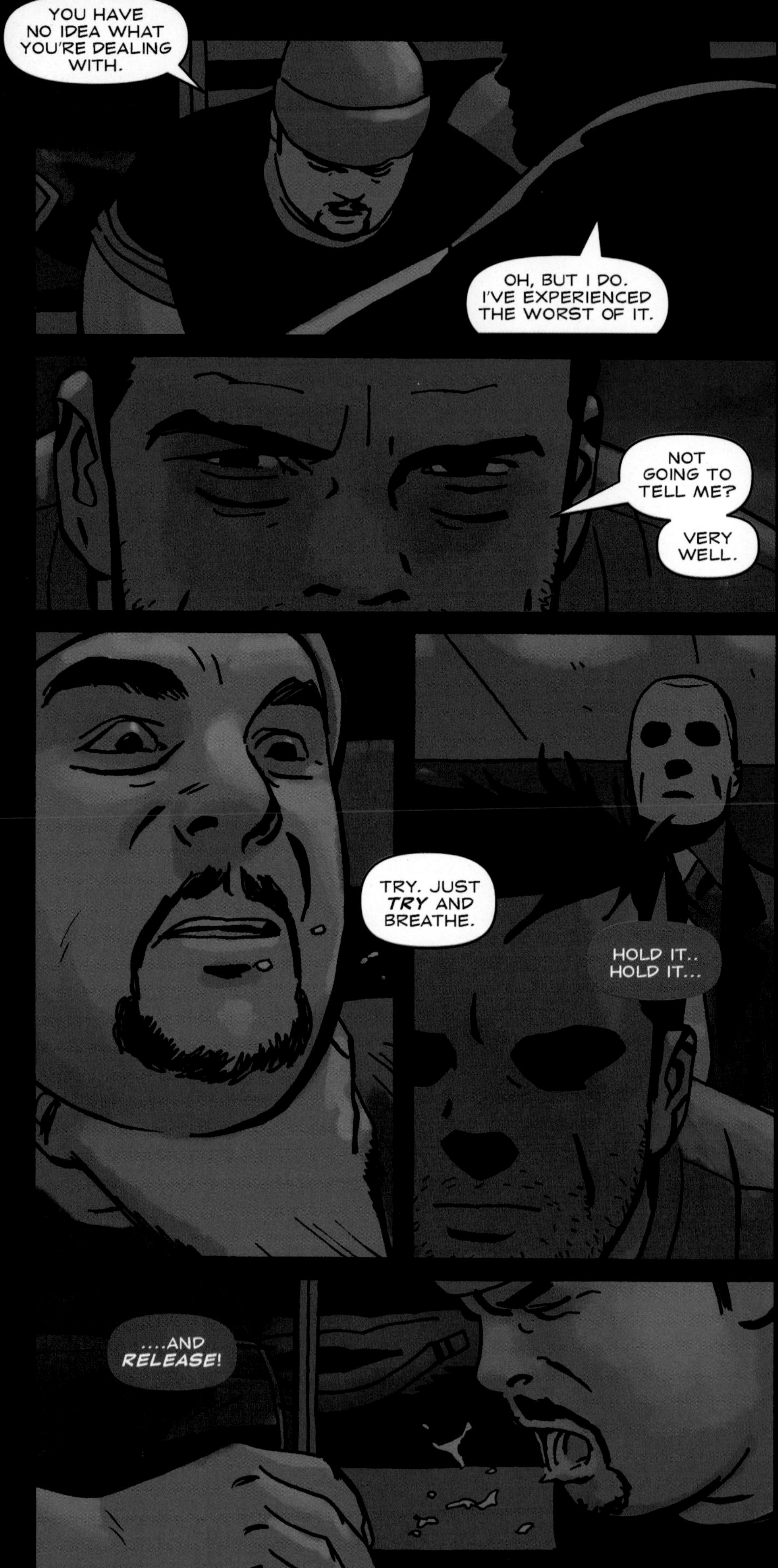
YOU HAVE NO IDEA WHAT YOU'RE DEALING WITH.
OH, BUT I DO. I'VE EXPERIENCED THE WORST OF IT.
NOT GOING TO TELL ME?
VERY WELL.
TRY. JUST *TRY* AND BREATHE.
HOLD IT.. HOLD IT...
....AND *RELEASE*!

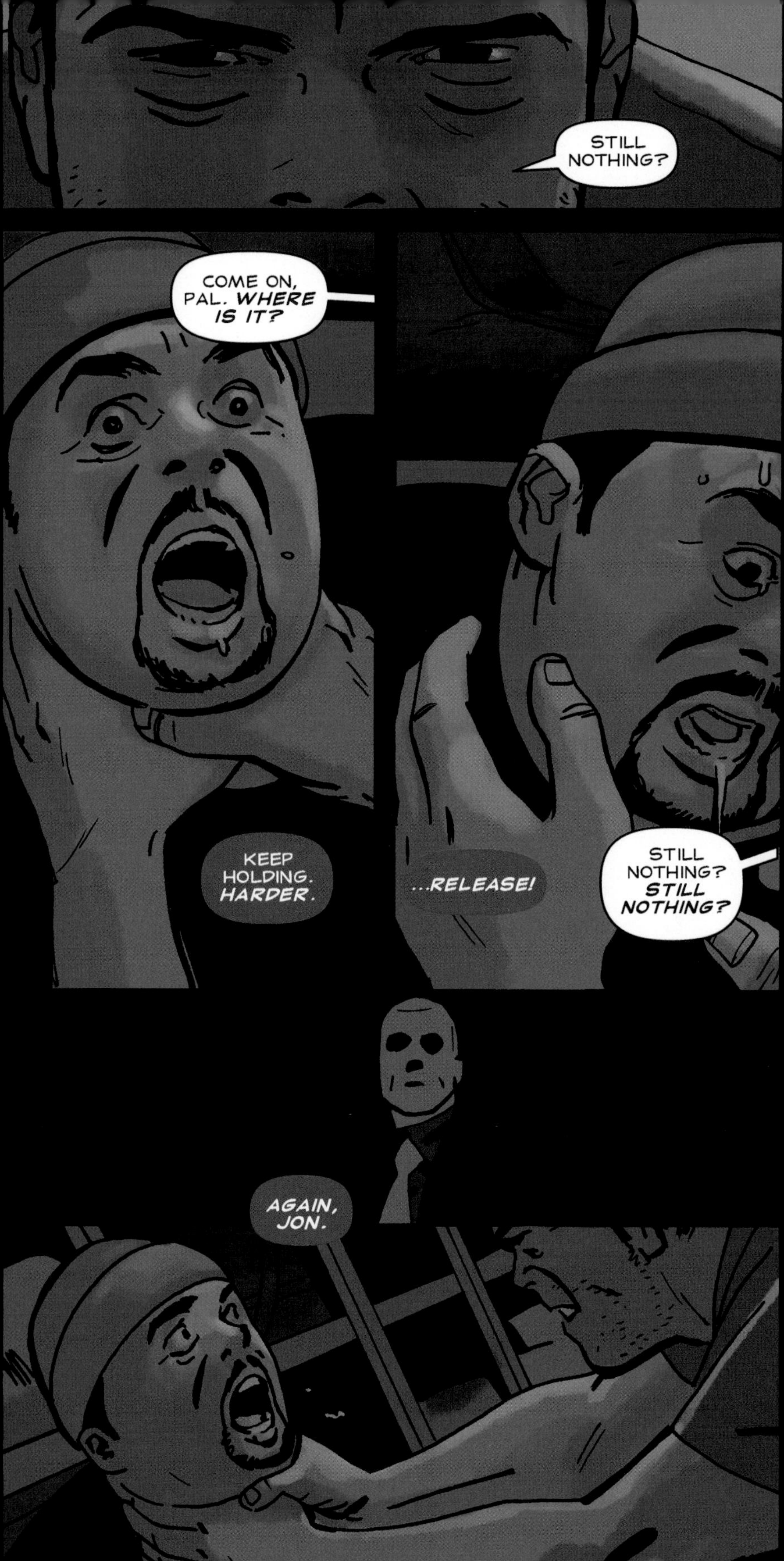
STILL NOTHING?
COME ON, PAL. WHERE IS IT?
KEEP HOLDING. HARDER.
...RELEASE!
STILL NOTHING? STILL NOTHING?
AGAIN, JON.

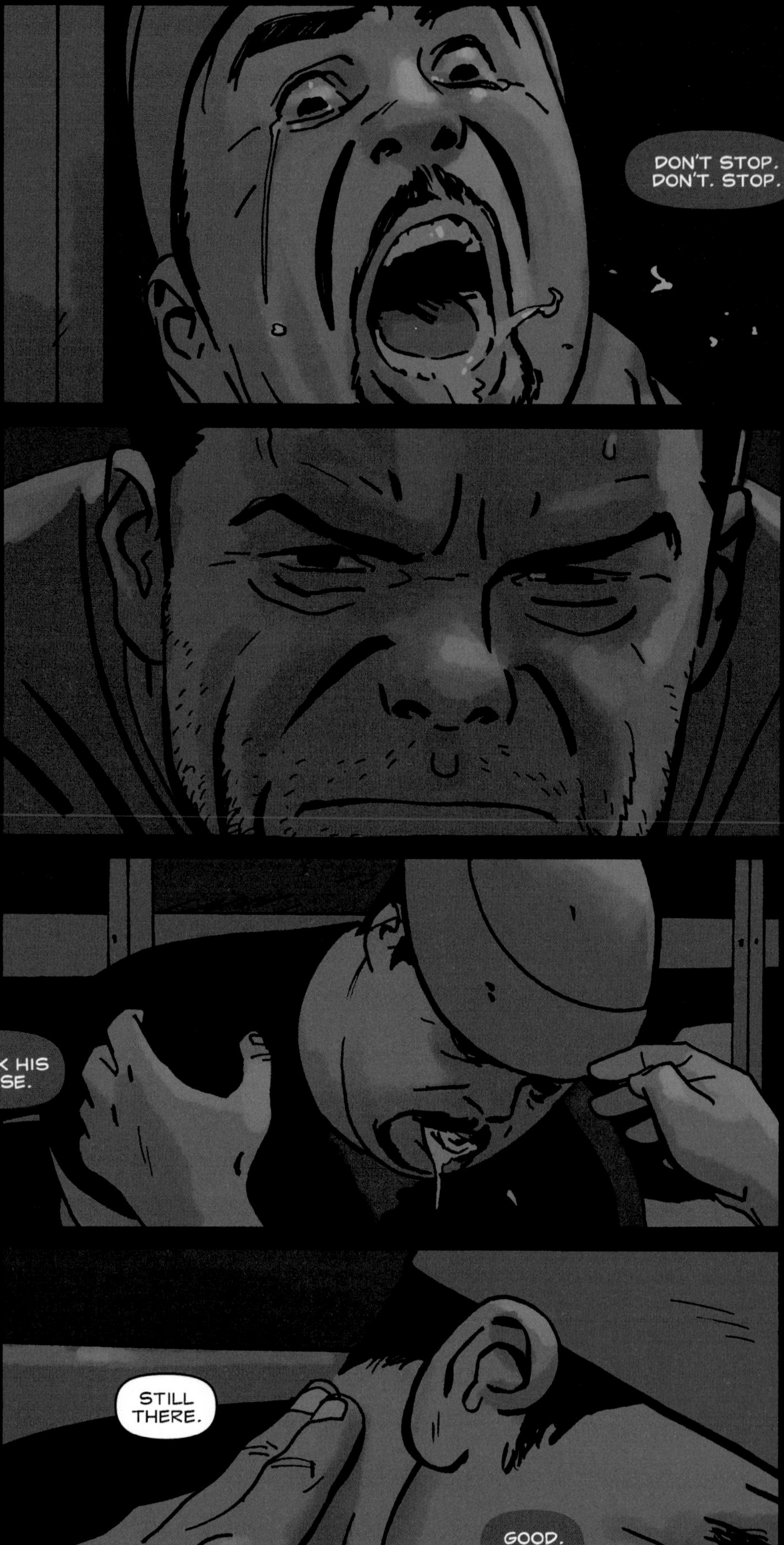
DON'T STOP.
DON'T. STOP.
CHECK HIS PULSE.
STILL THERE.
GOOD. DO IT.

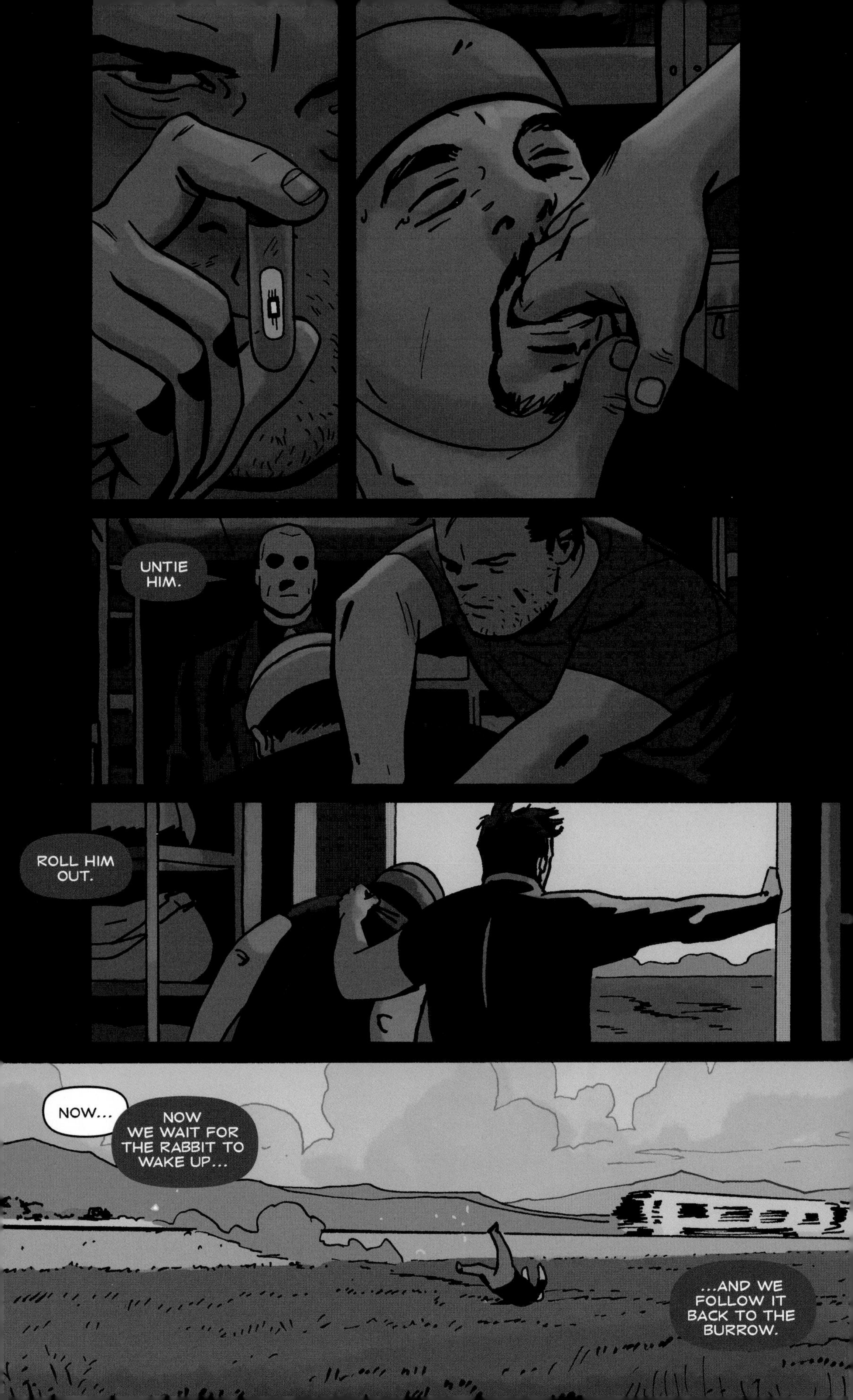
UNTIE HIM.
ROLL HIM OUT.
NOW...
NOW WE WAIT FOR THE RABBIT TO WAKE UP...
...AND WE FOLLOW IT BACK TO THE BURROW.

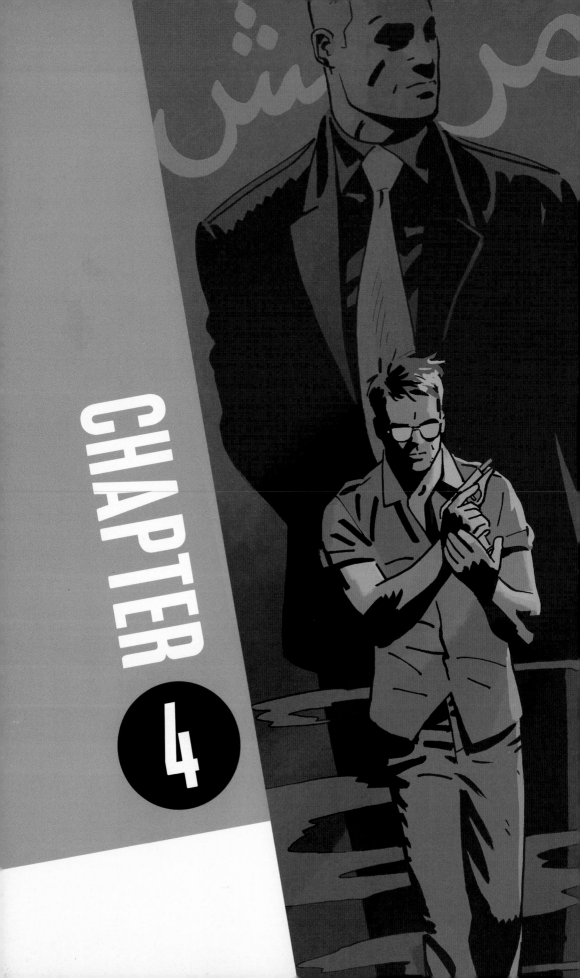

CHAPTER 4

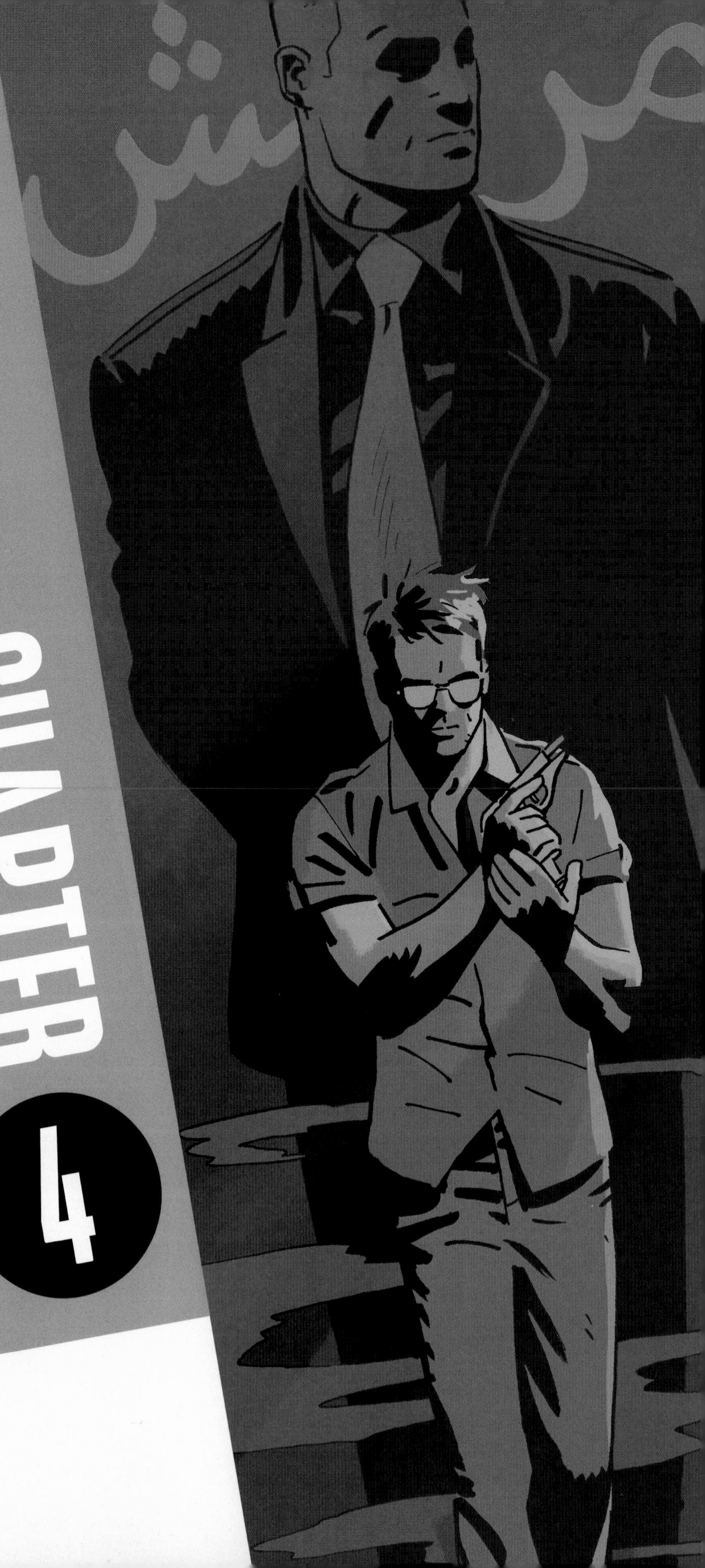

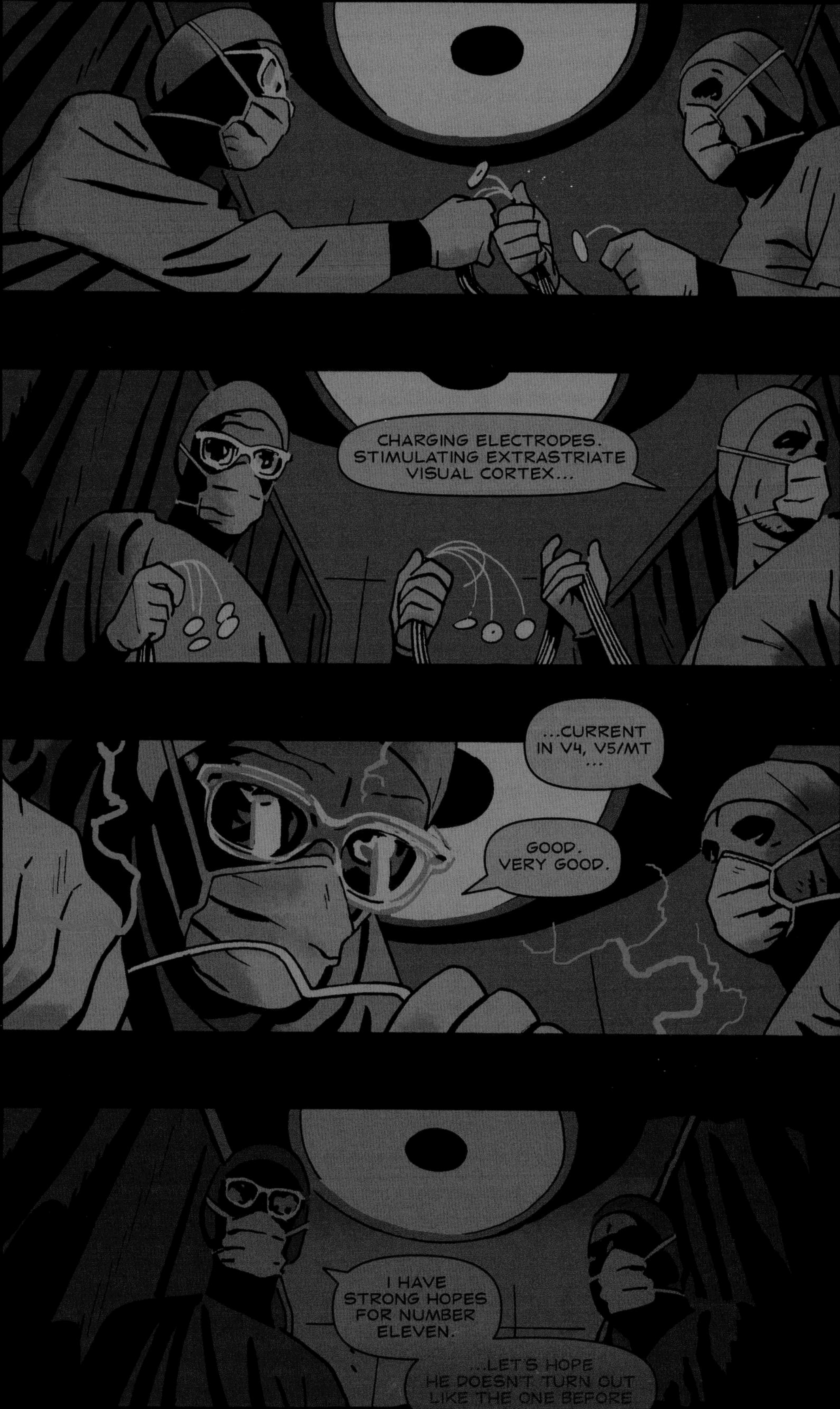
CHARGING ELECTRODES. STIMULATING EXTRASTRIATE VISUAL CORTEX...
...CURRENT IN V4, V5/MT ...
GOOD. VERY GOOD.
I HAVE STRONG HOPES FOR NUMBER ELEVEN.
...LET'S HOPE HE DOESN'T TURN OUT LIKE THE ONE BEFORE

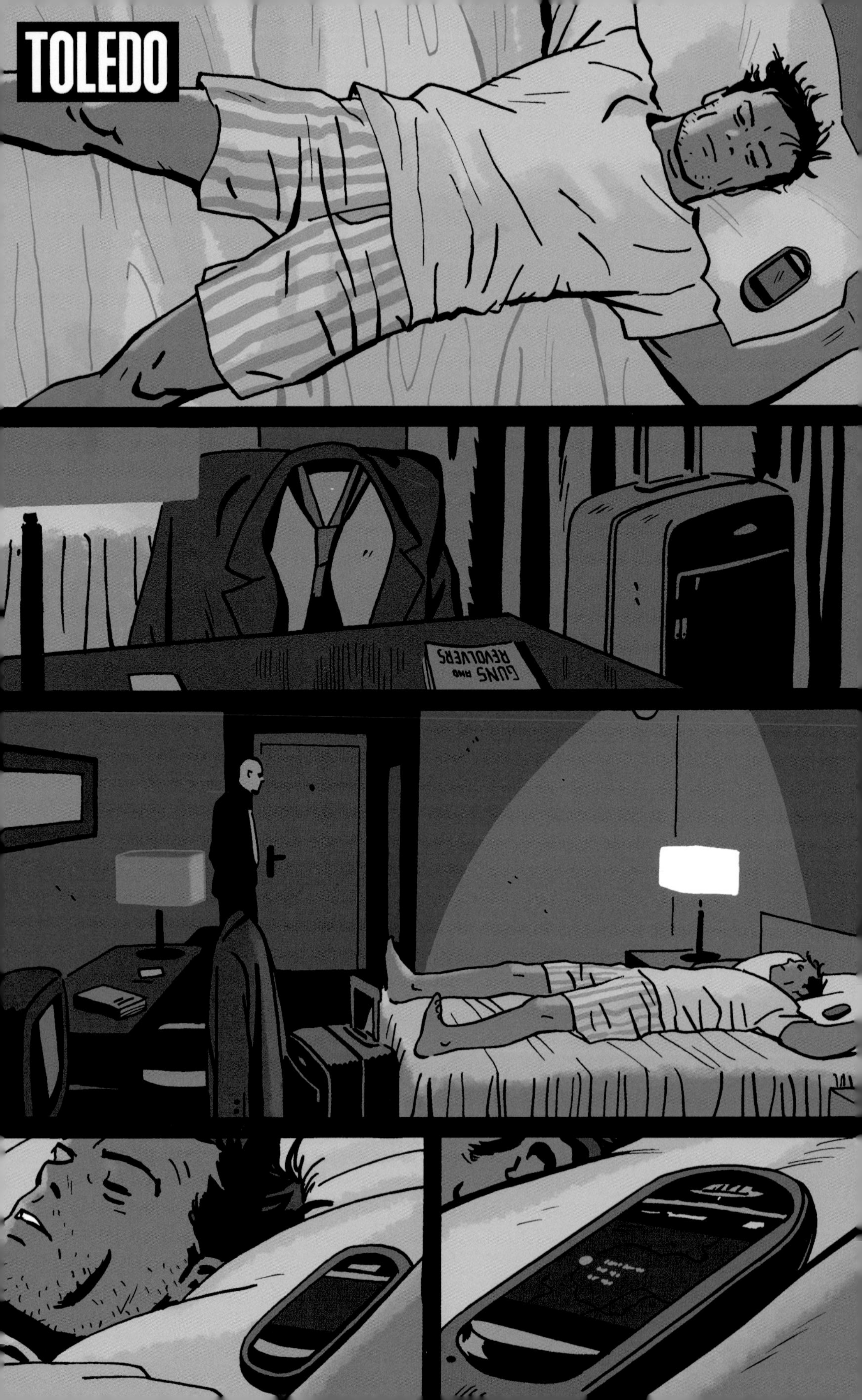
TOLEDO
GUNS AND REVOLVERS

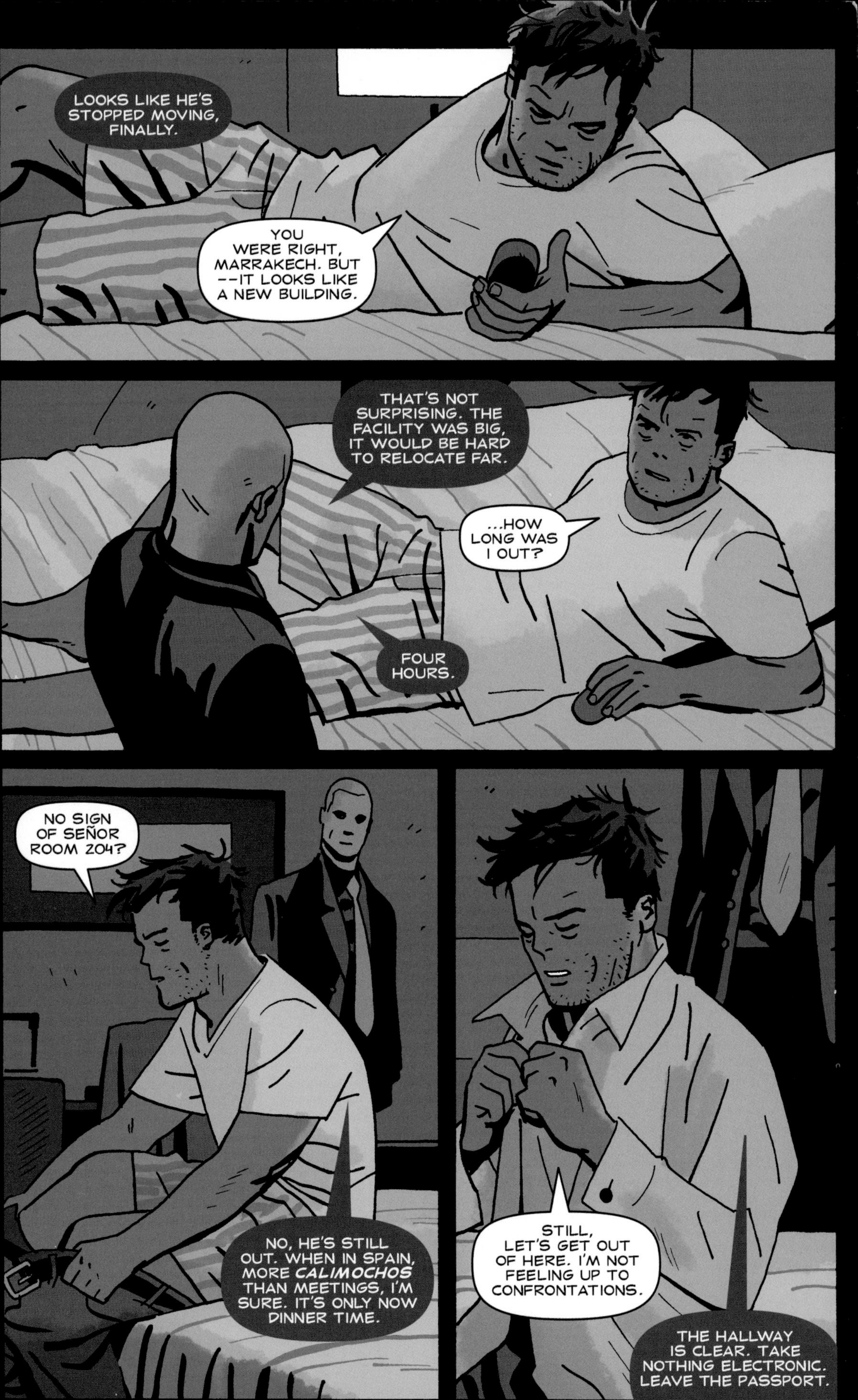
LOOKS LIKE HE'S STOPPED MOVING, FINALLY.
YOU WERE RIGHT, MARRAKECH. BUT --IT LOOKS LIKE A NEW BUILDING.
THAT'S NOT SURPRISING. THE FACILITY WAS BIG, IT WOULD BE HARD TO RELOCATE FAR.
...HOW LONG WAS I OUT?
FOUR HOURS.
NO SIGN OF SEÑOR ROOM 204?
NO, HE'S STILL OUT. WHEN IN SPAIN, MORE *CALIMOCHOS* THAN MEETINGS, I'M SURE. IT'S ONLY NOW DINNER TIME.
STILL, LET'S GET OUT OF HERE. I'M NOT FEELING UP TO CONFRONTATIONS.
THE HALLWAY IS CLEAR. TAKE NOTHING ELECTRONIC. LEAVE THE PASSPORT.

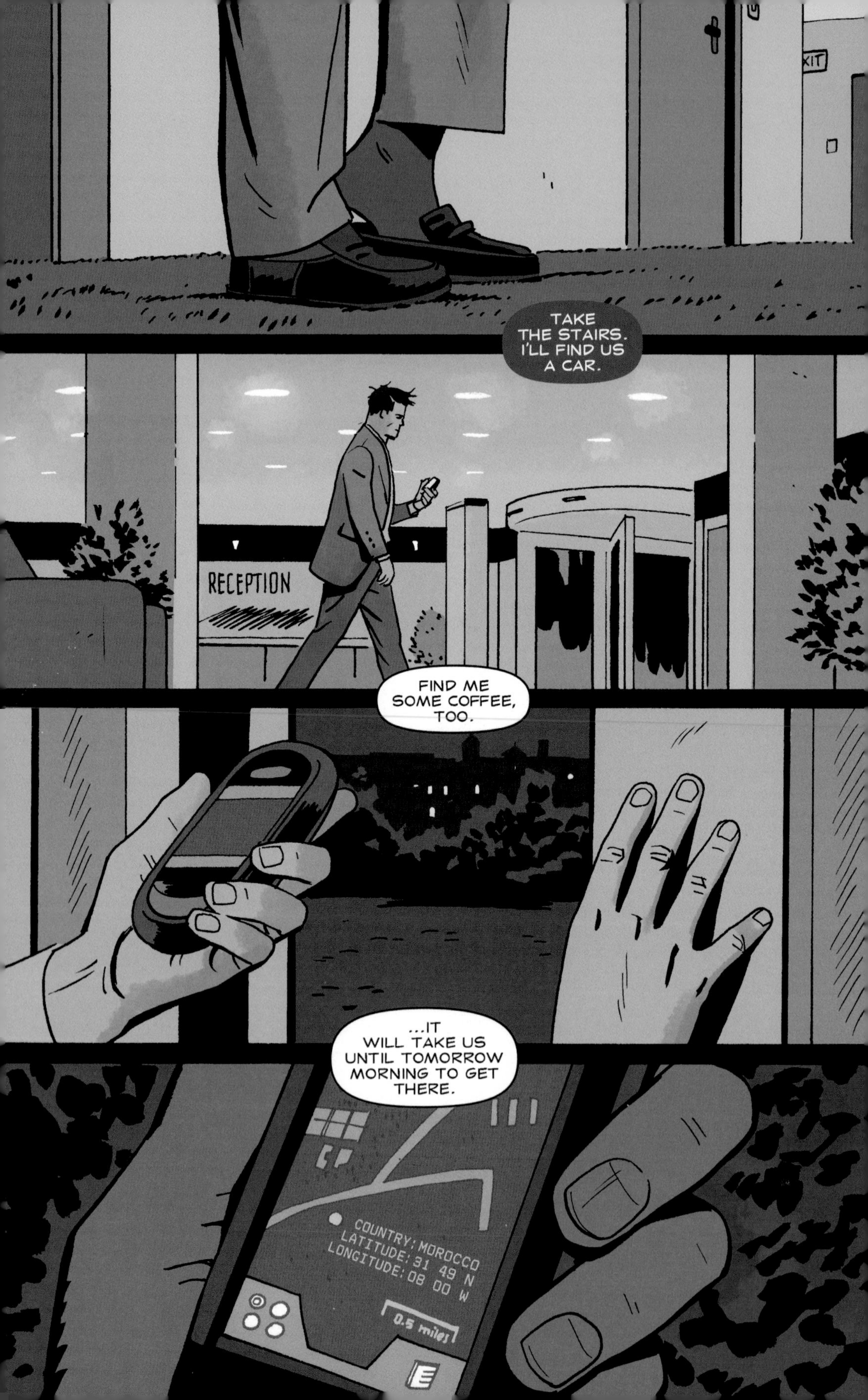
TAKE THE STAIRS. I'LL FIND US A CAR.
RECEPTION
FIND ME SOME COFFEE, TOO.
...IT WILL TAKE US UNTIL TOMORROW MORNING TO GET THERE.
COUNTRY: MOROCCO
LATITUDE: 31 49 N
LONGITUDE: 08 00 W
0.5 miles

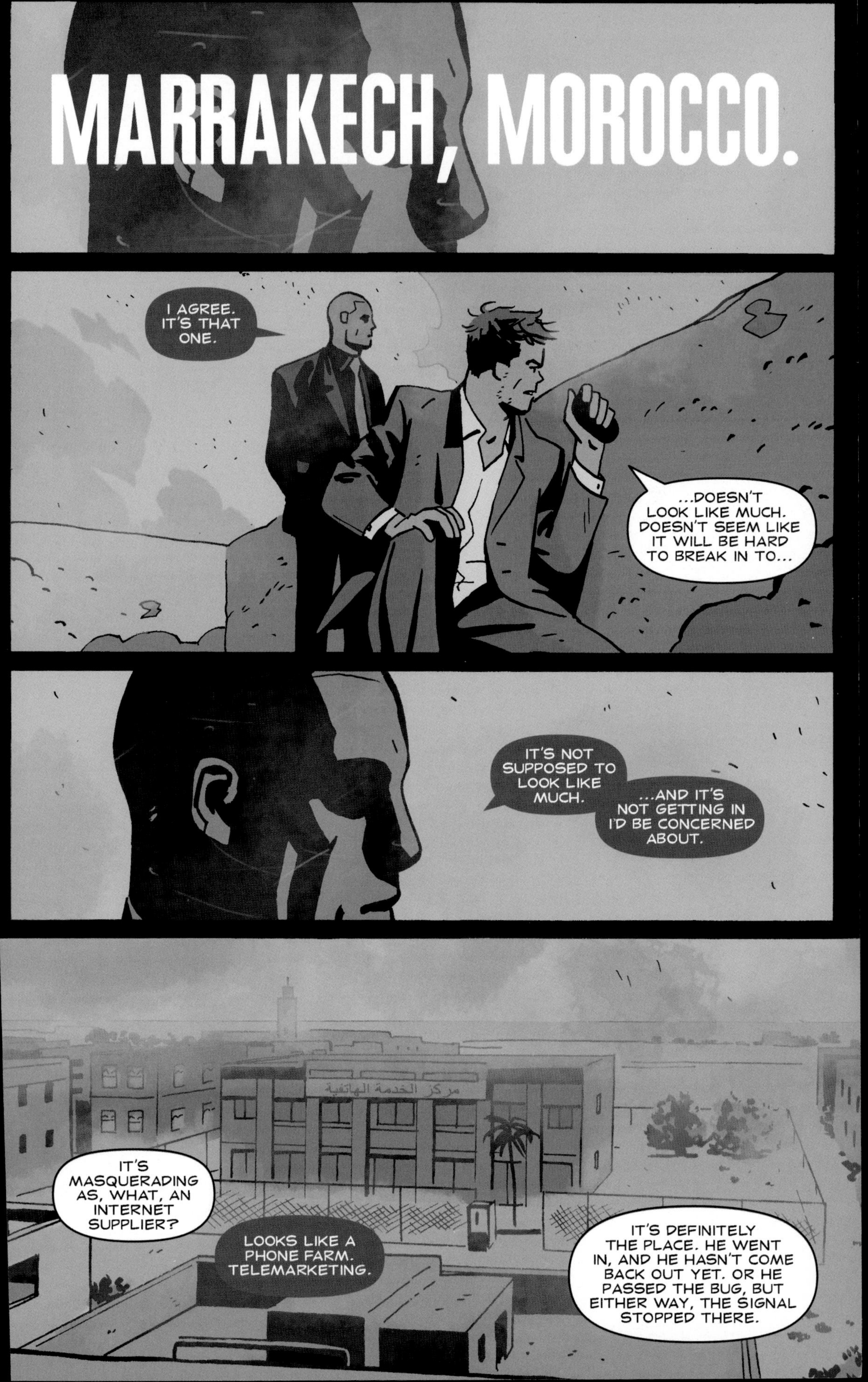
MARRAKECH, MOROCCO.
I AGREE. IT'S THAT ONE.
...DOESN'T LOOK LIKE MUCH. DOESN'T SEEM LIKE IT WILL BE HARD TO BREAK IN TO...
IT'S NOT SUPPOSED TO LOOK LIKE MUCH.
...AND IT'S NOT GETTING IN I'D BE CONCERNED ABOUT.
مركز الخدمة الهاتفية
IT'S MASQUERADING AS, WHAT, AN INTERNET SUPPLIER?
LOOKS LIKE A PHONE FARM. TELEMARKETING.
IT'S DEFINITELY THE PLACE. HE WENT IN, AND HE HASN'T COME BACK OUT YET. OR HE PASSED THE BUG, BUT EITHER WAY, THE SIGNAL STOPPED THERE.

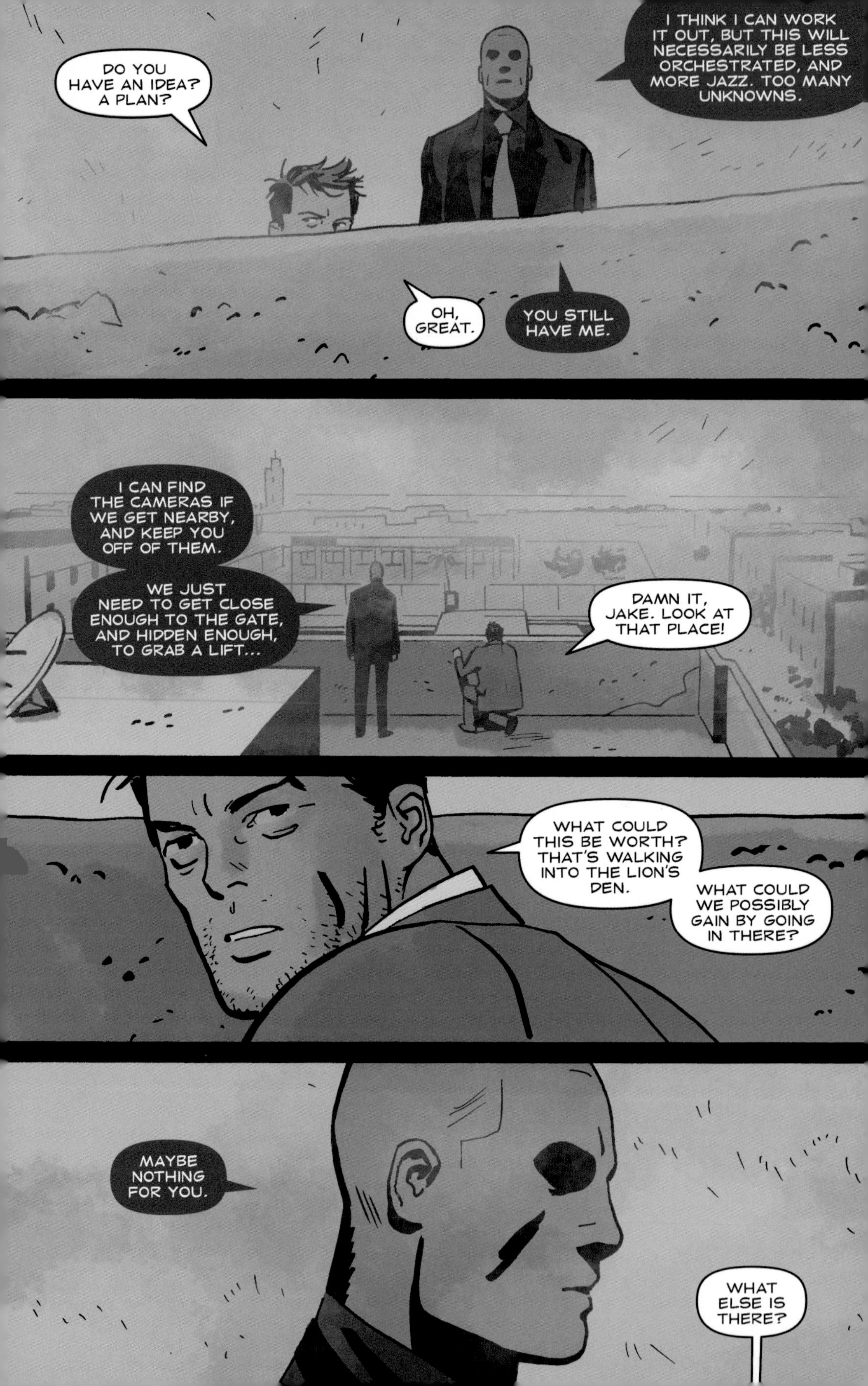
DO YOU HAVE AN IDEA? A PLAN?
I THINK I CAN WORK IT OUT, BUT THIS WILL NECESSARILY BE LESS ORCHESTRATED, AND MORE JAZZ. TOO MANY UNKNOWNS.
OH, GREAT.
YOU STILL HAVE ME.
I CAN FIND THE CAMERAS IF WE GET NEARBY, AND KEEP YOU OFF OF THEM.
WE JUST NEED TO GET CLOSE ENOUGH TO THE GATE, AND HIDDEN ENOUGH, TO GRAB A LIFT...
DAMN IT, JAKE. LOOK AT THAT PLACE!
WHAT COULD THIS BE WORTH? THAT'S WALKING INTO THE LION'S DEN.
WHAT COULD WE POSSIBLY GAIN BY GOING IN THERE?
MAYBE NOTHING FOR YOU.
WHAT ELSE IS THERE?

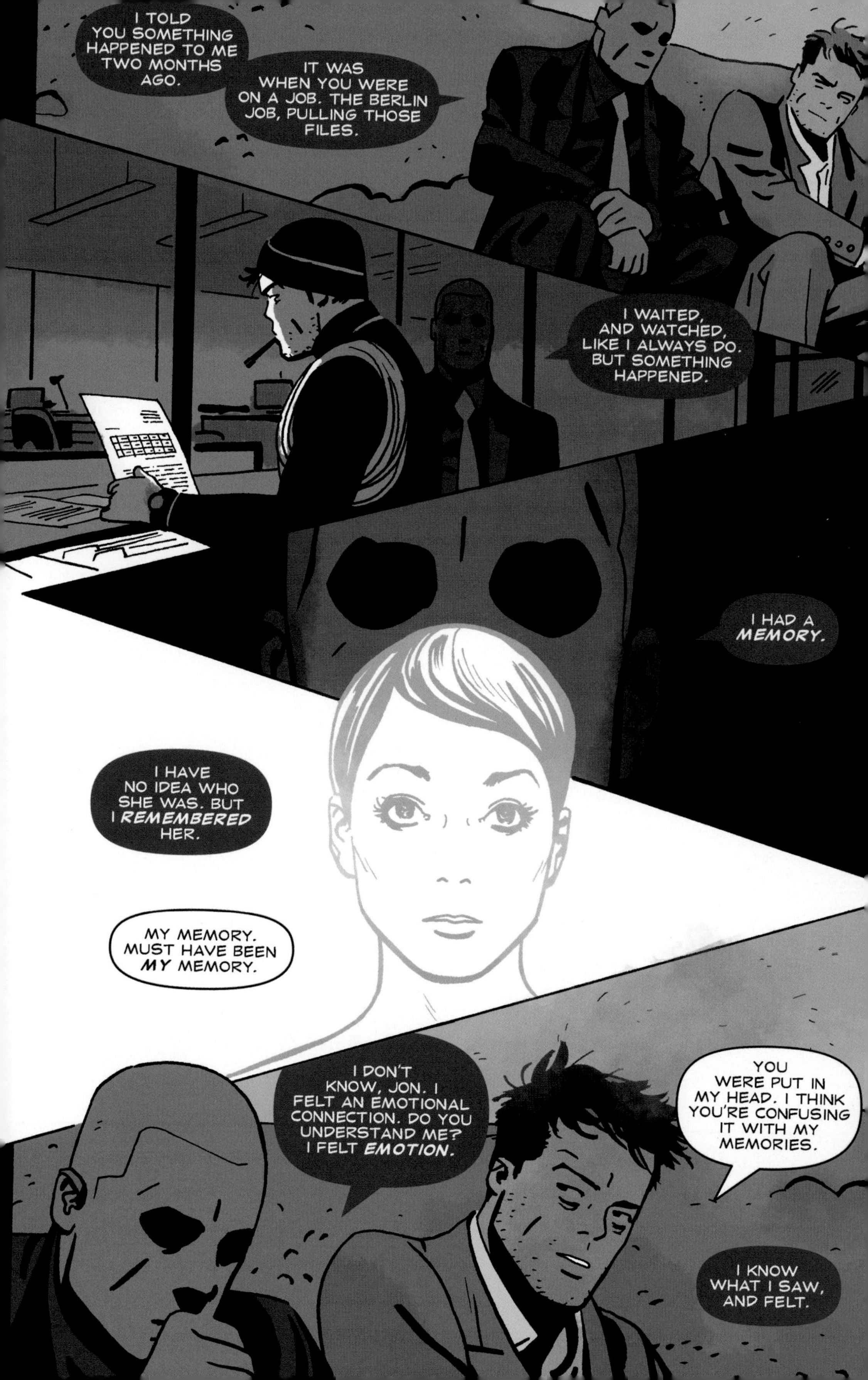
I TOLD YOU SOMETHING HAPPENED TO ME TWO MONTHS AGO.
IT WAS WHEN YOU WERE ON A JOB. THE BERLIN JOB, PULLING THOSE FILES.
I WAITED, AND WATCHED, LIKE I ALWAYS DO. BUT SOMETHING HAPPENED.
I HAD A MEMORY.
I HAVE NO IDEA WHO SHE WAS. BUT I REMEMBERED HER.
MY MEMORY. MUST HAVE BEEN MY MEMORY.
I DON'T KNOW, JON. I FELT AN EMOTIONAL CONNECTION. DO YOU UNDERSTAND ME? I FELT EMOTION.
YOU WERE PUT IN MY HEAD. I THINK YOU'RE CONFUSING IT WITH MY MEMORIES.
I KNOW WHAT I SAW, AND FELT.

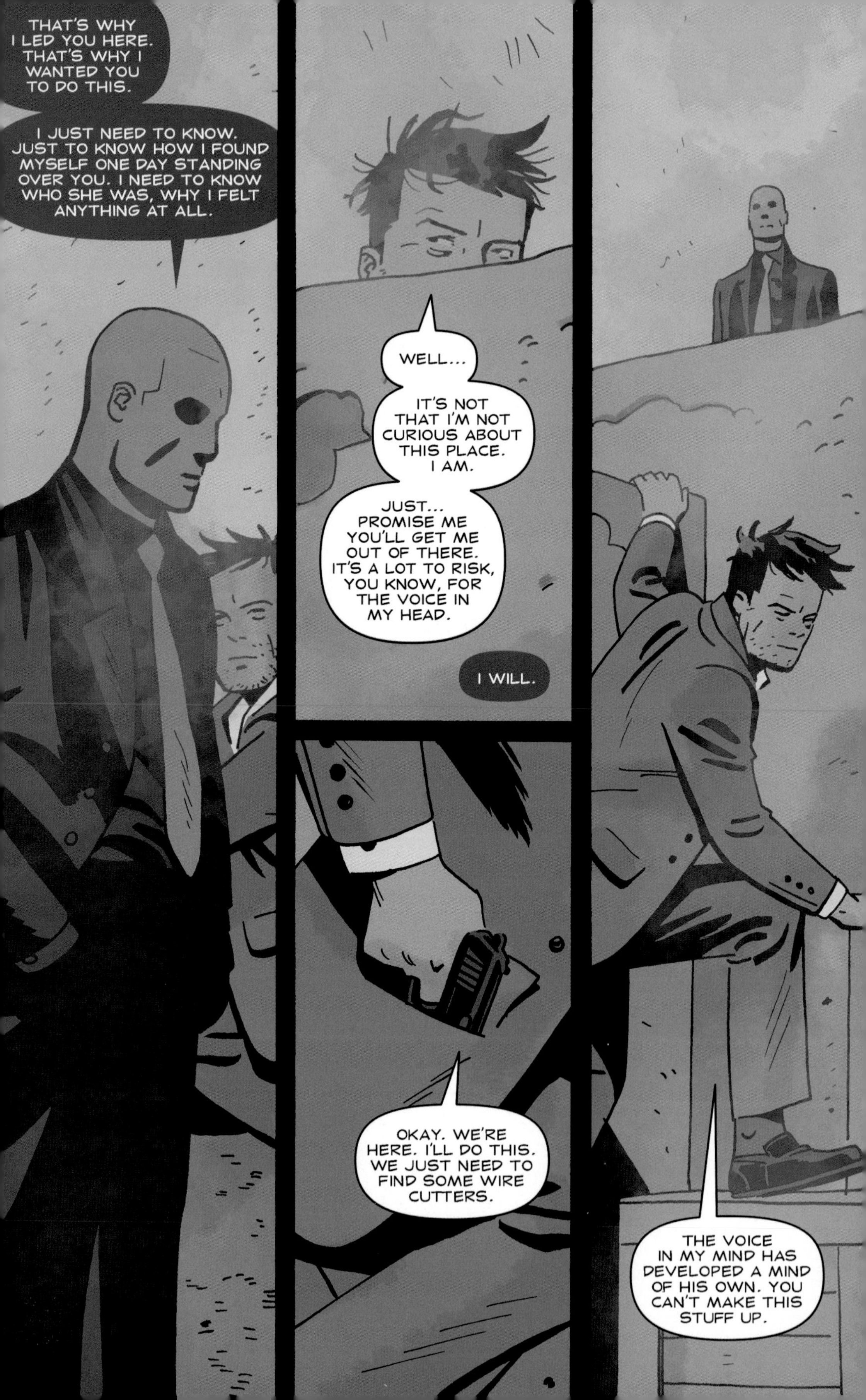
THAT'S WHY I LED YOU HERE. THAT'S WHY I WANTED YOU TO DO THIS.
I JUST NEED TO KNOW. JUST TO KNOW HOW I FOUND MYSELF ONE DAY STANDING OVER YOU. I NEED TO KNOW WHO SHE WAS, WHY I FELT ANYTHING AT ALL.
WELL...
IT'S NOT THAT I'M NOT CURIOUS ABOUT THIS PLACE. I AM.
JUST... PROMISE ME YOU'LL GET ME OUT OF THERE. IT'S A LOT TO RISK, YOU KNOW, FOR THE VOICE IN MY HEAD.
I WILL.
OKAY. WE'RE HERE. I'LL DO THIS. WE JUST NEED TO FIND SOME WIRE CUTTERS.
THE VOICE IN MY MIND HAS DEVELOPED A MIND OF HIS OWN. YOU CAN'T MAKE THIS STUFF UP.

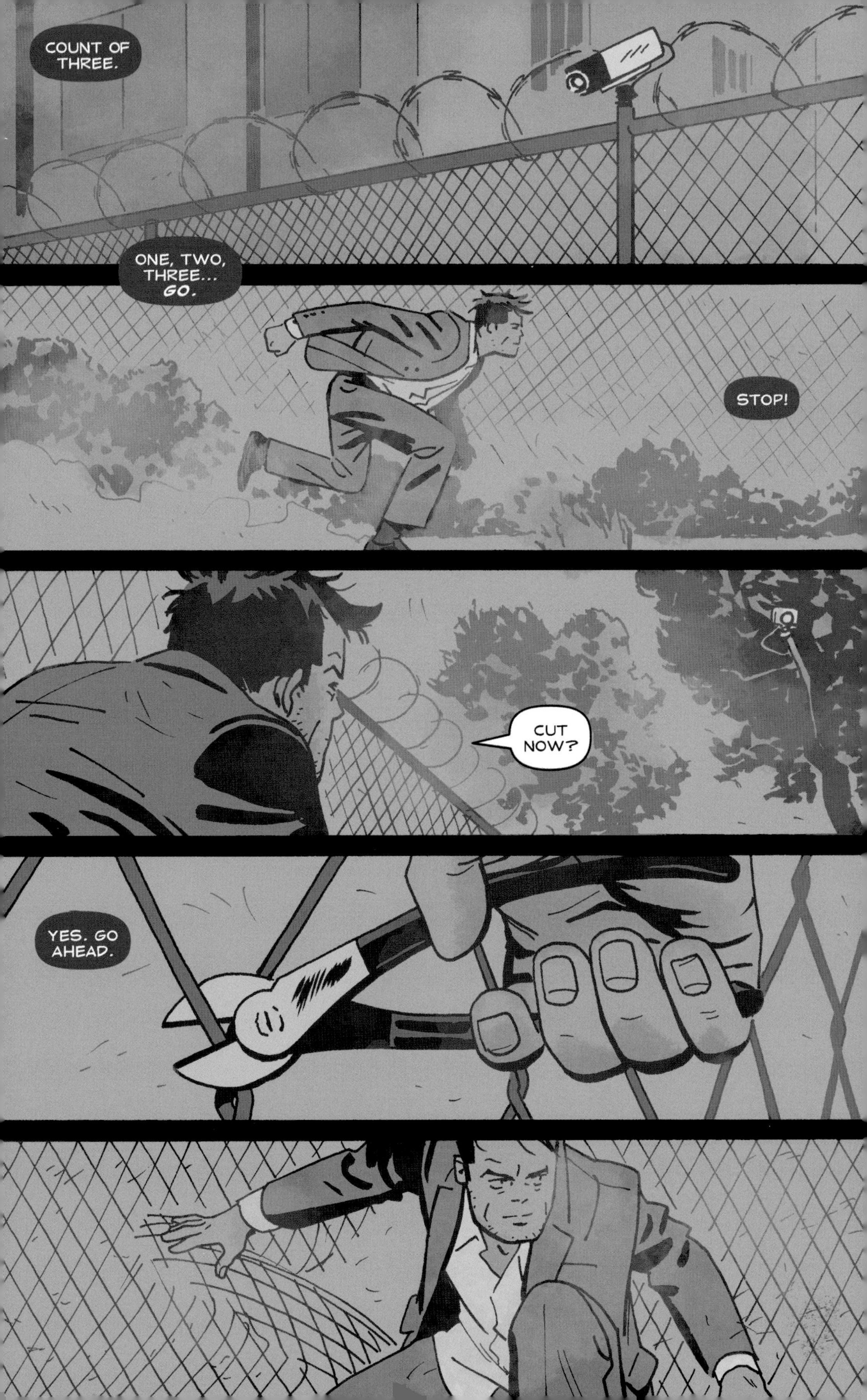
COUNT OF THREE.
ONE, TWO, THREE... GO.
STOP!
CUT NOW?
YES. GO AHEAD.

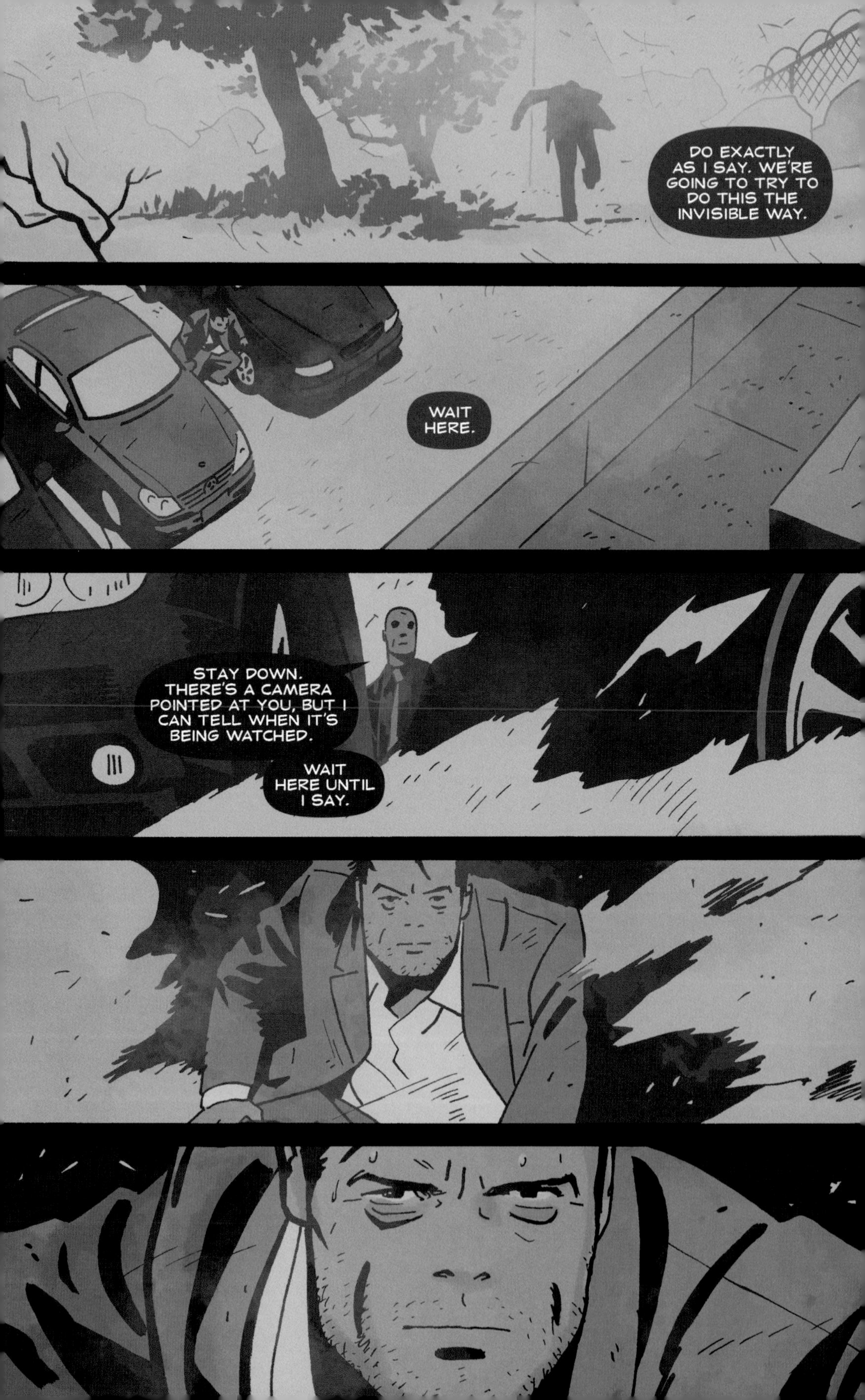
DO EXACTLY AS I SAY. WE'RE GOING TO TRY TO DO THIS THE INVISIBLE WAY.
WAIT HERE.
STAY DOWN. THERE'S A CAMERA POINTED AT YOU, BUT I CAN TELL WHEN IT'S BEING WATCHED.
WAIT HERE UNTIL I SAY.

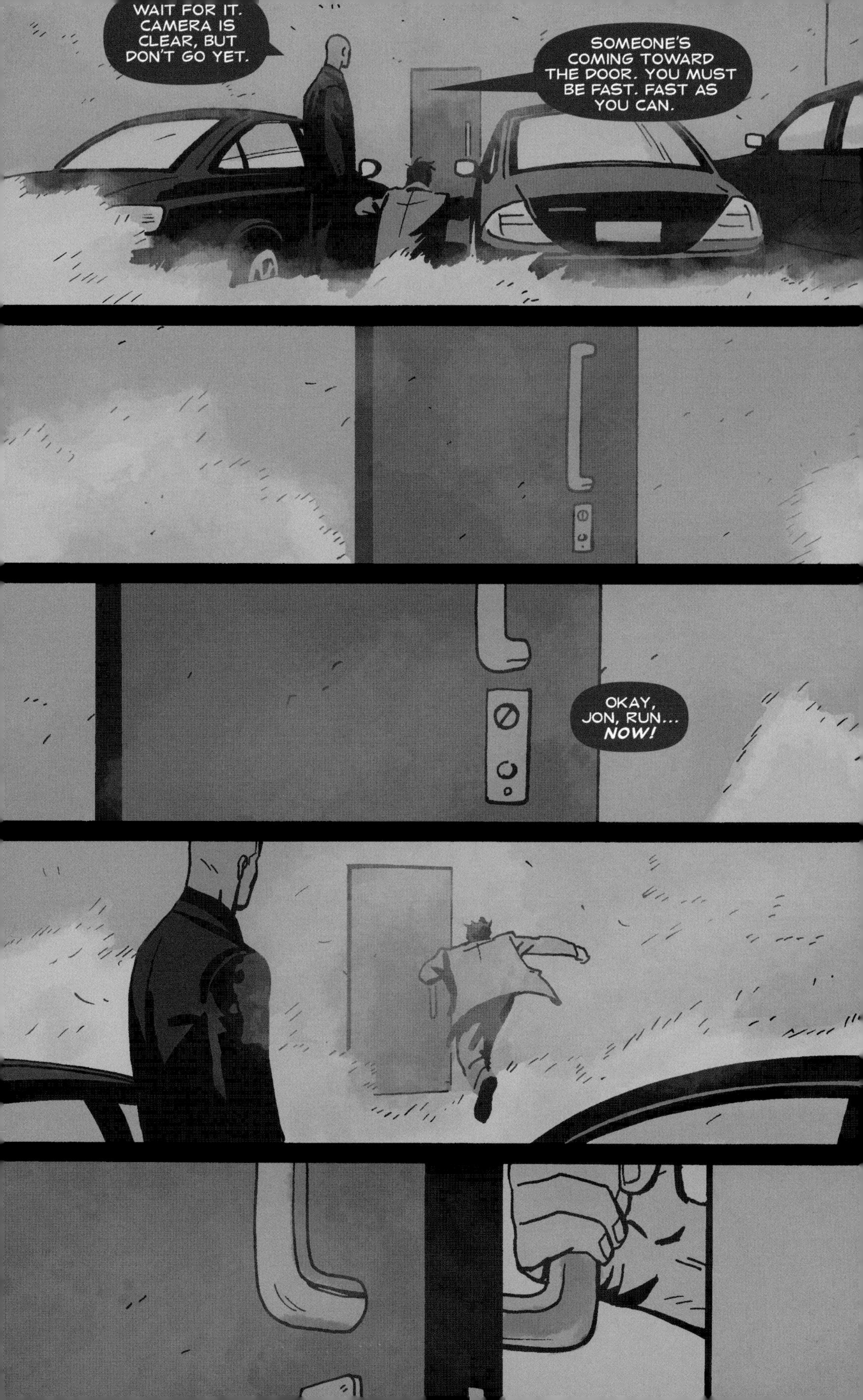
WAIT FOR IT. CAMERA IS CLEAR, BUT DON'T GO YET.
SOMEONE'S COMING TOWARD THE DOOR. YOU MUST BE FAST. FAST AS YOU CAN.
OKAY, JON, RUN... *NOW!*

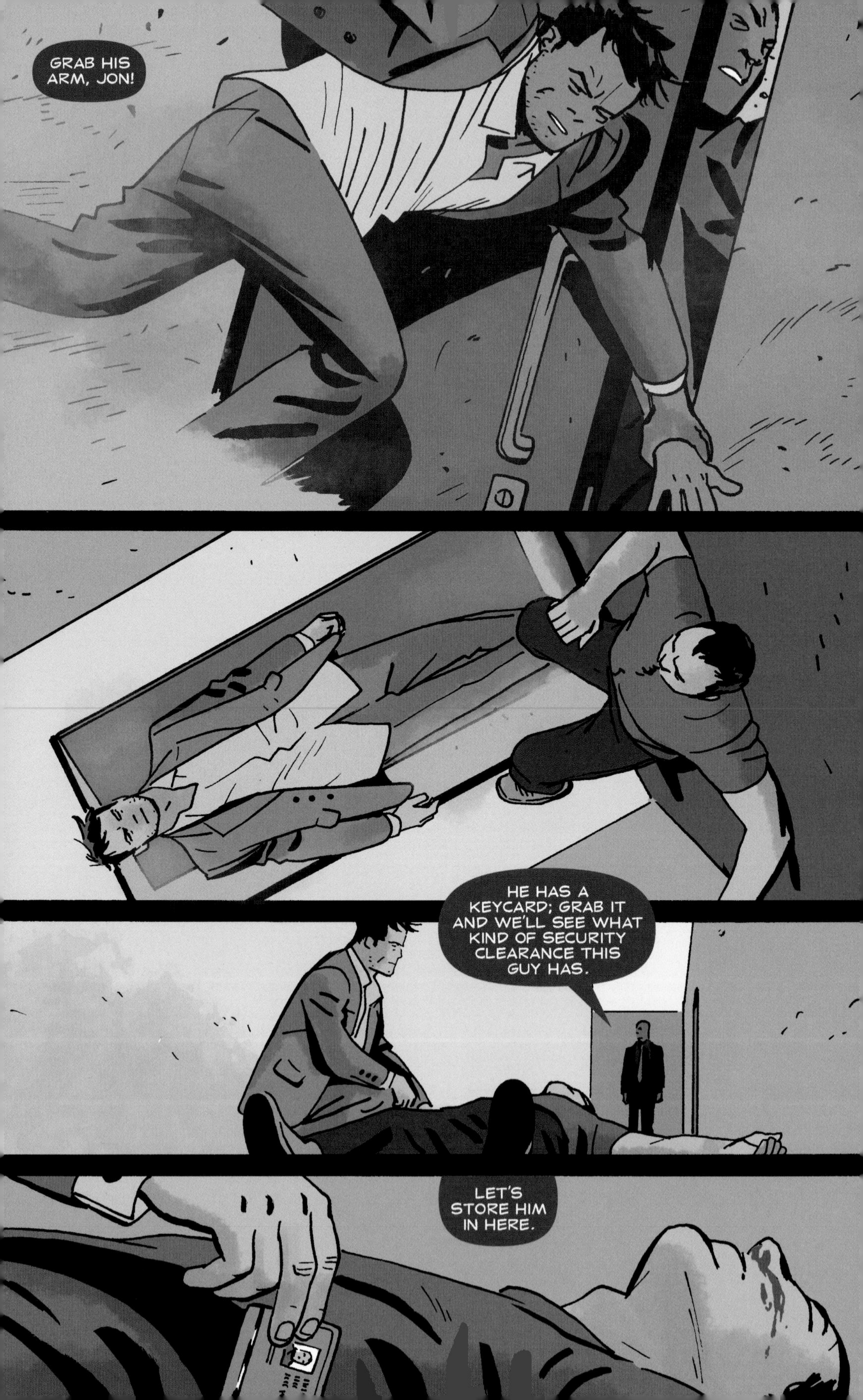
GRAB HIS ARM, JON!
HE HAS A KEYCARD; GRAB IT AND WE'LL SEE WHAT KIND OF SECURITY CLEARANCE THIS GUY HAS.
LET'S STORE HIM IN HERE.

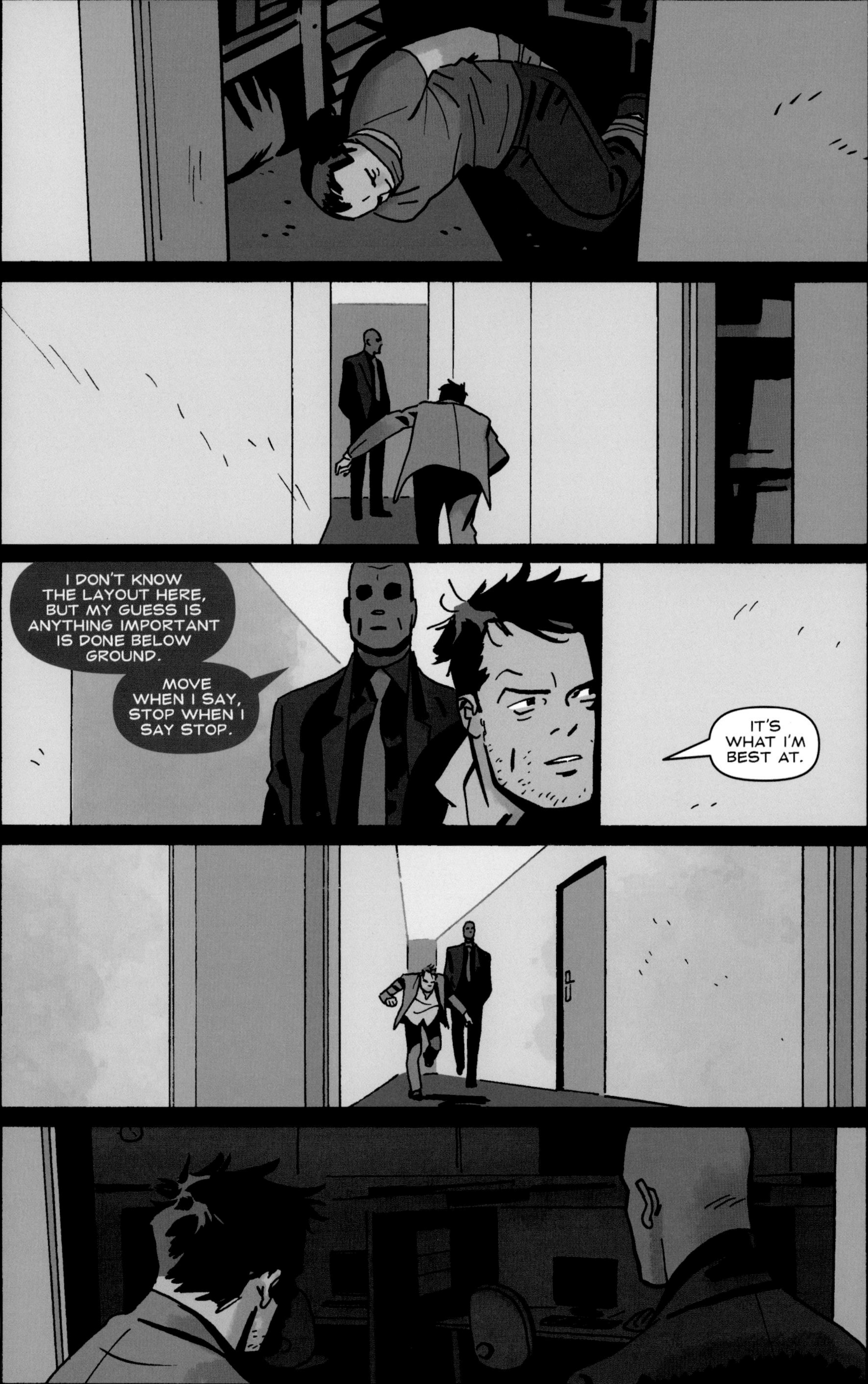
I DON'T KNOW THE LAYOUT HERE, BUT MY GUESS IS ANYTHING IMPORTANT IS DONE BELOW GROUND.
MOVE WHEN I SAY, STOP WHEN I SAY STOP.
IT'S WHAT I'M BEST AT.

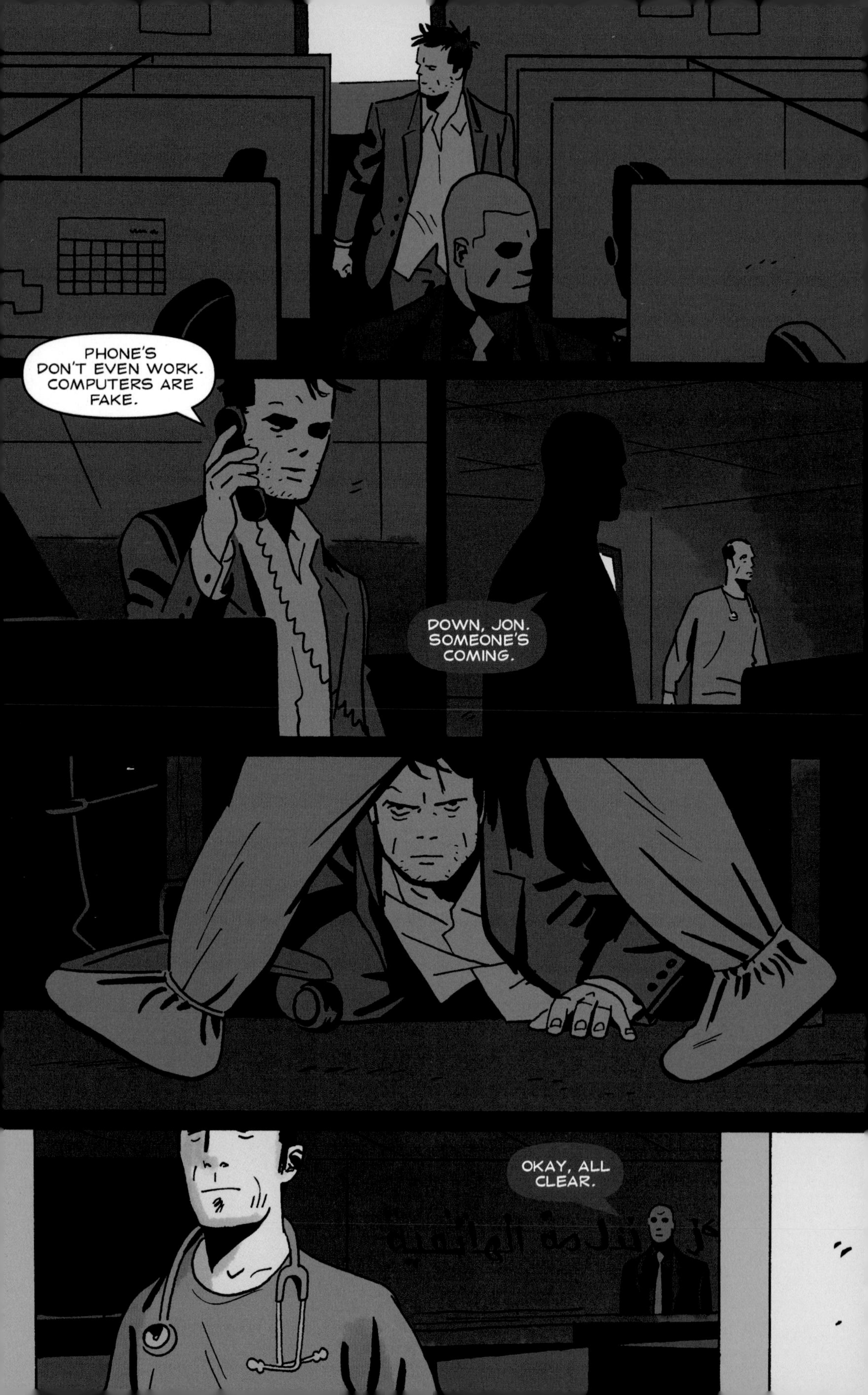
PHONE'S DON'T EVEN WORK. COMPUTERS ARE FAKE.
DOWN, JON. SOMEONE'S COMING.
OKAY, ALL CLEAR.

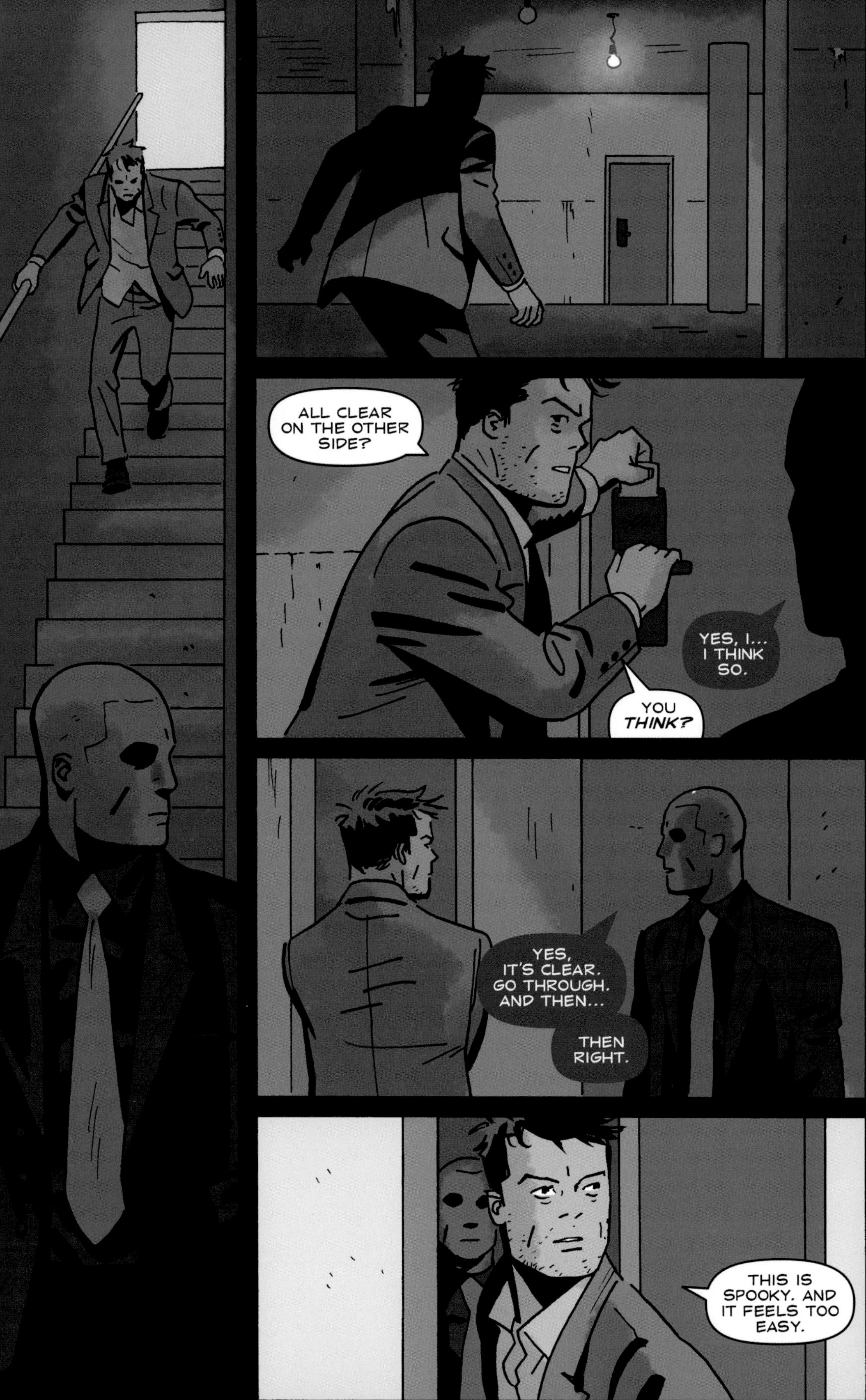
ALL CLEAR ON THE OTHER SIDE?
YES, I... I THINK SO.
YOU *THINK?*
YES, IT'S CLEAR. GO THROUGH. AND THEN...
THEN RIGHT.
THIS IS SPOOKY. AND IT FEELS TOO EASY.

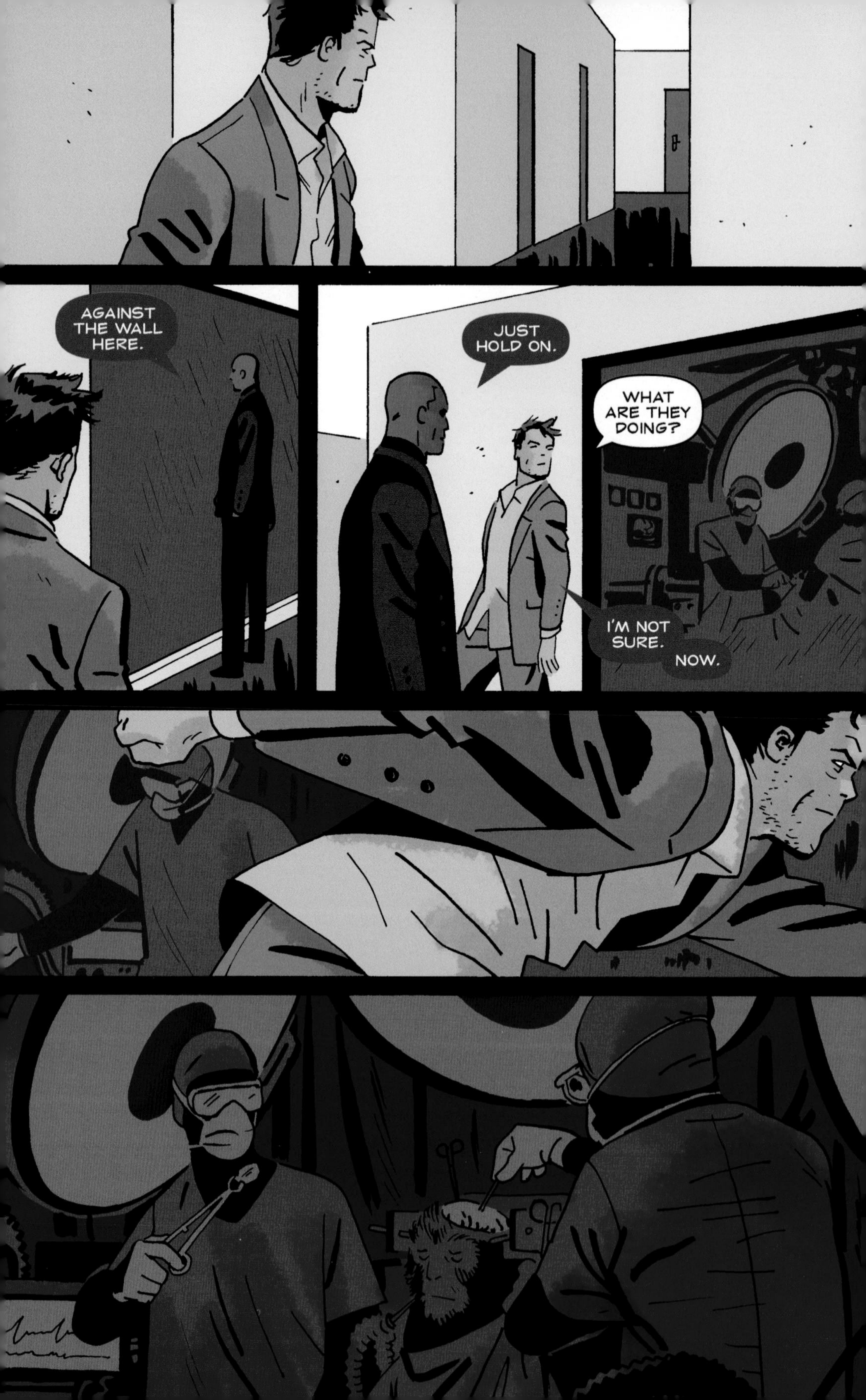
AGAINST THE WALL HERE.
JUST HOLD ON.
WHAT ARE THEY DOING?
I'M NOT SURE.
NOW.

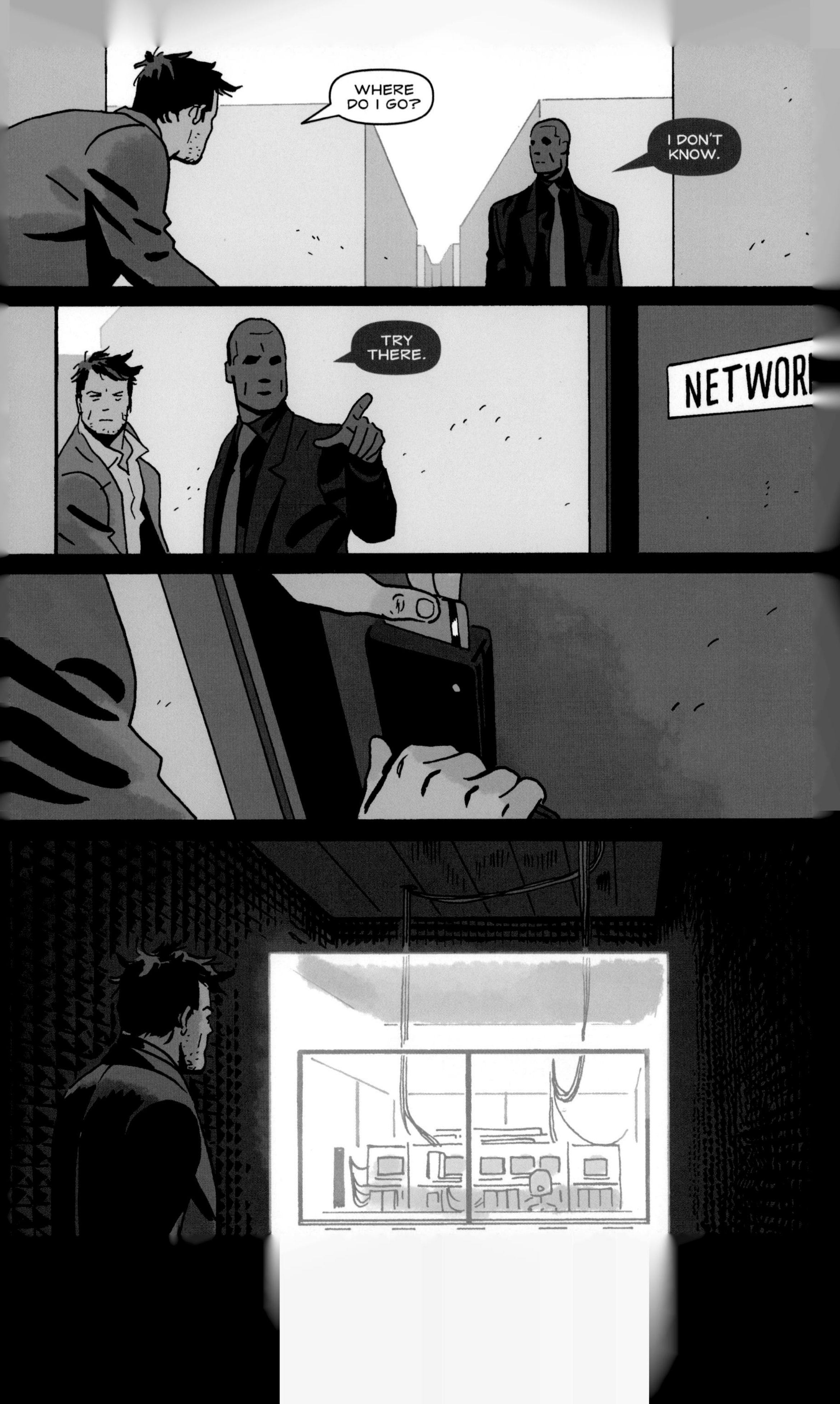
WHERE DO I GO?
I DON'T KNOW.
TRY THERE.
NETWOR

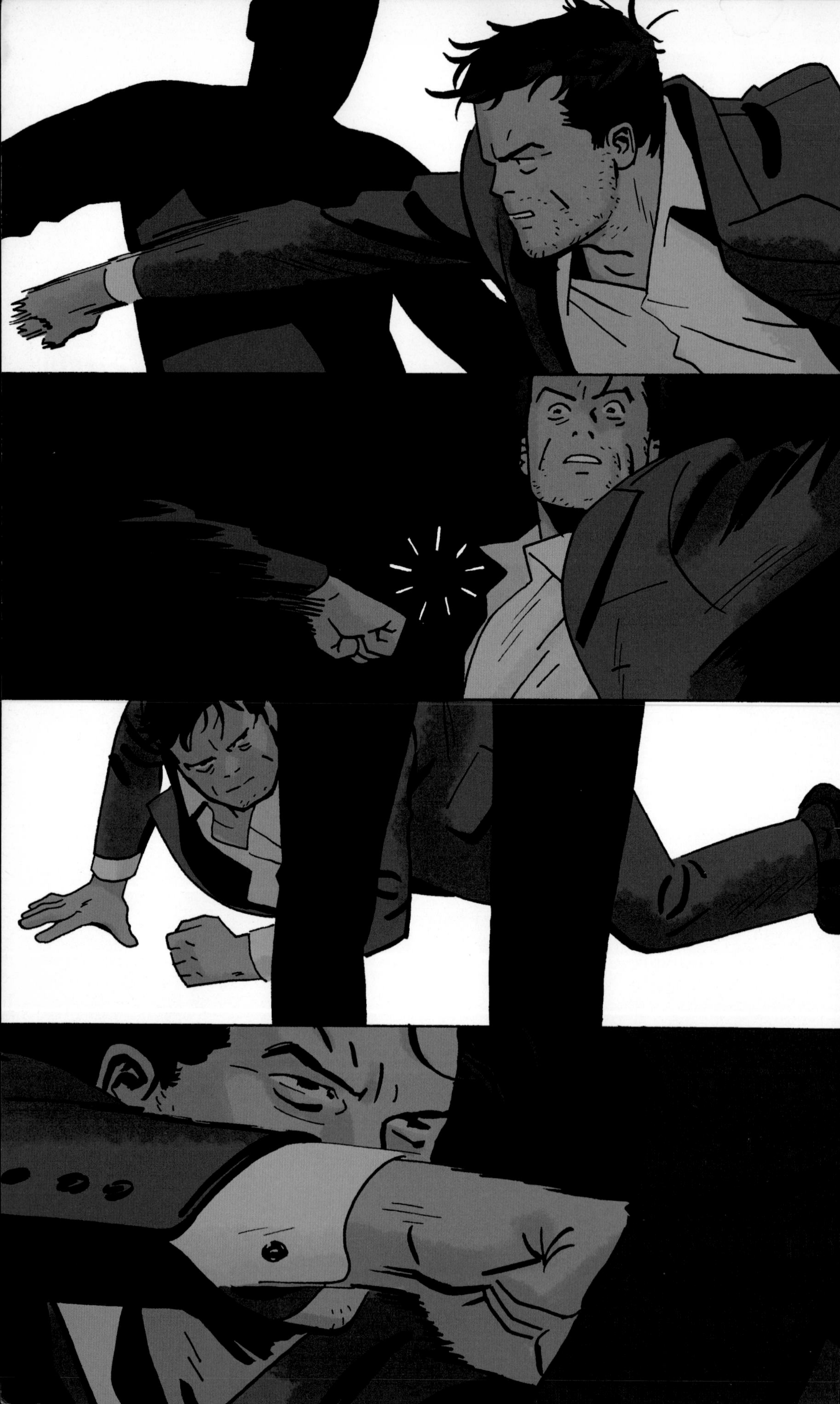

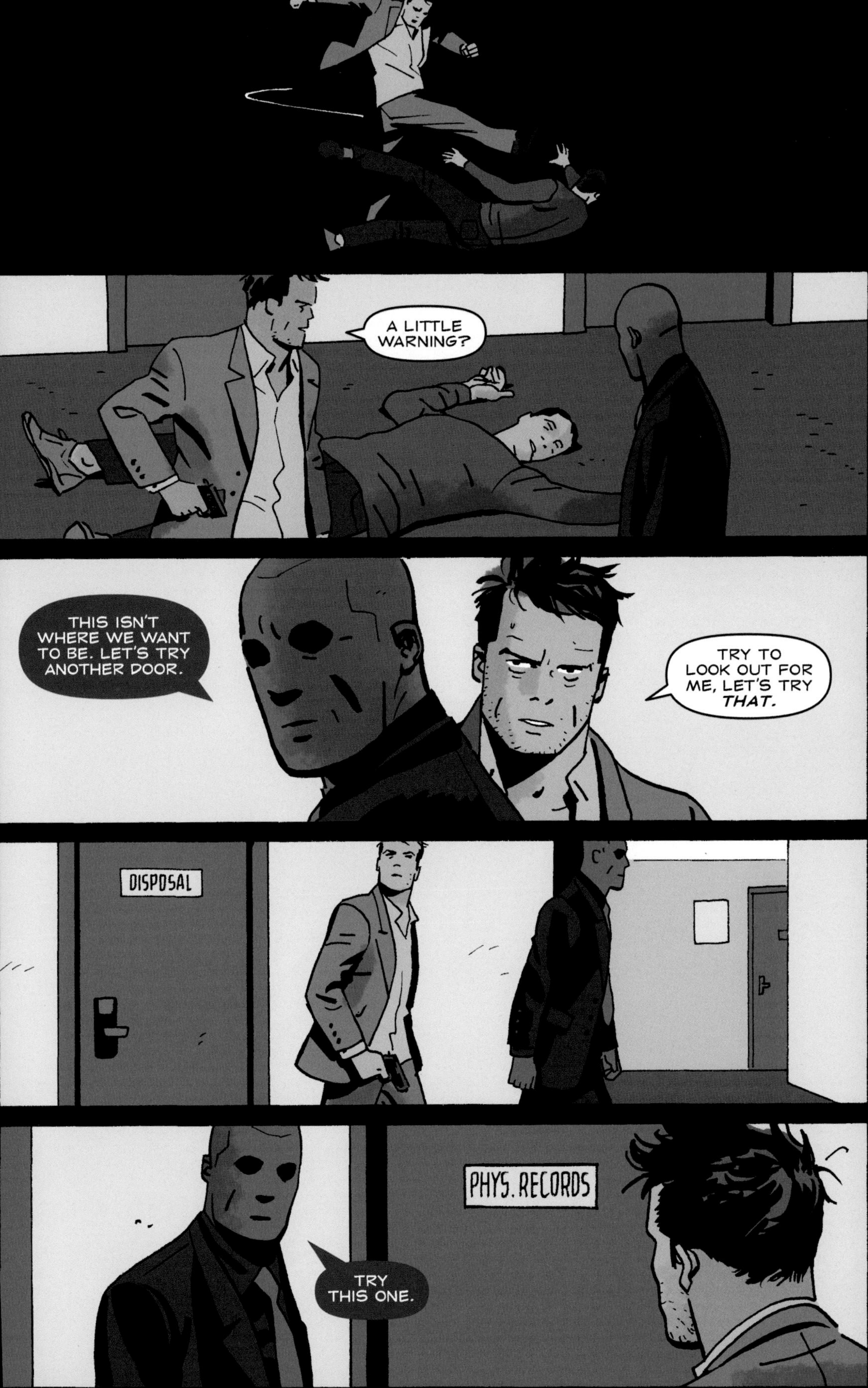
A LITTLE WARNING?
THIS ISN'T WHERE WE WANT TO BE. LET'S TRY ANOTHER DOOR.
TRY TO LOOK OUT FOR ME, LET'S TRY *THAT.*
DISPOSAL
PHYS. RECORDS
TRY THIS ONE.

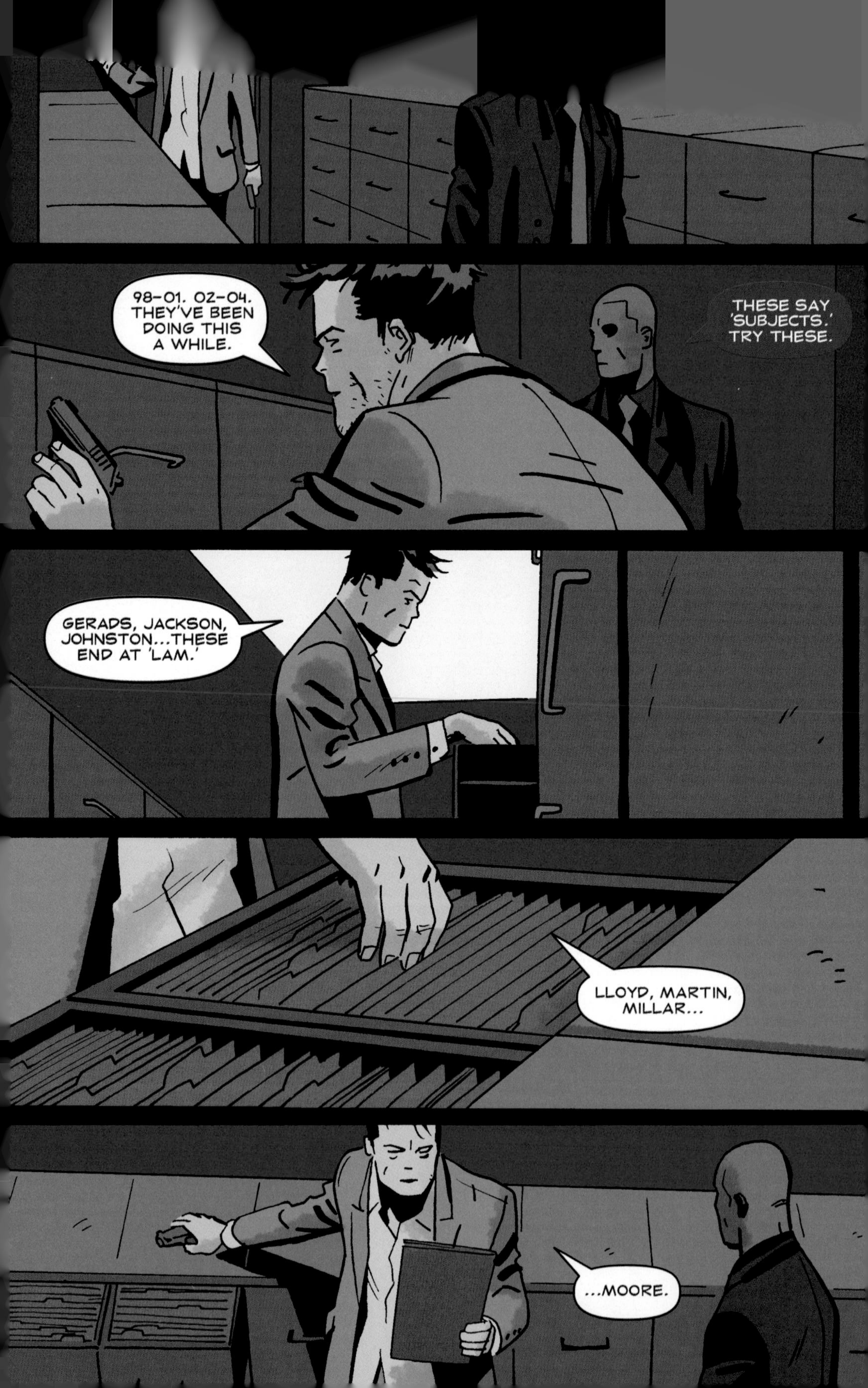
98-01. 02-04. THEY'VE BEEN DOING THIS A WHILE.
THESE SAY 'SUBJECTS.' TRY THESE.
GERADS, JACKSON, JOHNSTON...THESE END AT 'LAM.'
LLOYD, MARTIN, MILLAR...
...MOORE.

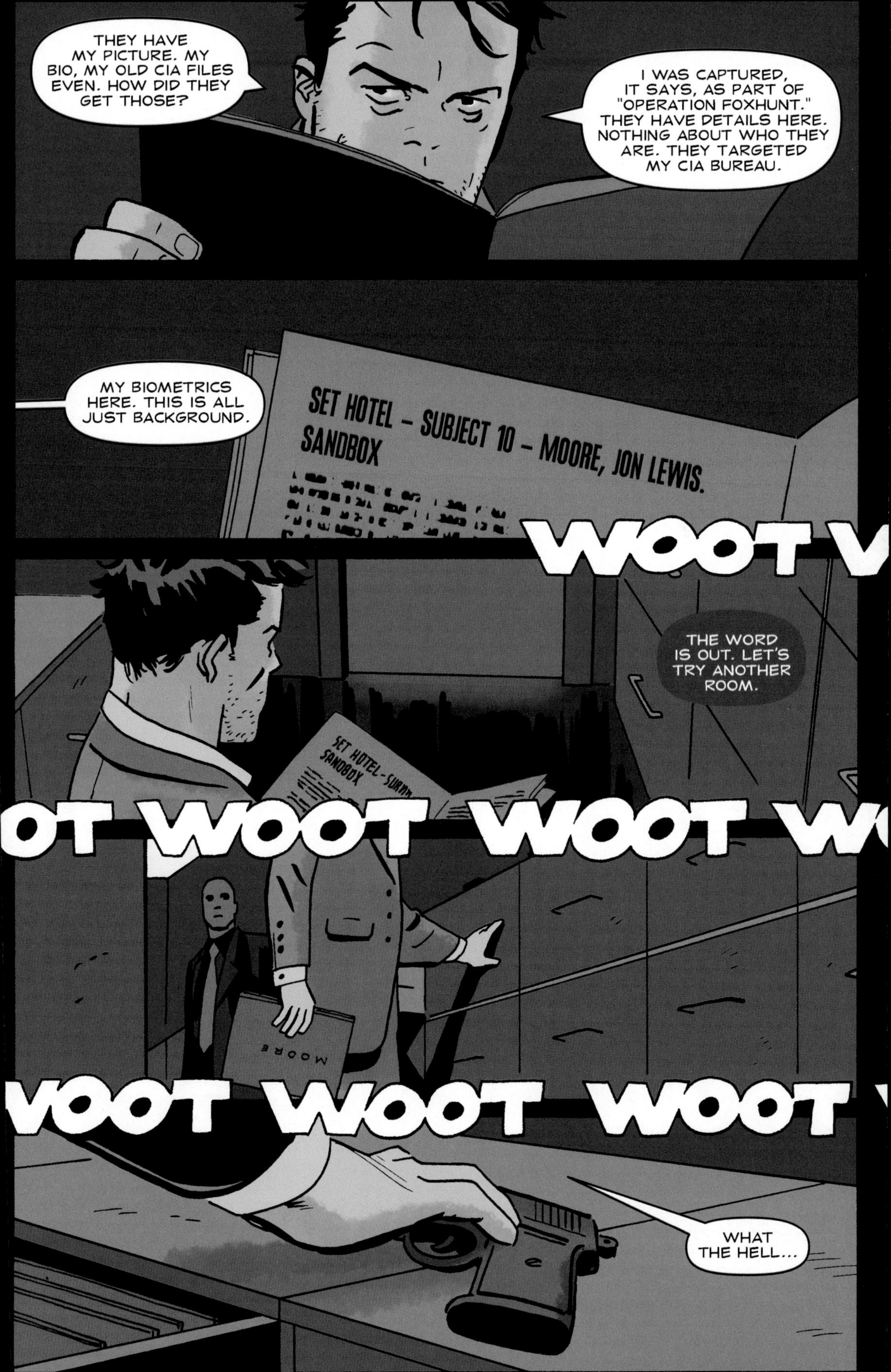
THEY HAVE MY PICTURE. MY BIO, MY OLD CIA FILES EVEN. HOW DID THEY GET THOSE?
I WAS CAPTURED, IT SAYS, AS PART OF "OPERATION FOXHUNT." THEY HAVE DETAILS HERE. NOTHING ABOUT WHO THEY ARE. THEY TARGETED MY CIA BUREAU.
MY BIOMETRICS HERE. THIS IS ALL JUST BACKGROUND.
SET HOTEL – SUBJECT 10 – MOORE, JON LEWIS.
SANDBOX
WOOT
THE WORD IS OUT. LET'S TRY ANOTHER ROOM.
SET HOTEL-
SANDBOX
WOOT WOOT
MOORE
WOOT WOOT WOOT
WHAT THE HELL...

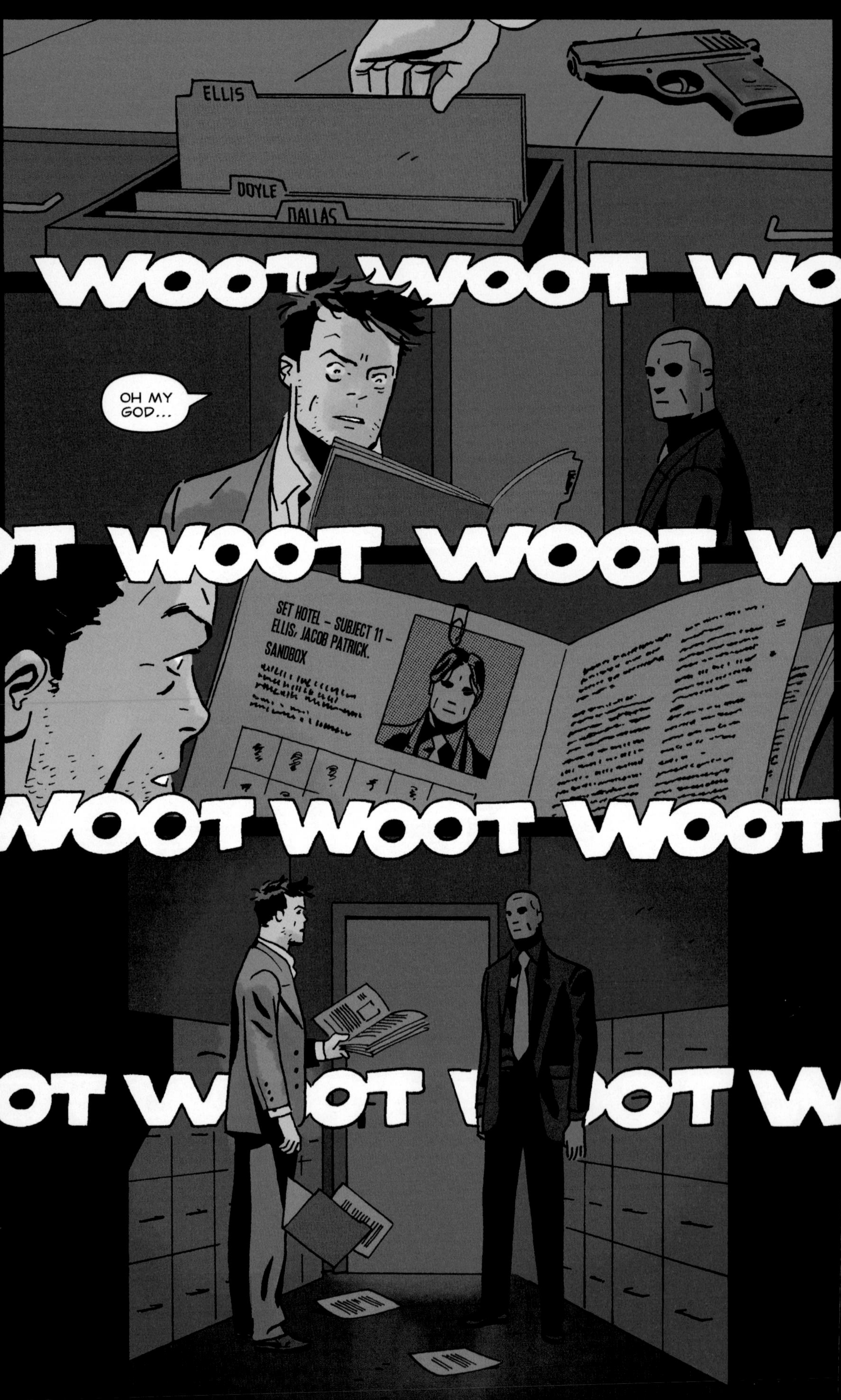
ELLIS
DOYLE
DALLAS
WOOT WOOT
OH MY GOD...
WOOT WOOT
SET HOTEL – SUBJECT 11 – ELLIS, JACOB PATRICK.
SANDBOX
WOOT WOOT WOOT

CHAPTER 5

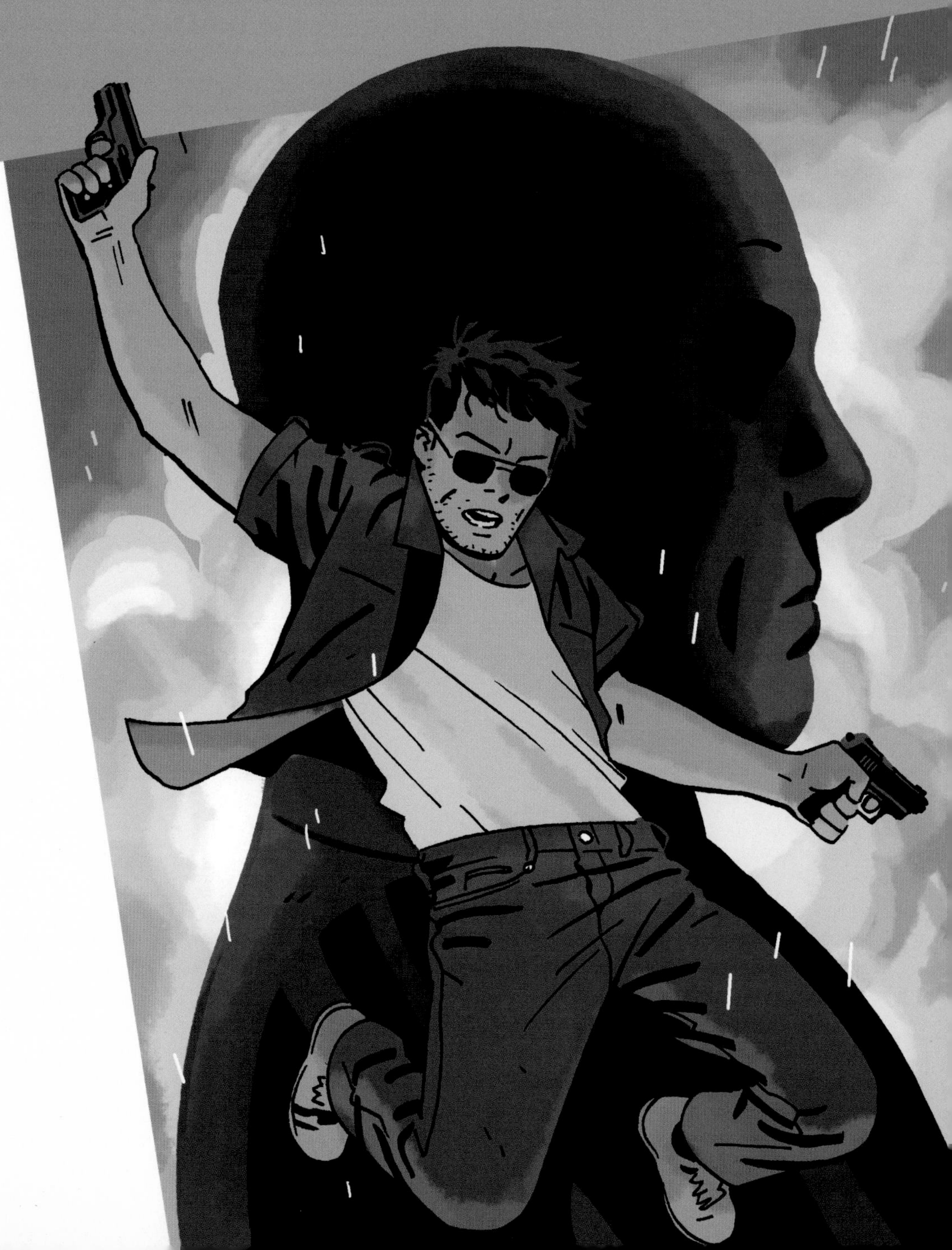

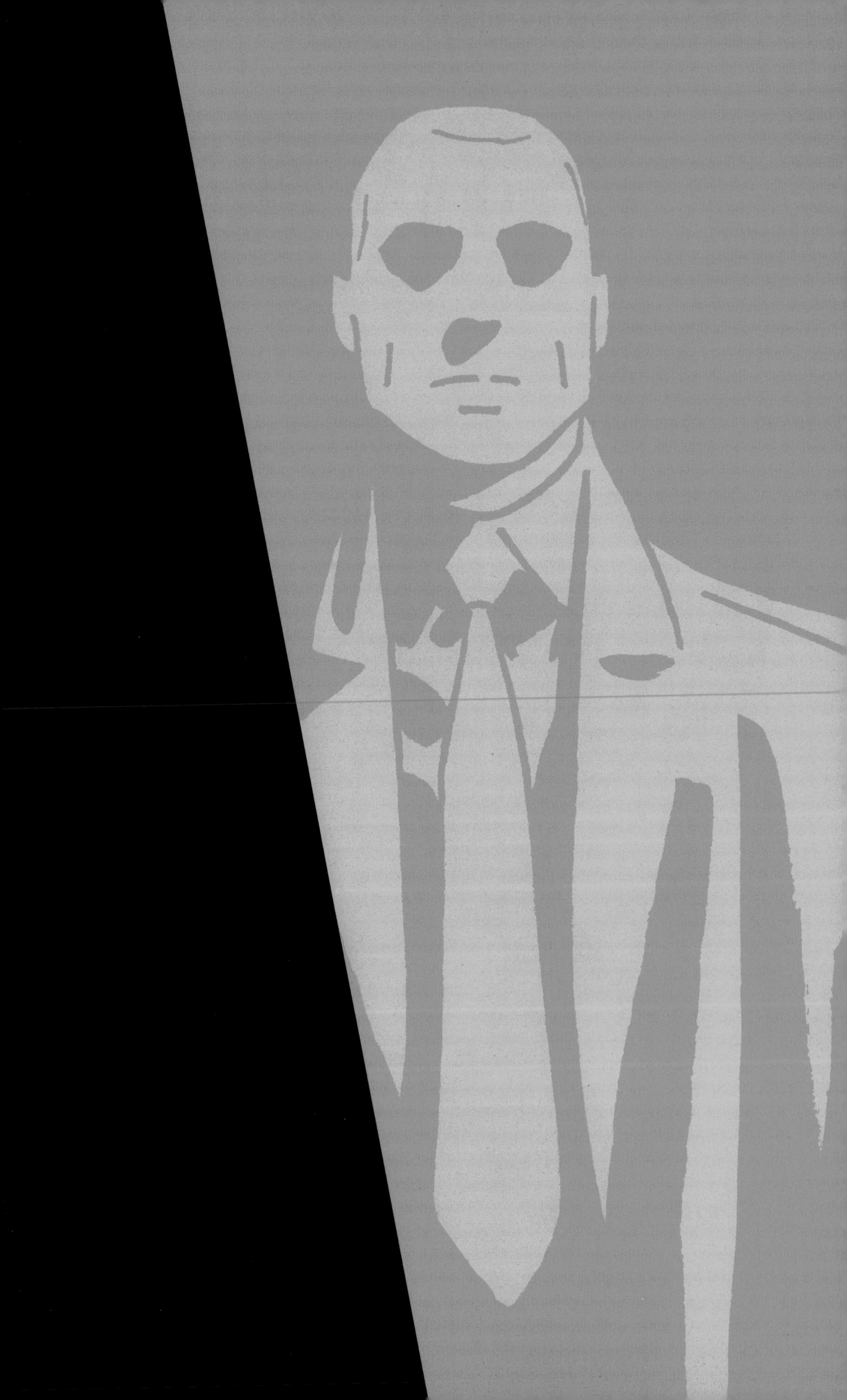

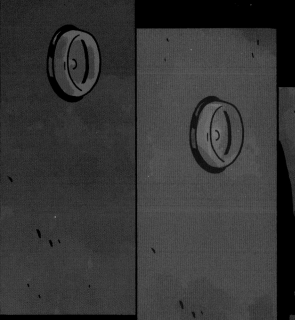

WE'RE BLOCKED IN. I CAN'T GO BACK THAT WAY.

WE CAN TRY ANOTHER WAY. THAT DOOR THERE, BEHIND YOU.

TRY? YOU KEEP *SAYING* THAT. IS IT THE WAY OUT, OR THE WAY FURTHER *IN*, JAKE?

LABS

I DON'T KNOW, JON. ...THINGS ARE LESS THAN CLEAR RIGHT NOW.

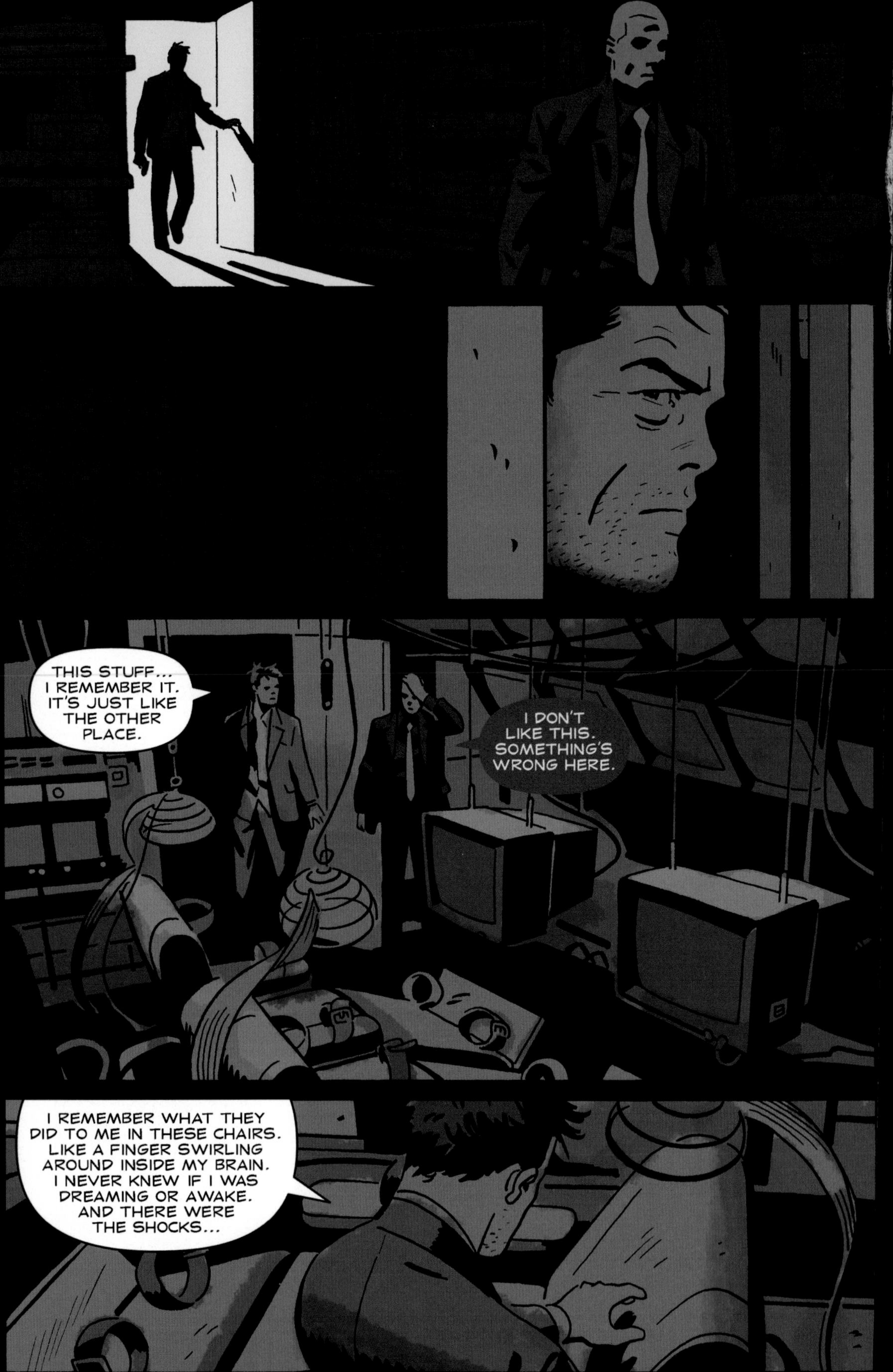
THIS STUFF... I REMEMBER IT. IT'S JUST LIKE THE OTHER PLACE.
I DON'T LIKE THIS. SOMETHING'S WRONG HERE.
I REMEMBER WHAT THEY DID TO ME IN THESE CHAIRS. LIKE A FINGER SWIRLING AROUND INSIDE MY BRAIN. I NEVER KNEW IF I WAS DREAMING OR AWAKE. AND THERE WERE THE SHOCKS...

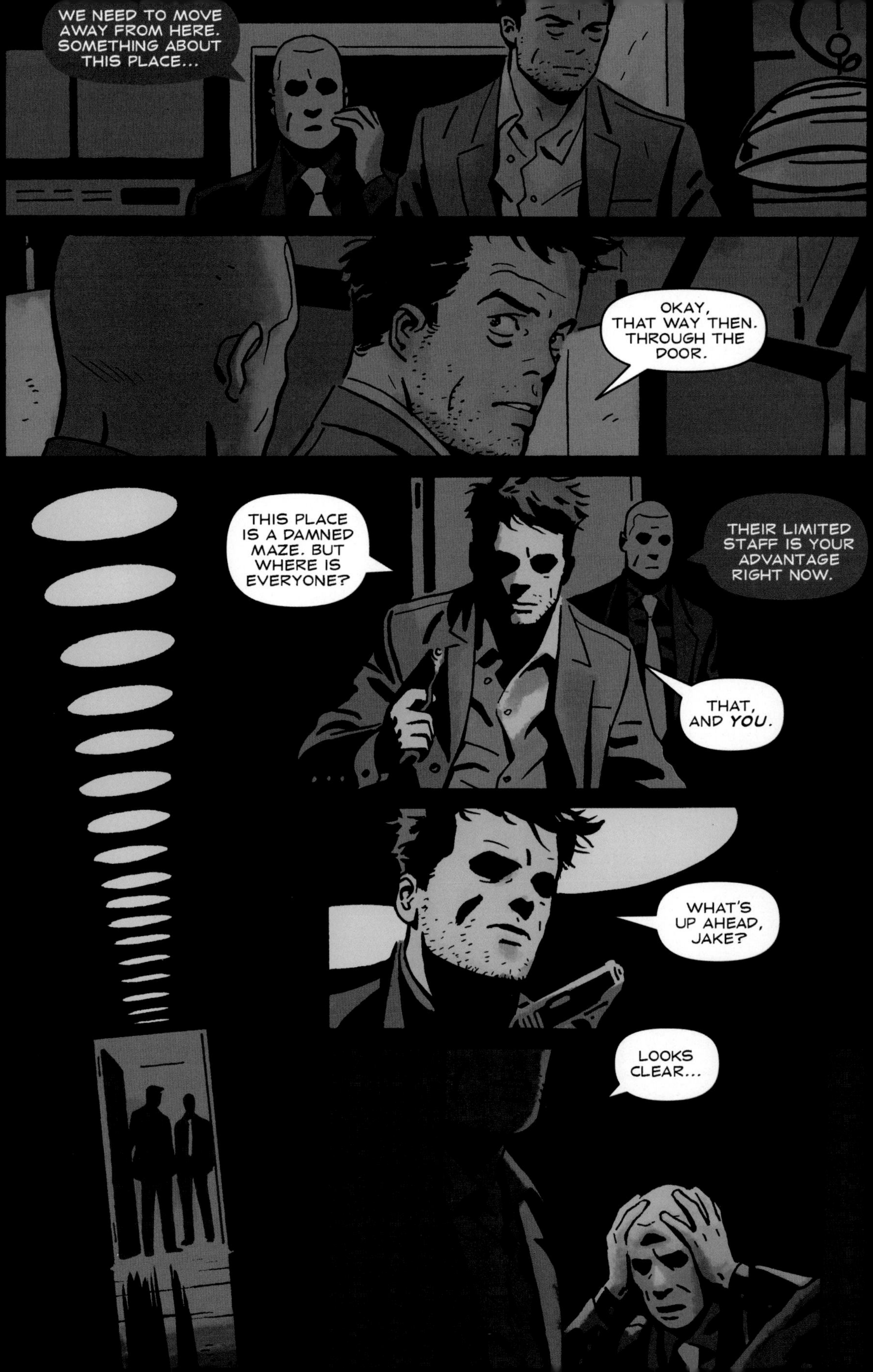
WE NEED TO MOVE AWAY FROM HERE. SOMETHING ABOUT THIS PLACE...
OKAY, THAT WAY THEN. THROUGH THE DOOR.
THIS PLACE IS A DAMNED MAZE. BUT WHERE IS EVERYONE?
THEIR LIMITED STAFF IS YOUR ADVANTAGE RIGHT NOW.
THAT, AND *YOU*.
WHAT'S UP AHEAD, JAKE?
LOOKS CLEAR...

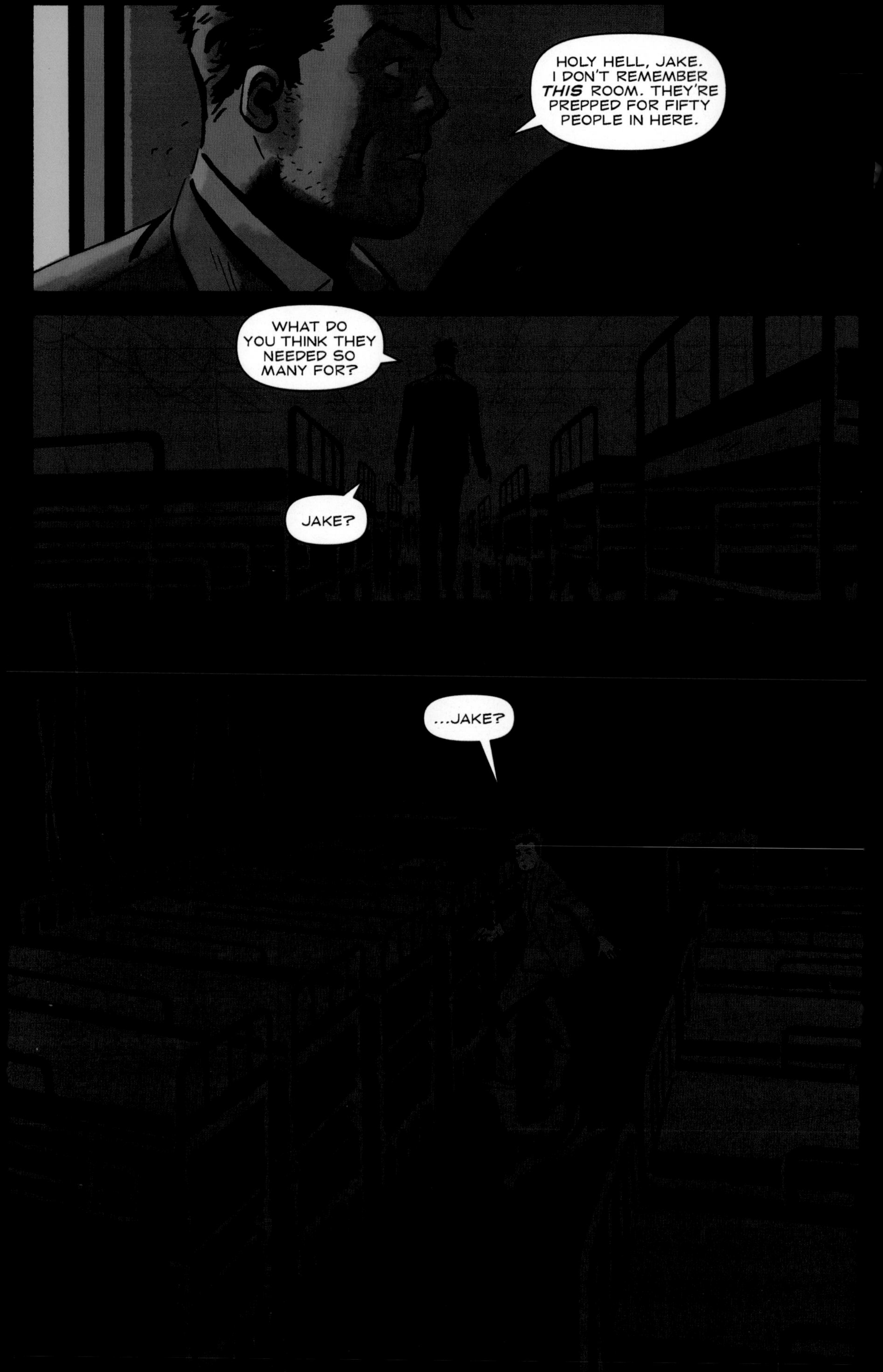
HOLY HELL, JAKE. I DON'T REMEMBER *THIS* ROOM. THEY'RE PREPPED FOR FIFTY PEOPLE IN HERE.
WHAT DO YOU THINK THEY NEEDED SO MANY FOR?
JAKE?
...JAKE?

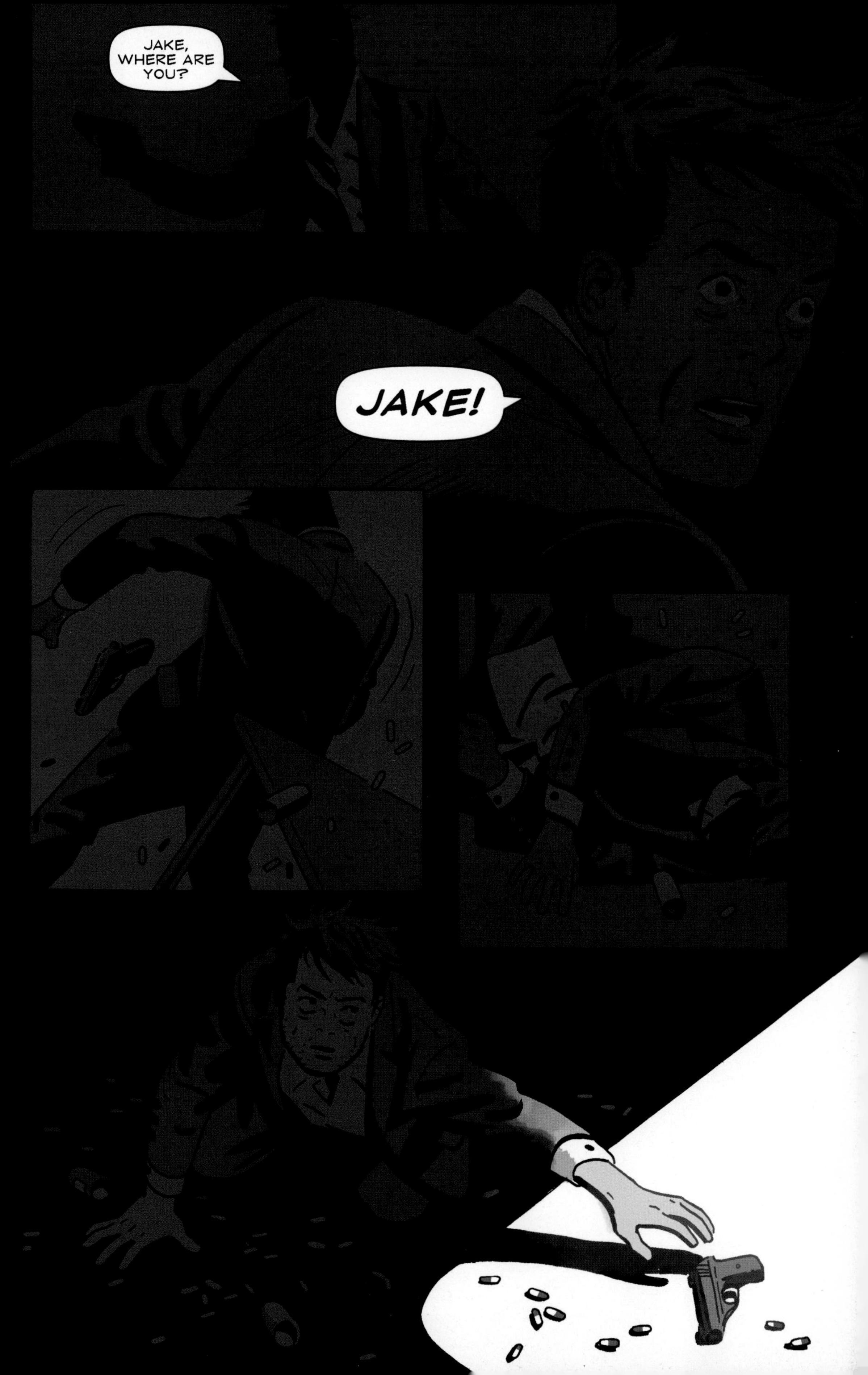
JAKE, WHERE ARE YOU?
JAKE!

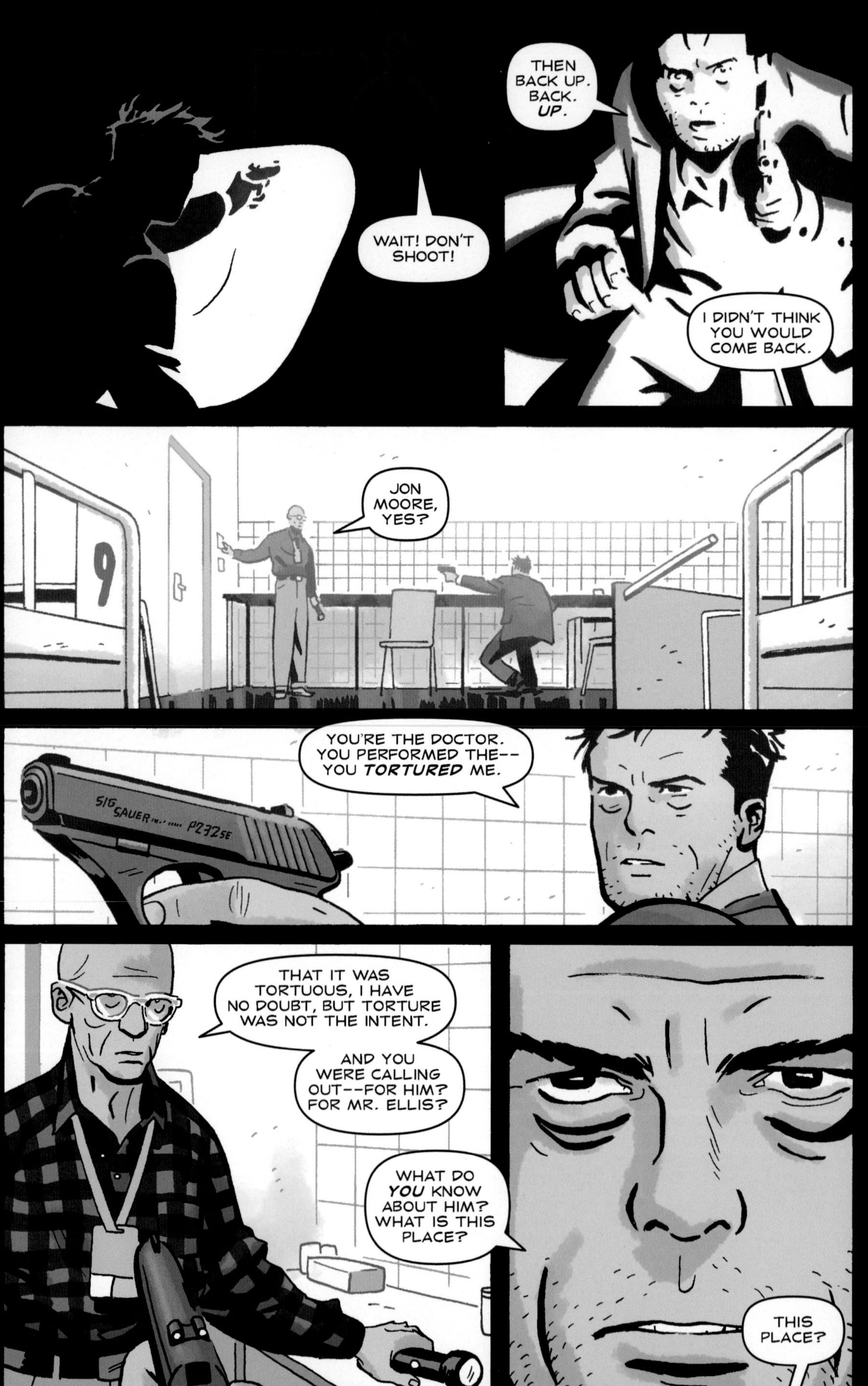
WAIT! DON'T SHOOT!
THEN BACK UP. BACK. *UP*.
I DIDN'T THINK YOU WOULD COME BACK.
JON MOORE, YES?
9
YOU'RE THE DOCTOR. YOU PERFORMED THE-- YOU *TORTURED* ME.
SIG SAUER
P232SE
THAT IT WAS TORTUOUS, I HAVE NO DOUBT, BUT TORTURE WAS NOT THE INTENT.
AND YOU WERE CALLING OUT--FOR HIM? FOR MR. ELLIS?
WHAT DO *YOU* KNOW ABOUT HIM? WHAT IS THIS PLACE?
THIS PLACE?

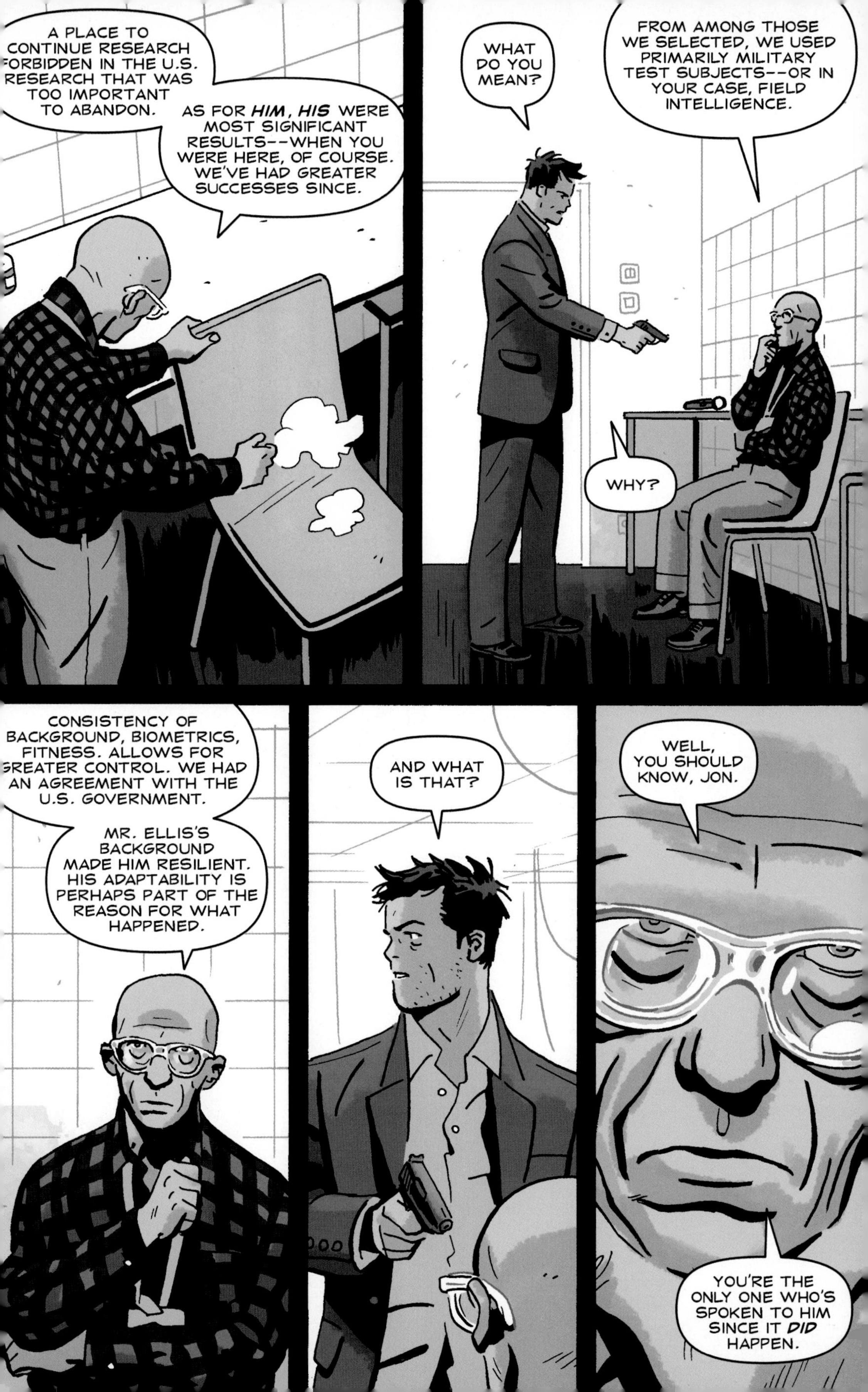
A PLACE TO CONTINUE RESEARCH FORBIDDEN IN THE U.S. RESEARCH THAT WAS TOO IMPORTANT TO ABANDON.
AS FOR *HIM*, *HIS* WERE MOST SIGNIFICANT RESULTS--WHEN YOU WERE HERE, OF COURSE. WE'VE HAD GREATER SUCCESSES SINCE.
WHAT DO YOU MEAN?
FROM AMONG THOSE WE SELECTED, WE USED PRIMARILY MILITARY TEST SUBJECTS--OR IN YOUR CASE, FIELD INTELLIGENCE.
WHY?
CONSISTENCY OF BACKGROUND, BIOMETRICS, FITNESS. ALLOWS FOR GREATER CONTROL. WE HAD AN AGREEMENT WITH THE U.S. GOVERNMENT.
MR. ELLIS'S BACKGROUND MADE HIM RESILIENT. HIS ADAPTABILITY IS PERHAPS PART OF THE REASON FOR WHAT HAPPENED.
AND WHAT IS THAT?
WELL, YOU SHOULD KNOW, JON.
YOU'RE THE ONLY ONE WHO'S SPOKEN TO HIM SINCE IT *DID* HAPPEN.

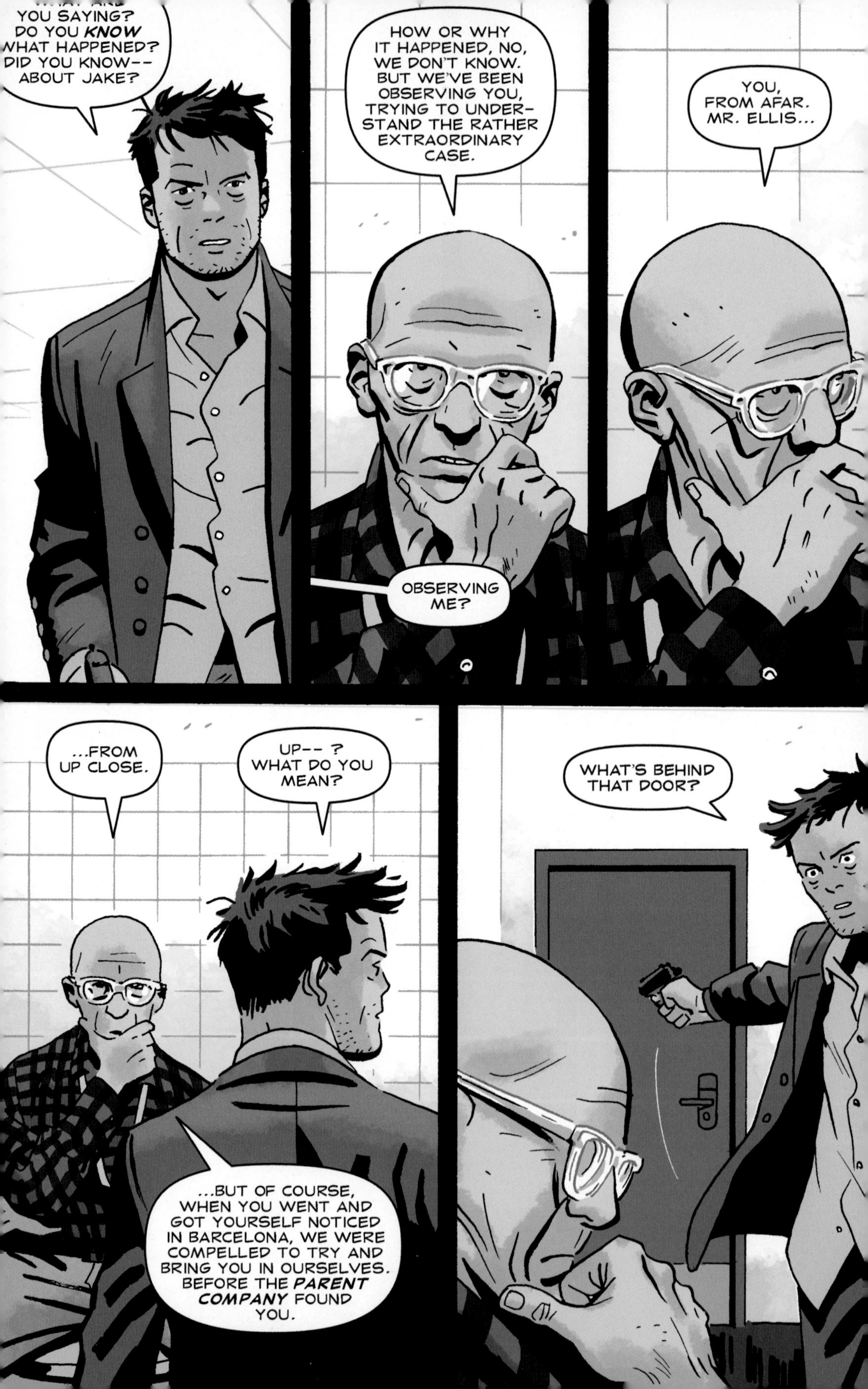
YOU SAYING? DO YOU KNOW WHAT HAPPENED? DID YOU KNOW-- ABOUT JAKE?
HOW OR WHY IT HAPPENED, NO, WE DON'T KNOW. BUT WE'VE BEEN OBSERVING YOU, TRYING TO UNDERSTAND THE RATHER EXTRAORDINARY CASE.
OBSERVING ME?
YOU, FROM AFAR. MR. ELLIS...
...FROM UP CLOSE.
UP-- ? WHAT DO YOU MEAN?
...BUT OF COURSE, WHEN YOU WENT AND GOT YOURSELF NOTICED IN BARCELONA, WE WERE COMPELLED TO TRY AND BRING YOU IN OURSELVES. BEFORE THE PARENT COMPANY FOUND YOU.
WHAT'S BEHIND THAT DOOR?

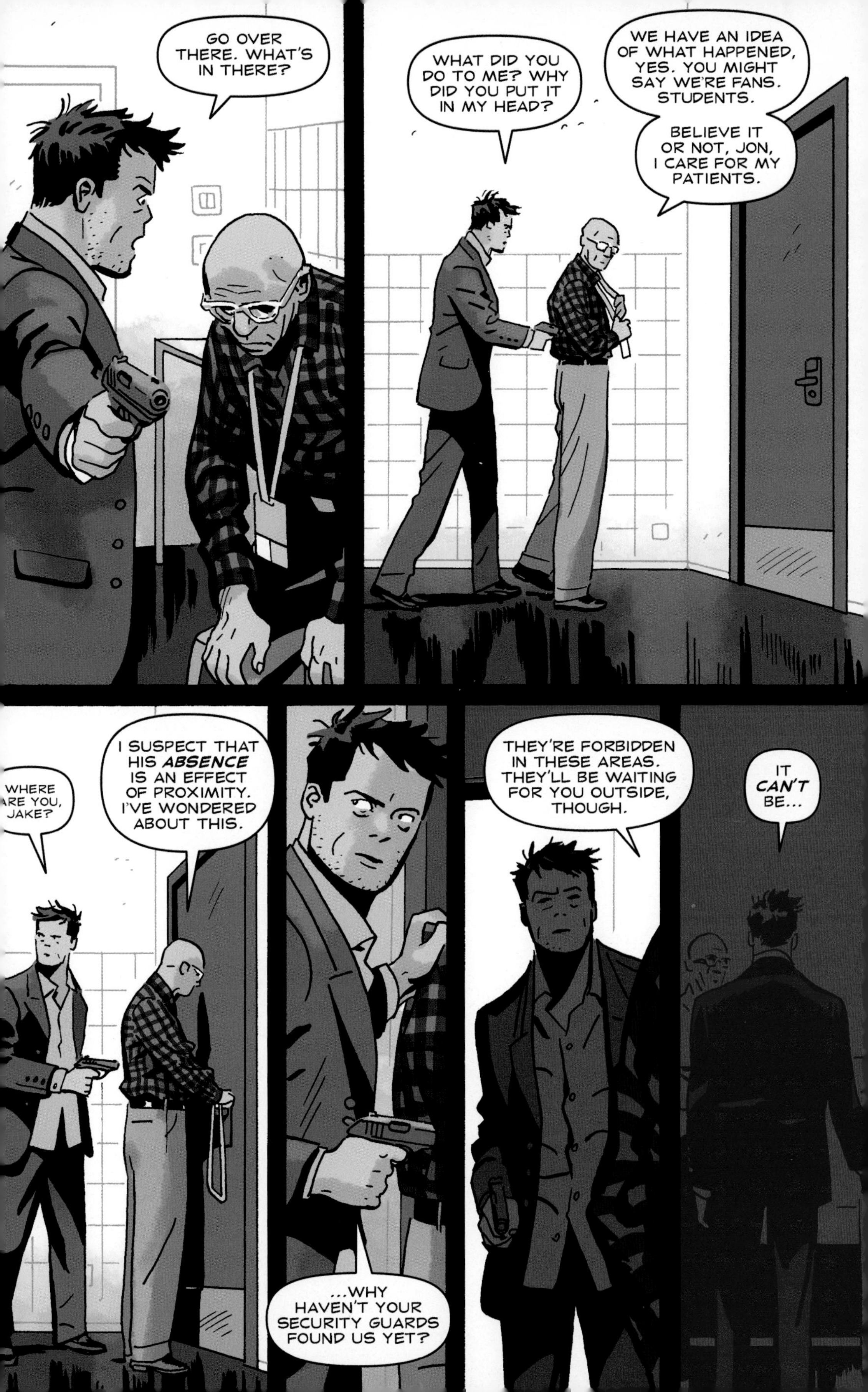
GO OVER THERE. WHAT'S IN THERE?
WHAT DID YOU DO TO ME? WHY DID YOU PUT IT IN MY HEAD?
WE HAVE AN IDEA OF WHAT HAPPENED, YES. YOU MIGHT SAY WE'RE FANS. STUDENTS.
BELIEVE IT OR NOT, JON, I CARE FOR MY PATIENTS.
WHERE ARE YOU, JAKE?
I SUSPECT THAT HIS *ABSENCE* IS AN EFFECT OF PROXIMITY. I'VE WONDERED ABOUT THIS.
...WHY HAVEN'T YOUR SECURITY GUARDS FOUND US YET?
THEY'RE FORBIDDEN IN THESE AREAS. THEY'LL BE WAITING FOR YOU OUTSIDE, THOUGH.
IT *CAN'T* BE...

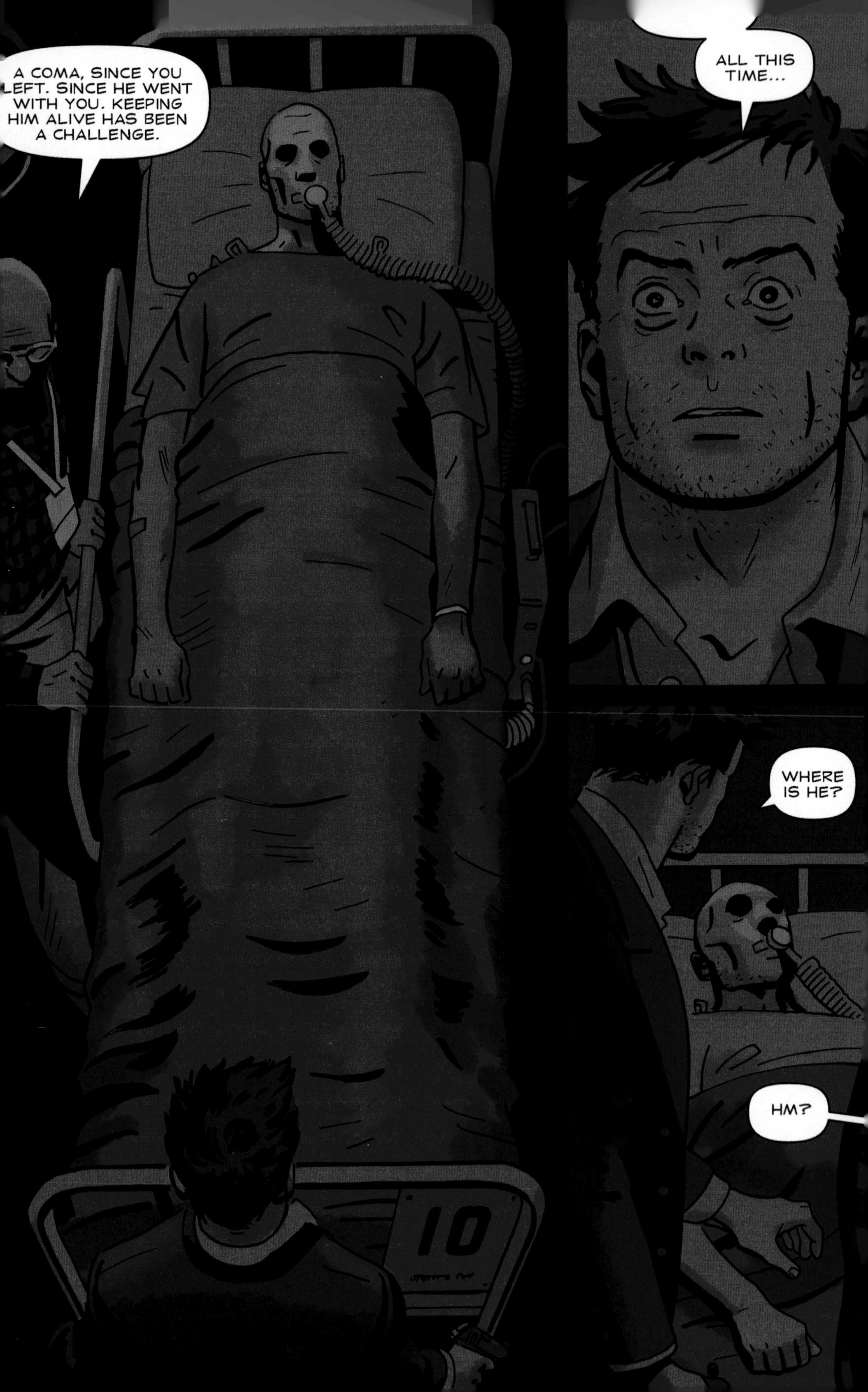
A COMA, SINCE YOU LEFT. SINCE HE WENT WITH YOU. KEEPING HIM ALIVE HAS BEEN A CHALLENGE.
ALL THIS TIME...
WHERE IS HE?
HM?
10

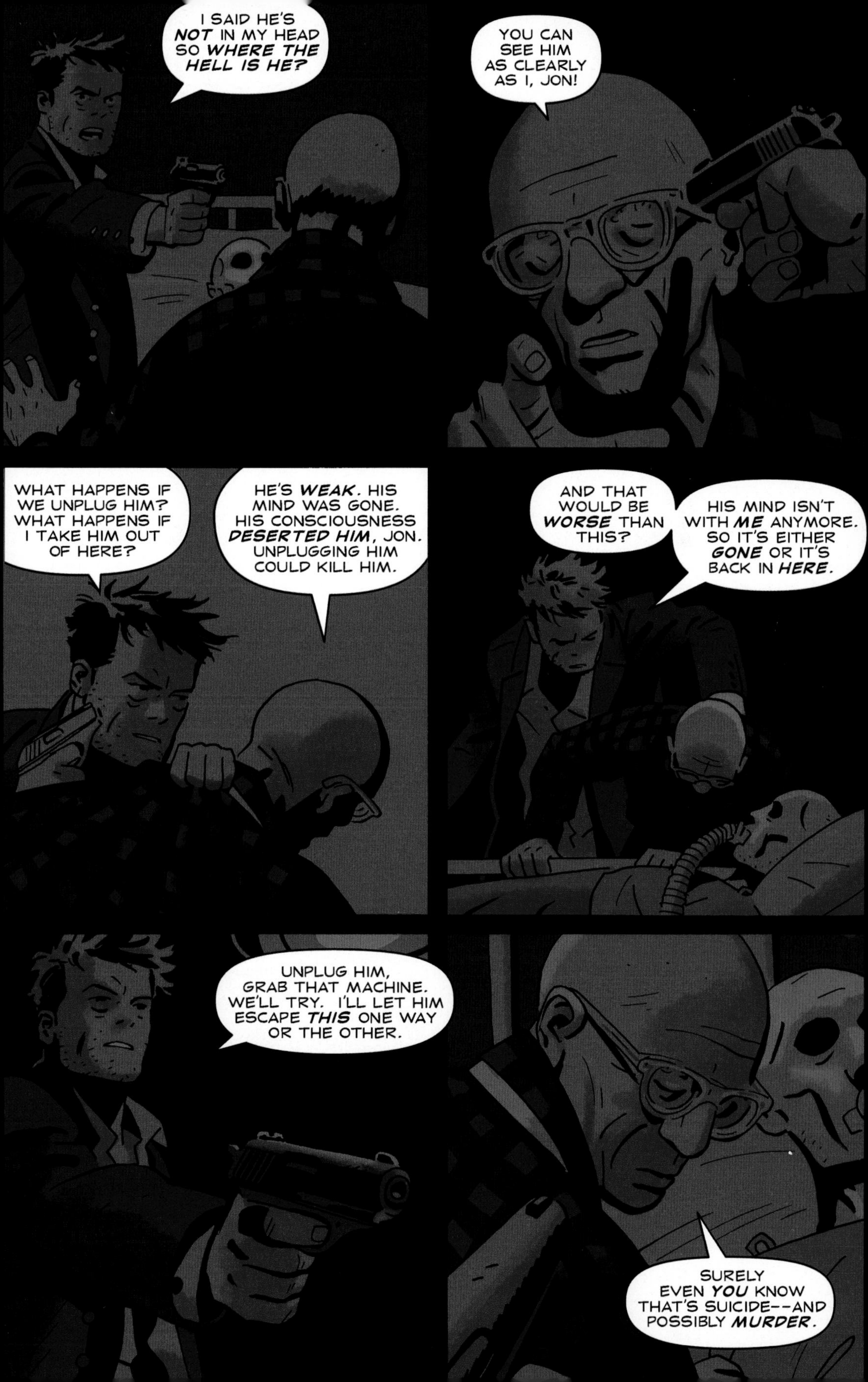

I SAID HE'S *NOT* IN MY HEAD SO *WHERE THE HELL IS HE?*
YOU CAN SEE HIM AS CLEARLY AS I, JON!
WHAT HAPPENS IF WE UNPLUG HIM? WHAT HAPPENS IF I TAKE HIM OUT OF HERE?
HE'S *WEAK*. HIS MIND WAS GONE. HIS CONSCIOUSNESS *DESERTED HIM*, JON. UNPLUGGING HIM COULD KILL HIM.
AND THAT WOULD BE *WORSE* THAN THIS?
HIS MIND ISN'T WITH *ME* ANYMORE. SO IT'S EITHER *GONE* OR IT'S BACK IN *HERE*.
UNPLUG HIM, GRAB THAT MACHINE. WE'LL TRY. I'LL LET HIM ESCAPE *THIS* ONE WAY OR THE OTHER.
SURELY EVEN *YOU* KNOW THAT'S SUICIDE--AND POSSIBLY *MURDER*.

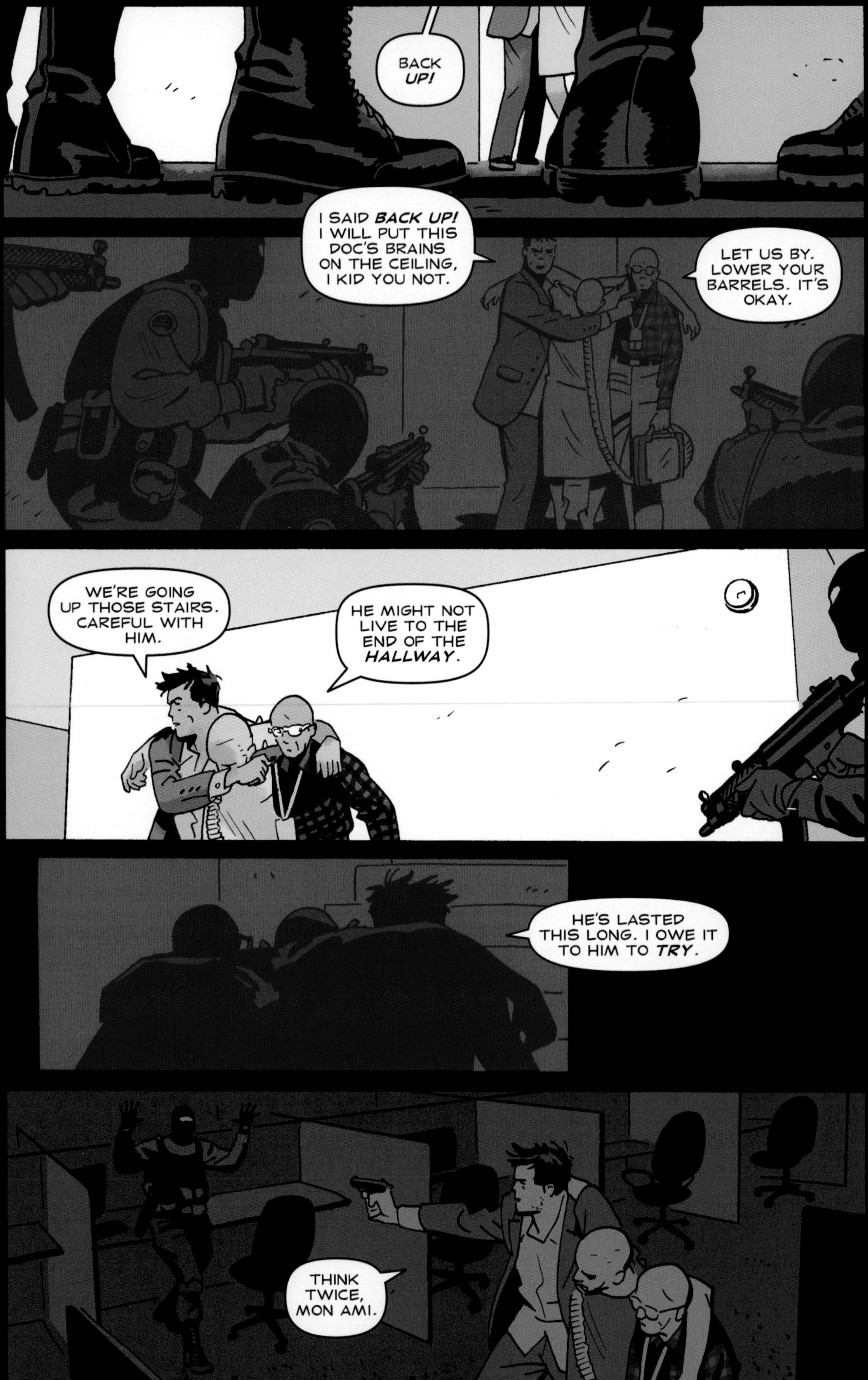
BACK UP!
I SAID BACK UP! I WILL PUT THIS DOC'S BRAINS ON THE CEILING, I KID YOU NOT.
LET US BY. LOWER YOUR BARRELS. IT'S OKAY.
WE'RE GOING UP THOSE STAIRS. CAREFUL WITH HIM.
HE MIGHT NOT LIVE TO THE END OF THE HALLWAY.
HE'S LASTED THIS LONG. I OWE IT TO HIM TO TRY.
THINK TWICE, MON AMI.

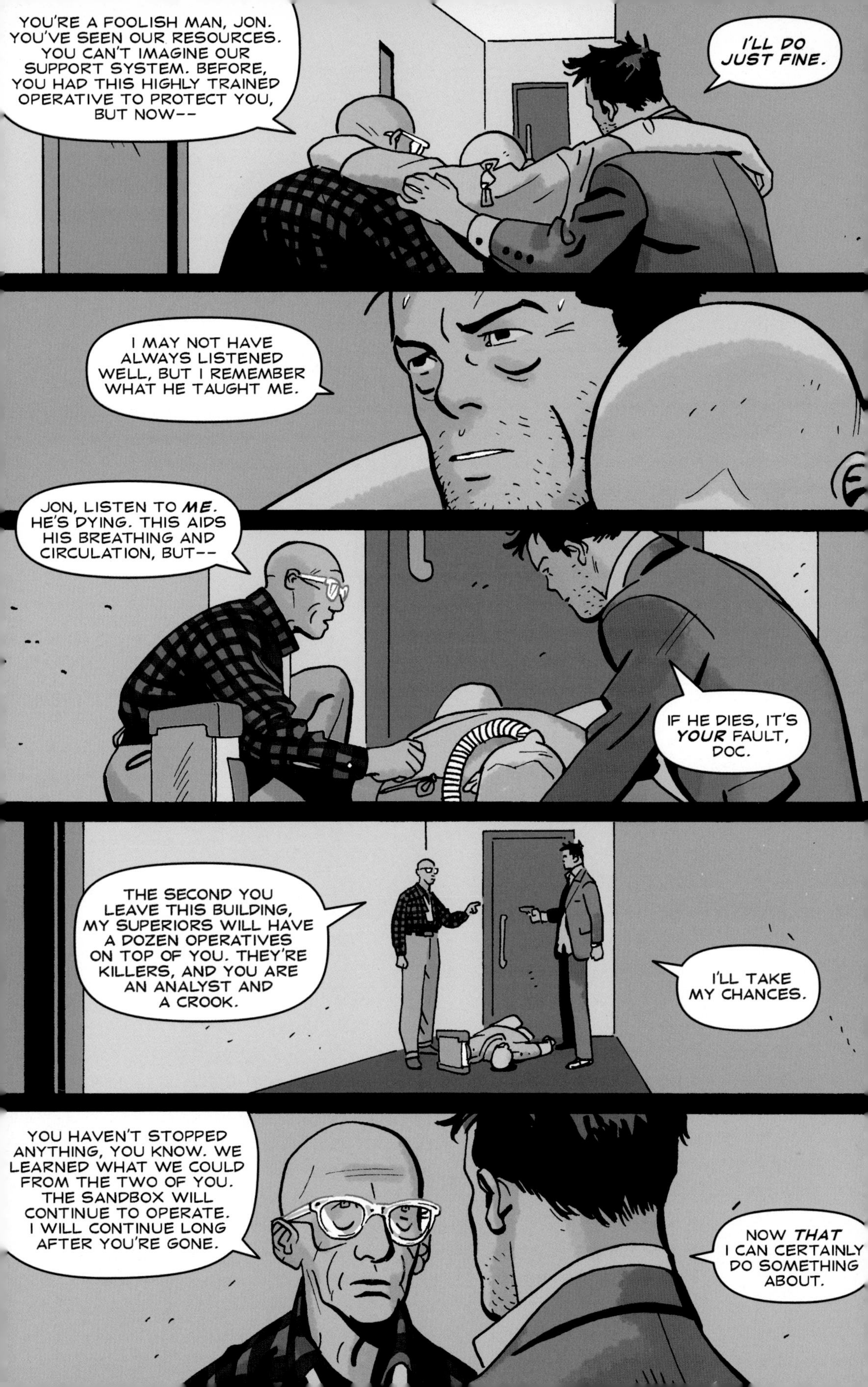
YOU'RE A FOOLISH MAN, JON. YOU'VE SEEN OUR RESOURCES. YOU CAN'T IMAGINE OUR SUPPORT SYSTEM. BEFORE, YOU HAD THIS HIGHLY TRAINED OPERATIVE TO PROTECT YOU, BUT NOW--
I'LL DO JUST FINE.
I MAY NOT HAVE ALWAYS LISTENED WELL, BUT I REMEMBER WHAT HE TAUGHT ME.
JON, LISTEN TO ME. HE'S DYING. THIS AIDS HIS BREATHING AND CIRCULATION, BUT--
IF HE DIES, IT'S YOUR FAULT, DOC.
THE SECOND YOU LEAVE THIS BUILDING, MY SUPERIORS WILL HAVE A DOZEN OPERATIVES ON TOP OF YOU. THEY'RE KILLERS, AND YOU ARE AN ANALYST AND A CROOK.
I'LL TAKE MY CHANCES.
YOU HAVEN'T STOPPED ANYTHING, YOU KNOW. WE LEARNED WHAT WE COULD FROM THE TWO OF YOU. THE SANDBOX WILL CONTINUE TO OPERATE. I WILL CONTINUE LONG AFTER YOU'RE GONE.
NOW THAT I CAN CERTAINLY DO SOMETHING ABOUT.

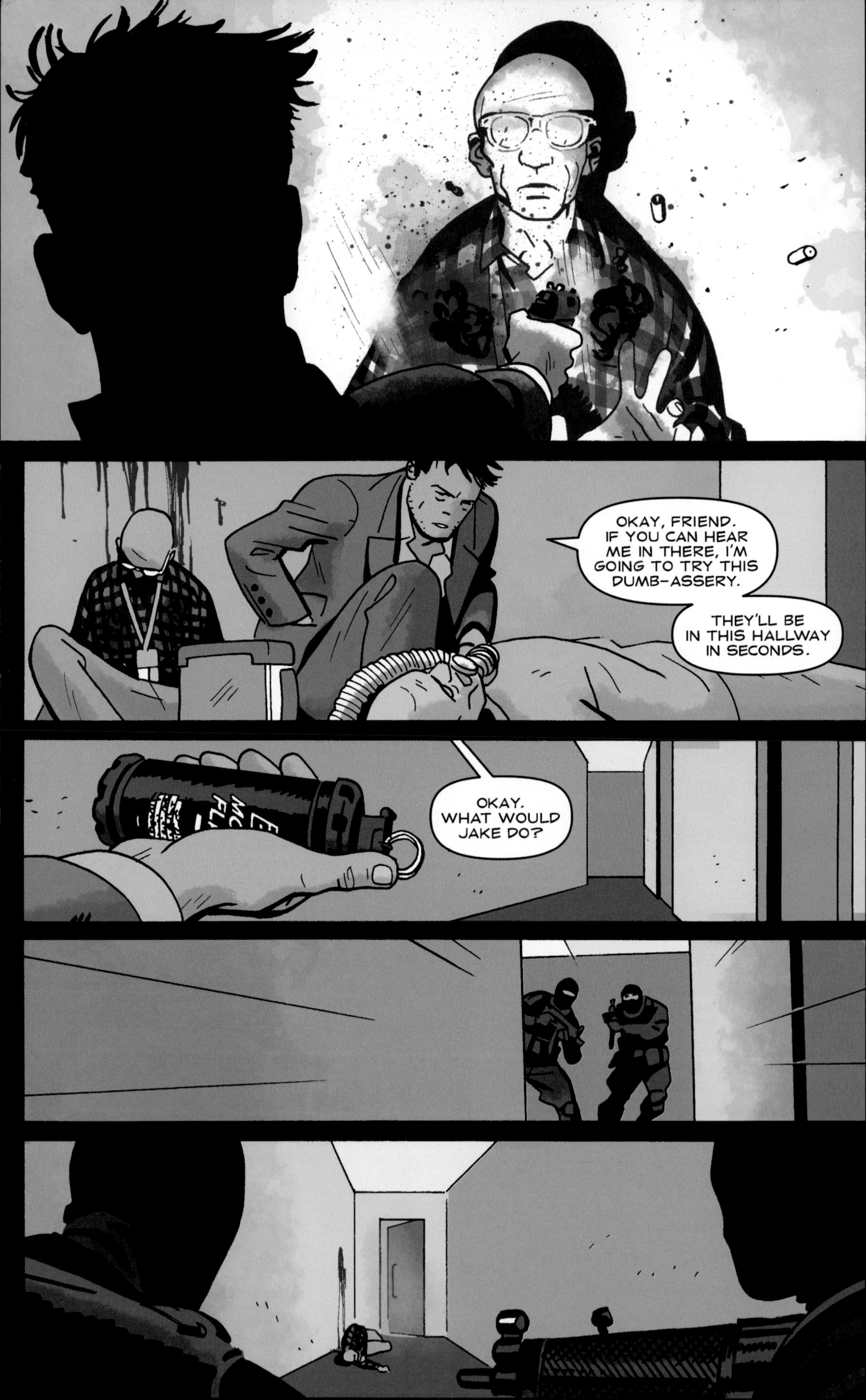
OKAY, FRIEND. IF YOU CAN HEAR ME IN THERE, I'M GOING TO TRY THIS DUMB-ASSERY.
THEY'LL BE IN THIS HALLWAY IN SECONDS.
OKAY. WHAT WOULD JAKE DO?

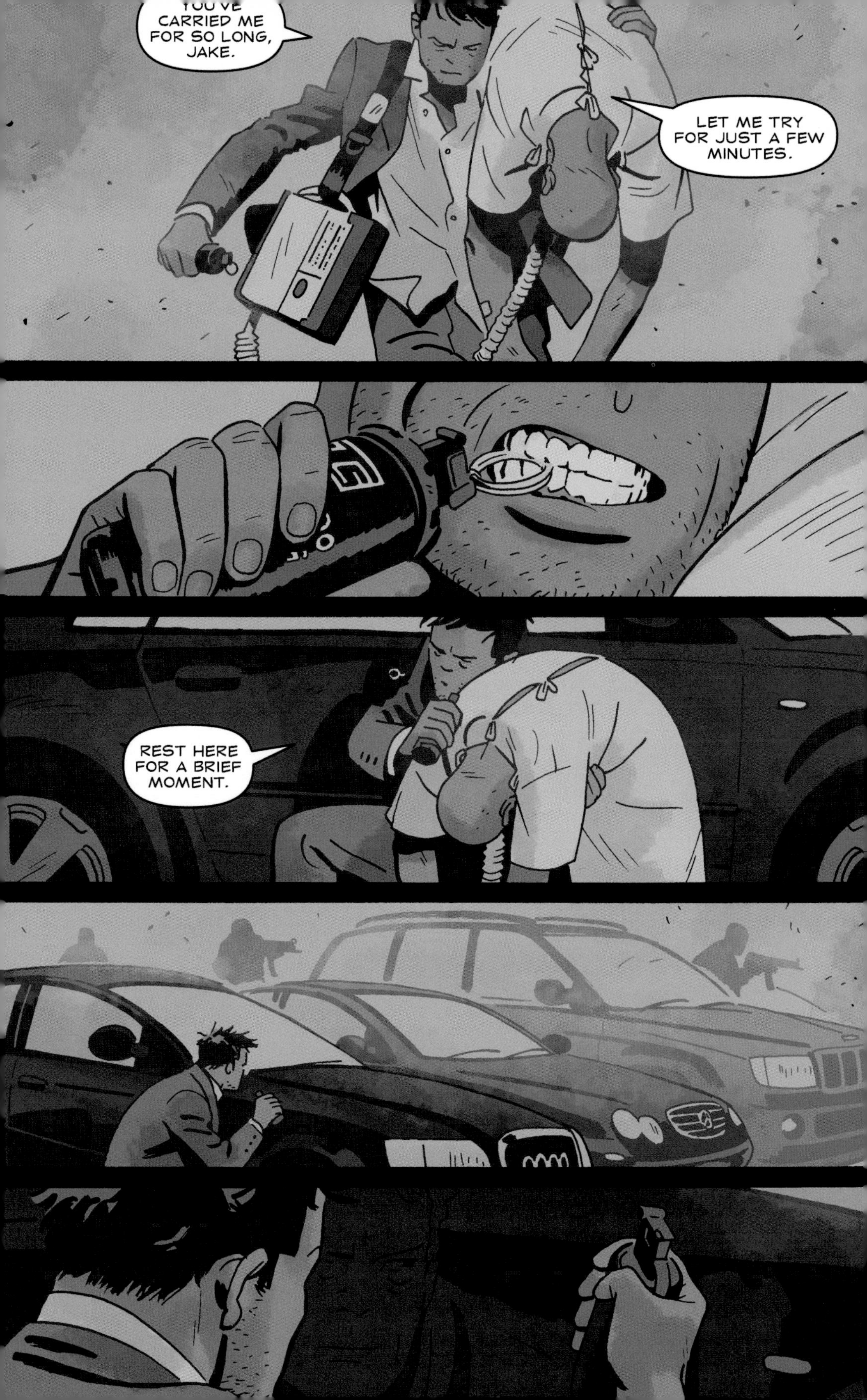
CARRIED ME FOR SO LONG, JAKE.
LET ME TRY FOR JUST A FEW MINUTES.
REST HERE FOR A BRIEF MOMENT.

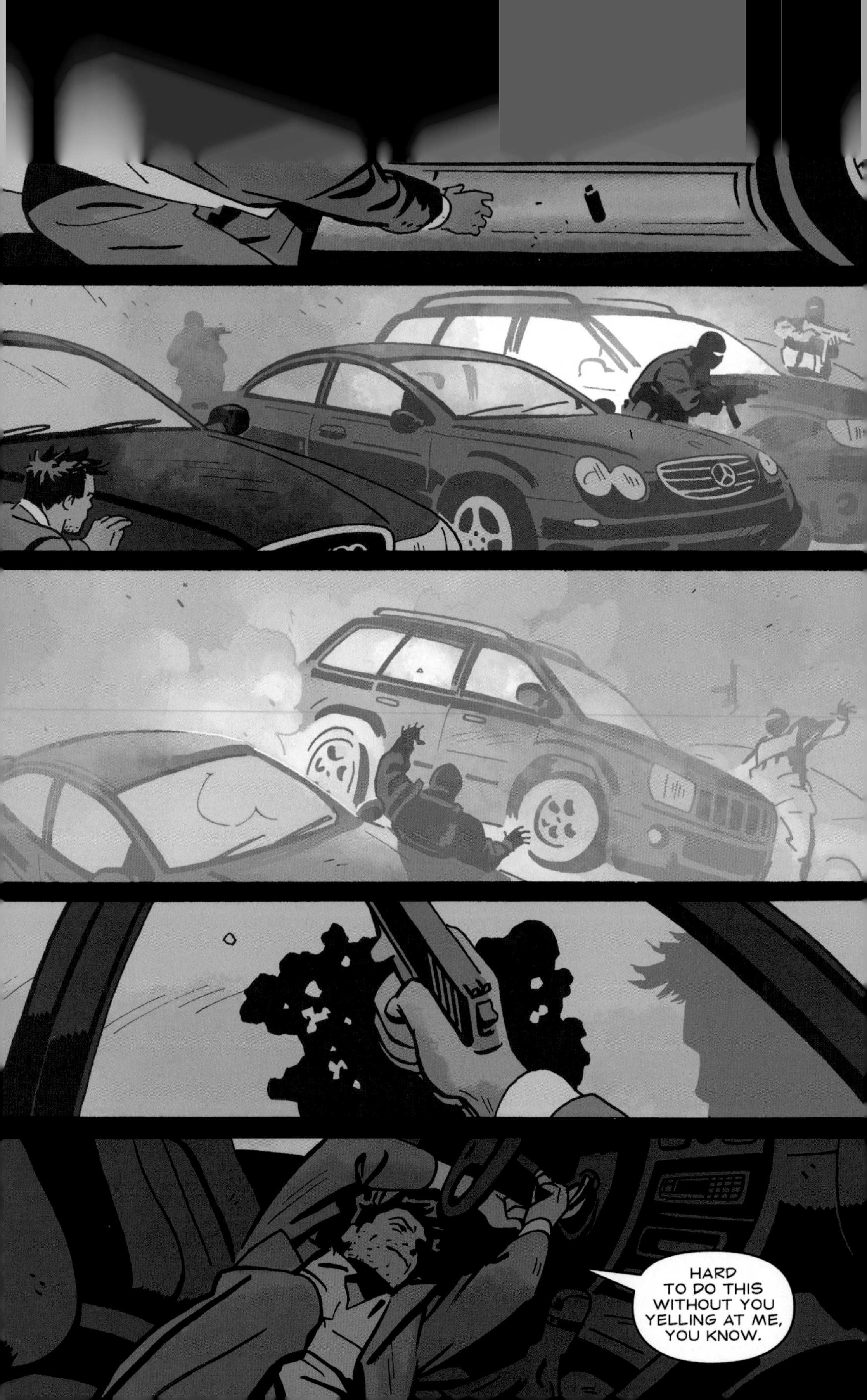
HARD TO DO THIS WITHOUT YOU YELLING AT ME, YOU KNOW.

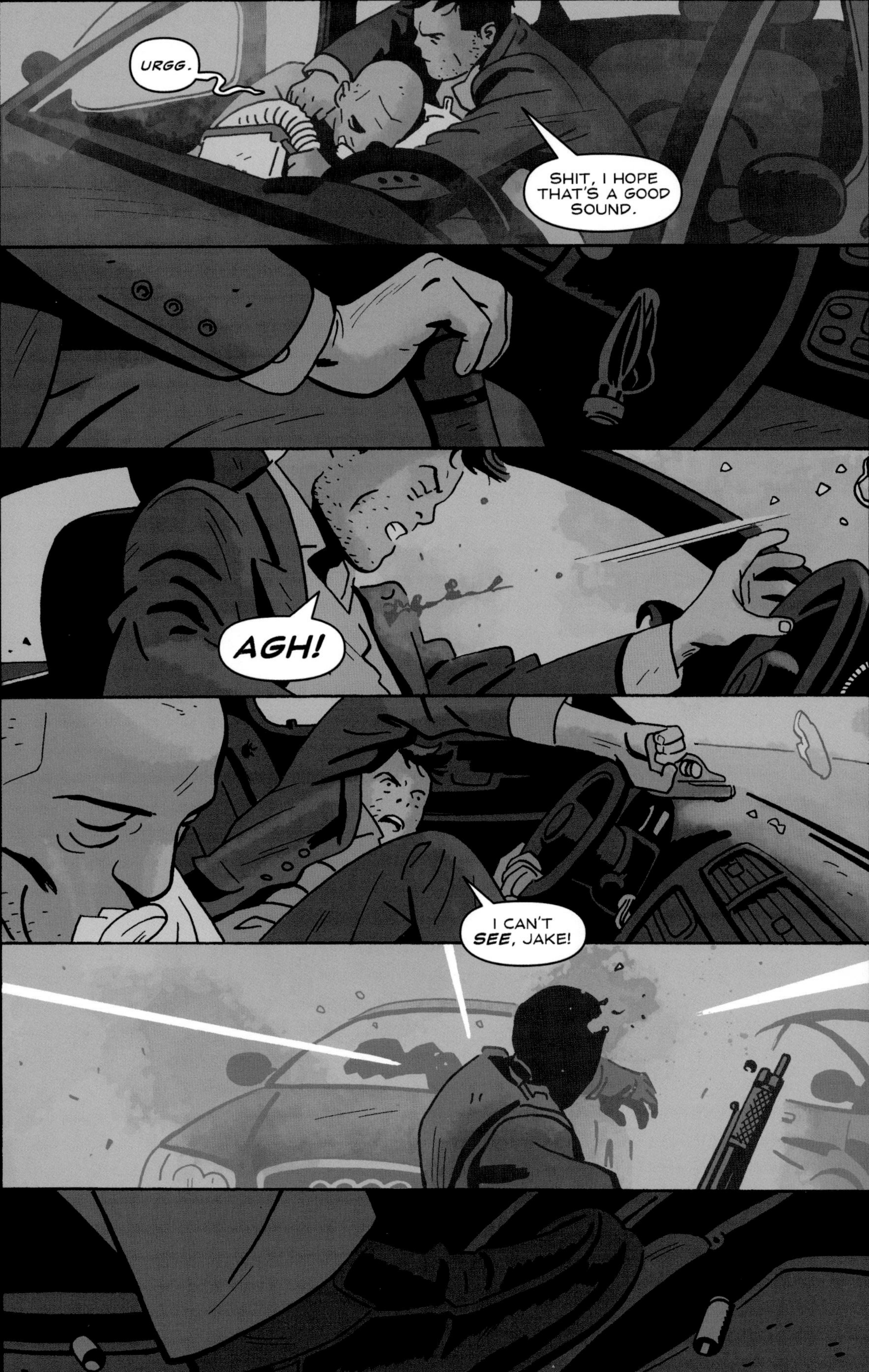
URGG.
SHIT, I HOPE THAT'S A GOOD SOUND.
AGH!
I CAN'T SEE, JAKE!

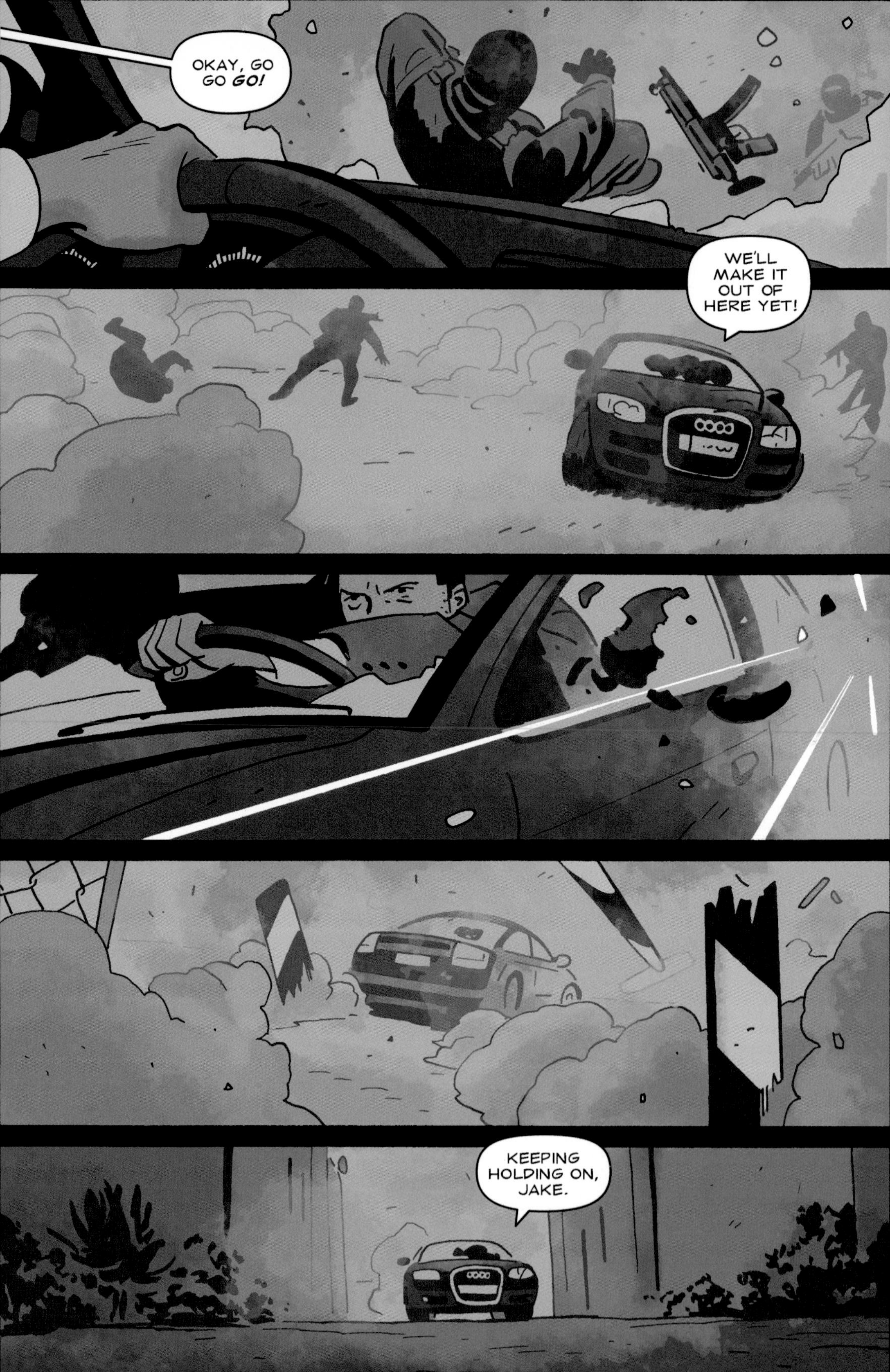
OKAY, GO GO *GO!*
WE'LL MAKE IT OUT OF HERE YET!
KEEPING HOLDING ON, JAKE.

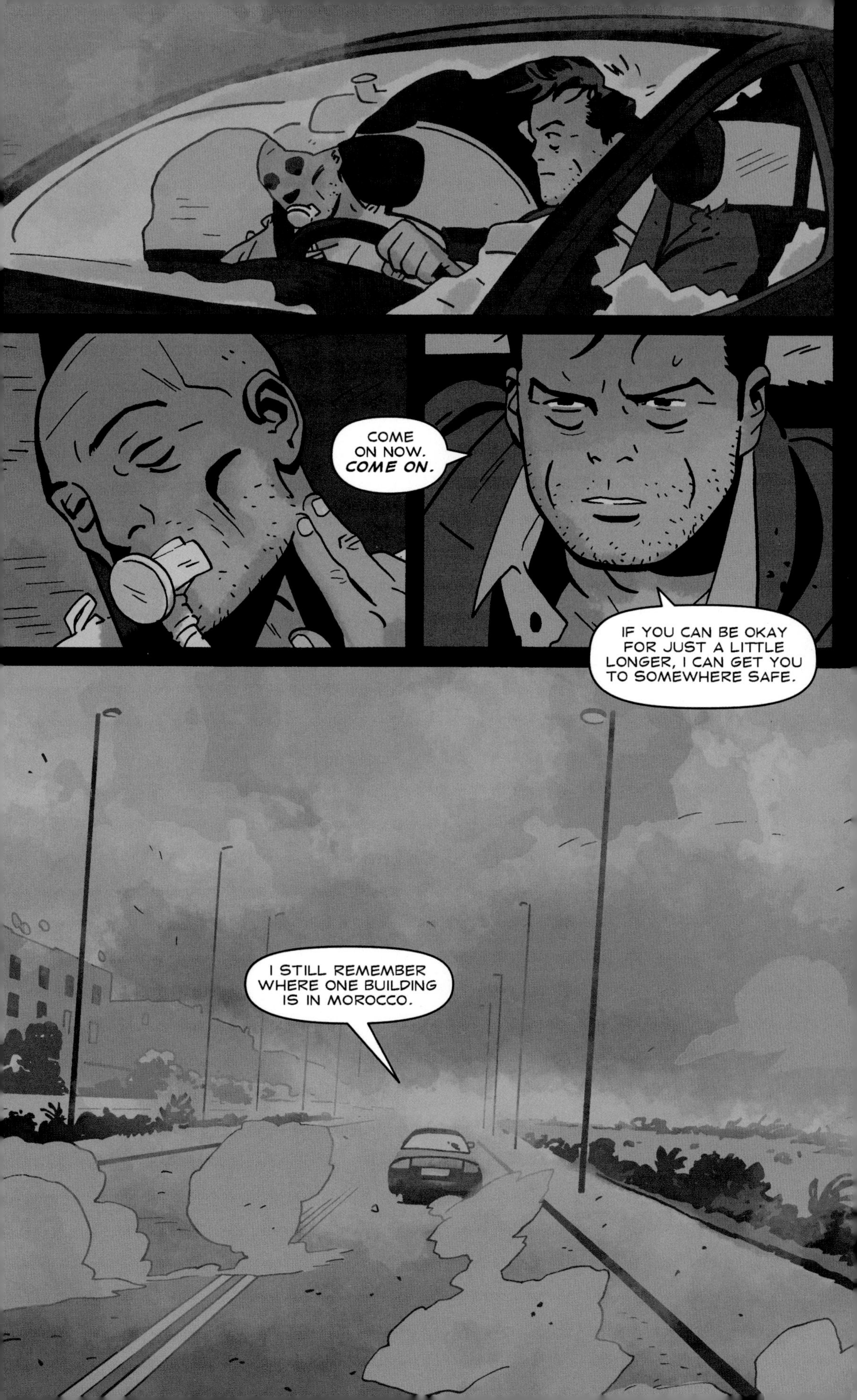
COME ON NOW. COME ON.
IF YOU CAN BE OKAY FOR JUST A LITTLE LONGER, I CAN GET YOU TO SOMEWHERE SAFE.
I STILL REMEMBER WHERE ONE BUILDING IS IN MOROCCO.

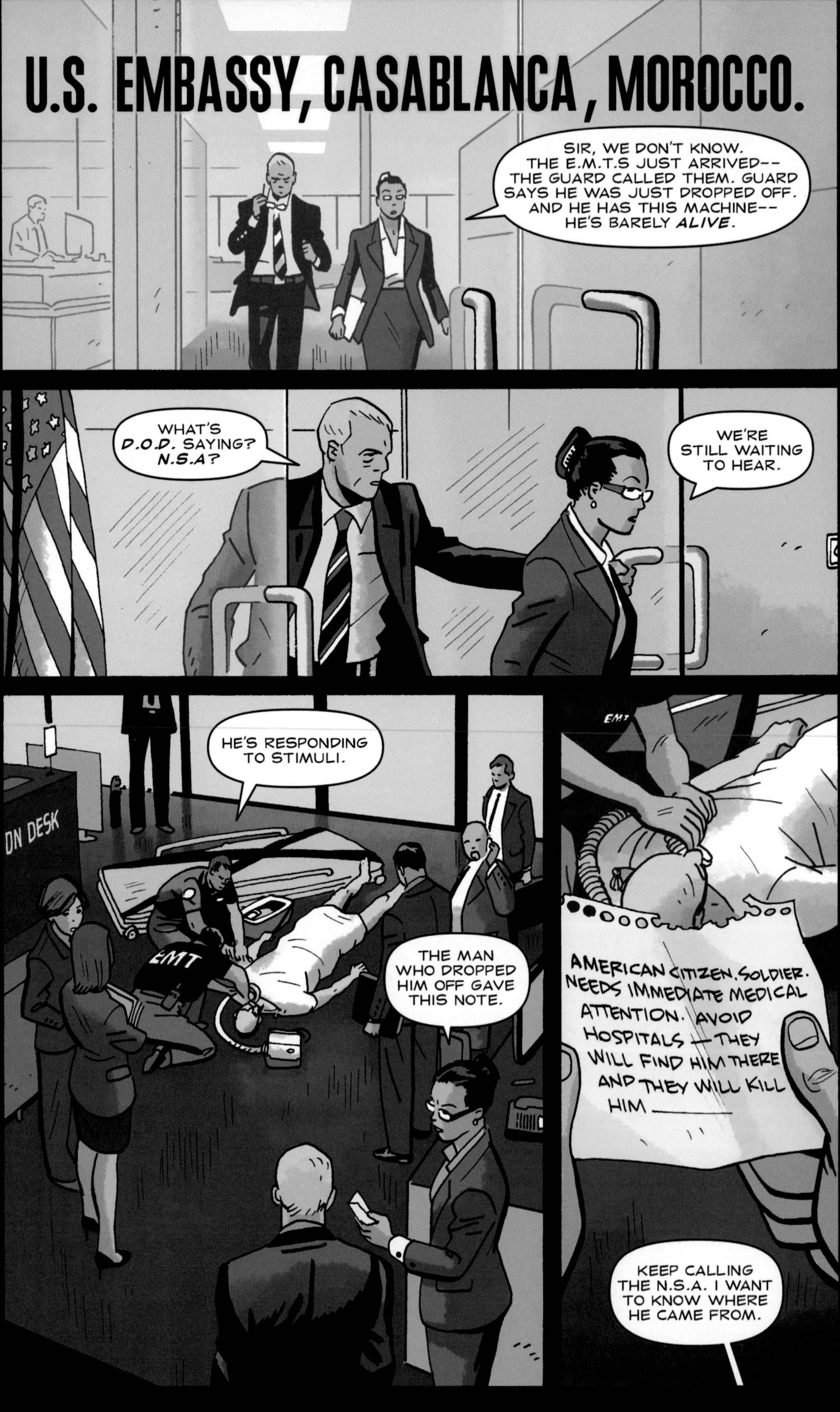
U.S. EMBASSY, CASABLANCA, MOROCCO.
SIR, WE DON'T KNOW. THE E.M.T.S JUST ARRIVED-- THE GUARD CALLED THEM. GUARD SAYS HE WAS JUST DROPPED OFF. AND HE HAS THIS MACHINE-- HE'S BARELY ALIVE.
WHAT'S D.O.D. SAYING? N.S.A?
WE'RE STILL WAITING TO HEAR.
HE'S RESPONDING TO STIMULI.
ON DESK
EMT
THE MAN WHO DROPPED HIM OFF GAVE THIS NOTE.
EMT
AMERICAN CITIZEN. SOLDIER. NEEDS IMMEDIATE MEDICAL ATTENTION. AVOID HOSPITALS — THEY WILL FIND HIM THERE AND THEY WILL KILL HIM ______
KEEP CALLING THE N.S.A. I WANT TO KNOW WHERE HE CAME FROM.

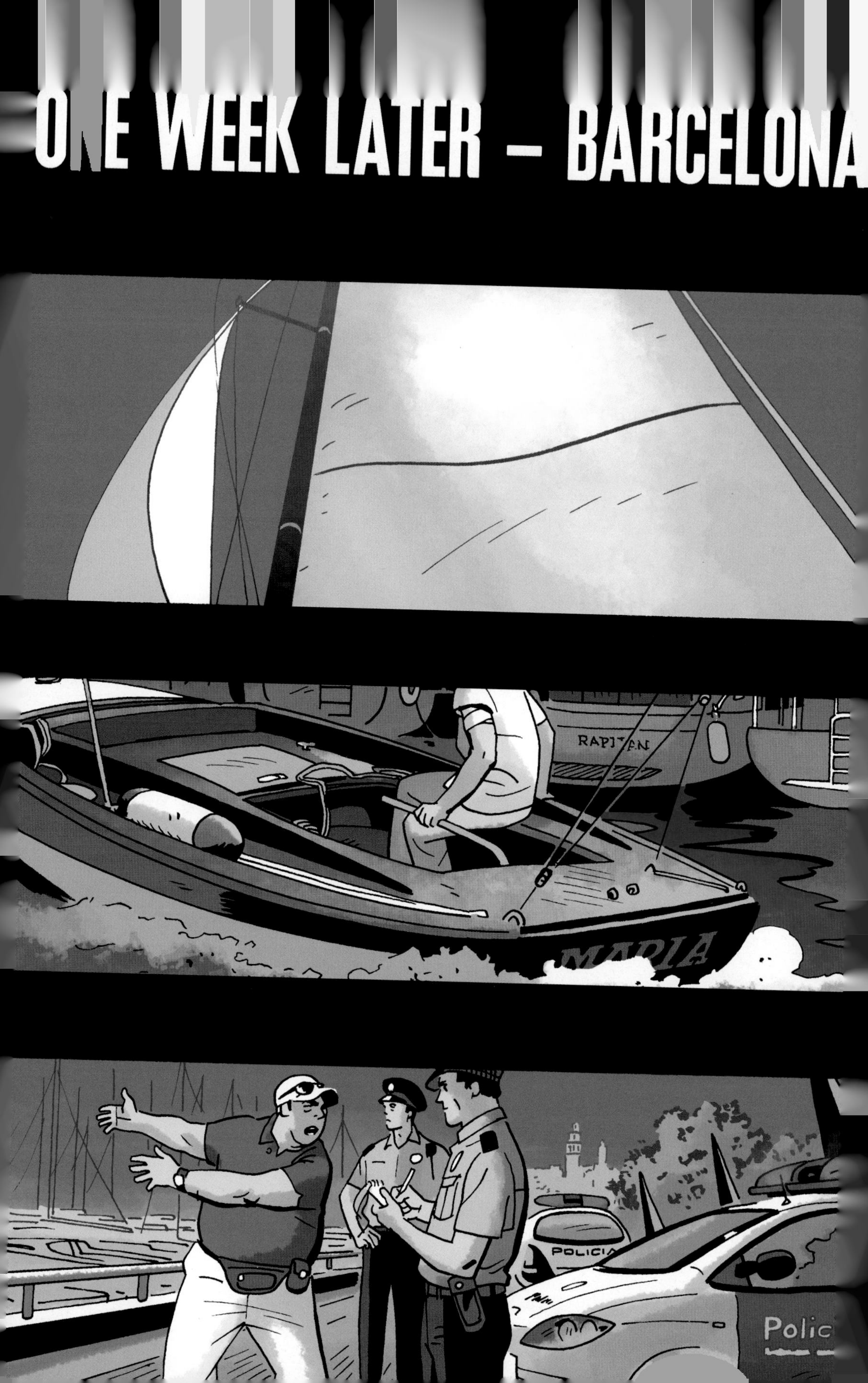
ONE WEEK LATER – BARCELONA
RAPITAN
MARIA
POLICIA
Polic

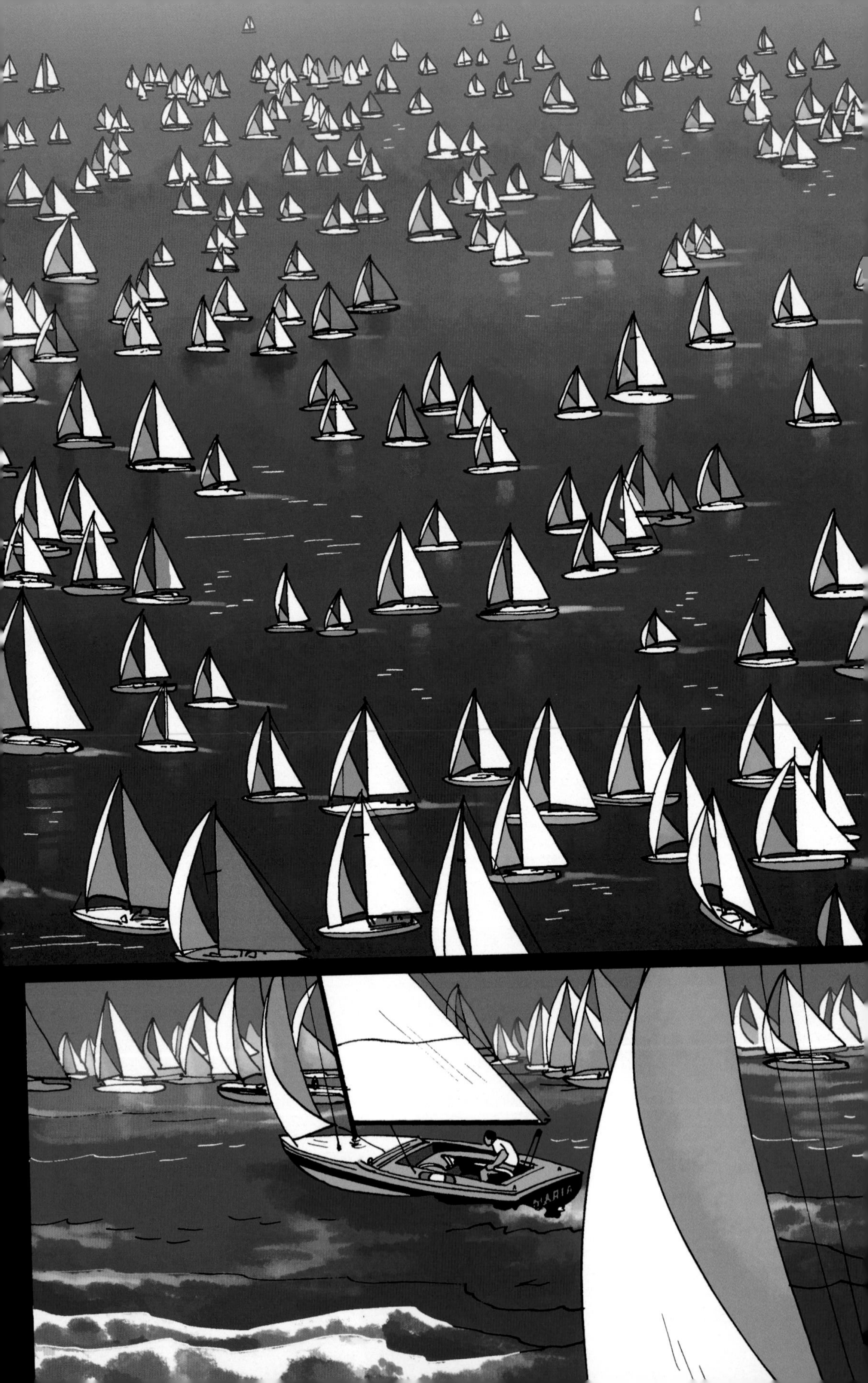

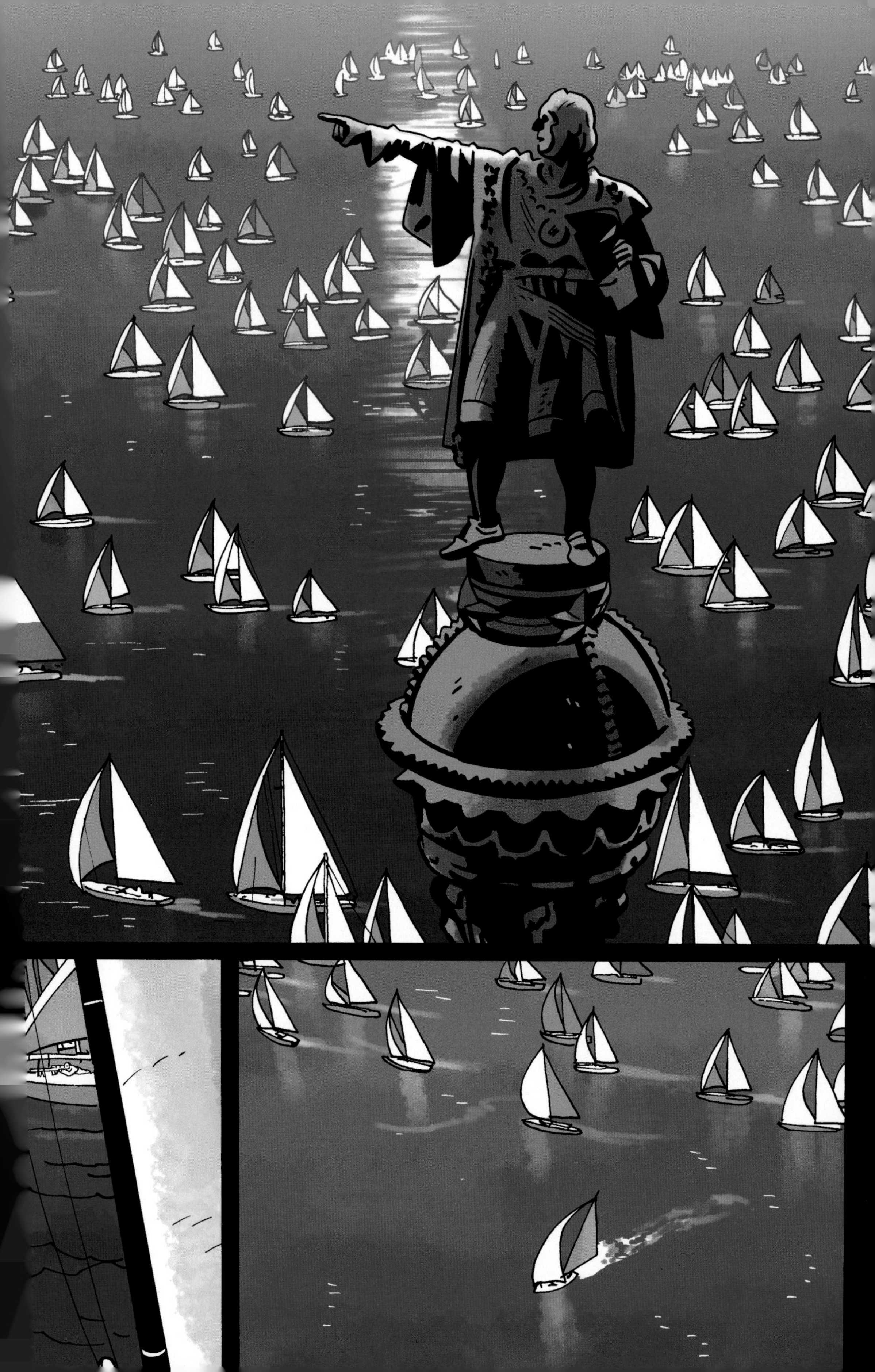

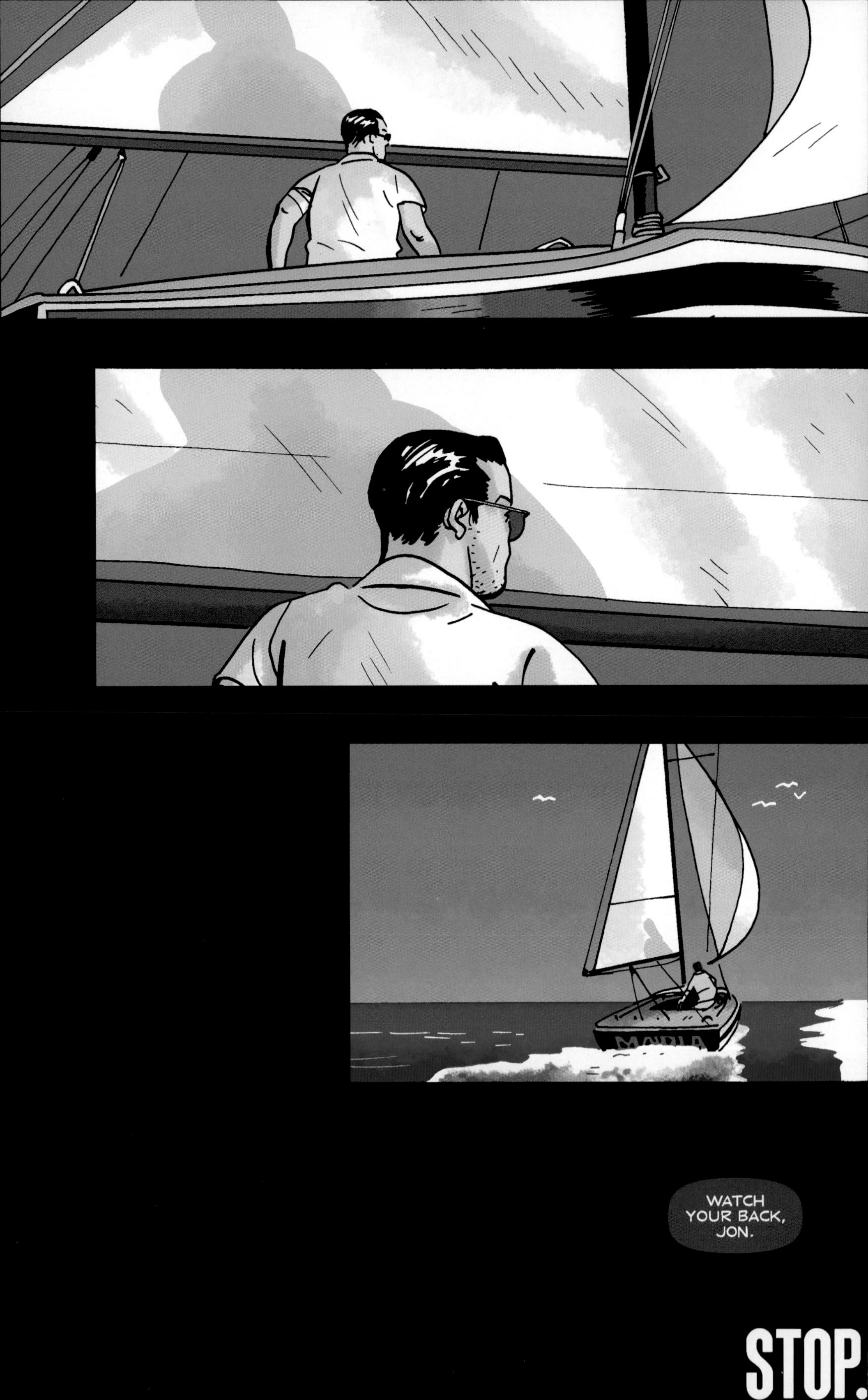
WATCH YOUR BACK, JON.
STOP.

COVER CONCEPTS

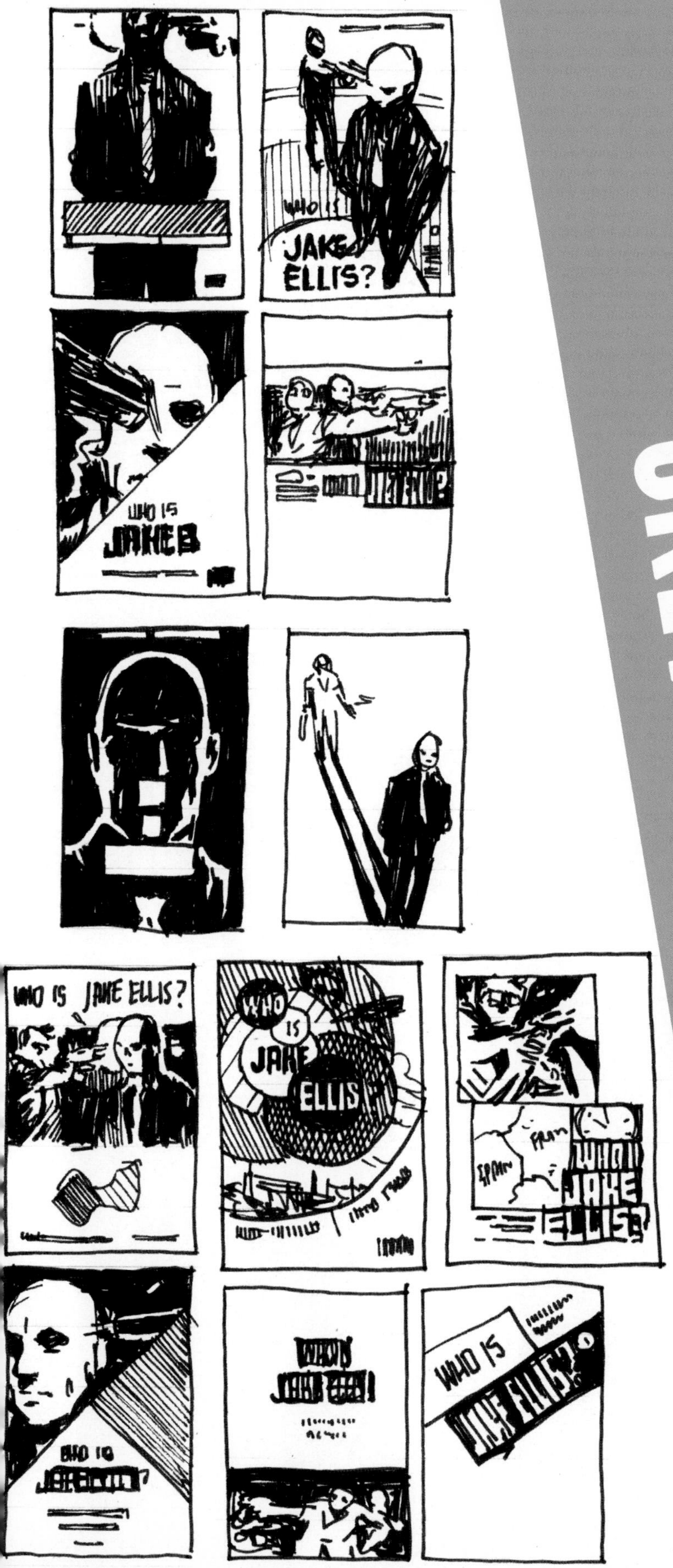
WHO
JAKE
ELLIS?
WHO IS
WHO IS JAKE ELLIS?
WHO
IS
JAKE
ELLIS
WHO IS

SKETCHBOOK

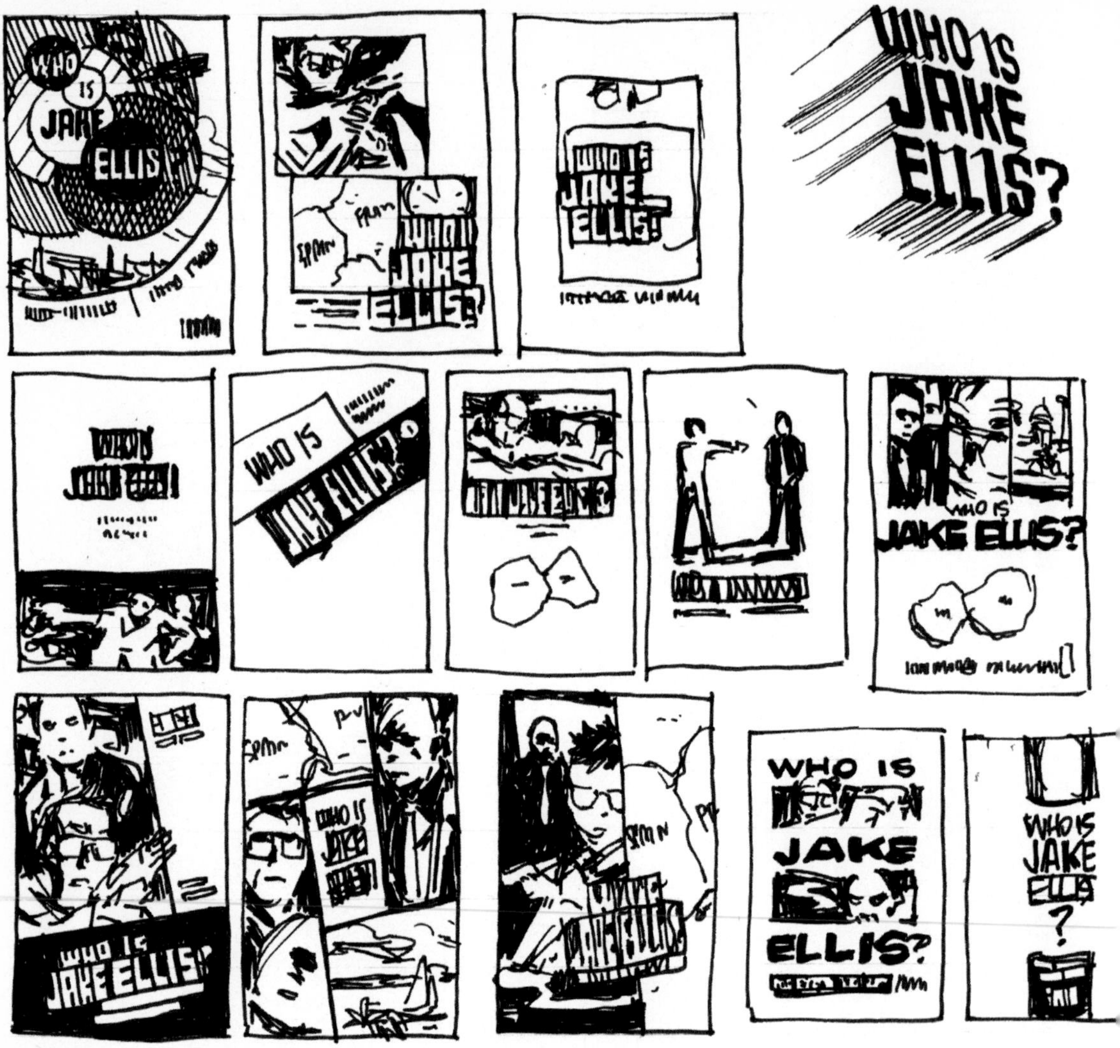
WHO IS
JAKE
ELLIS?

COVER CONCEPTS

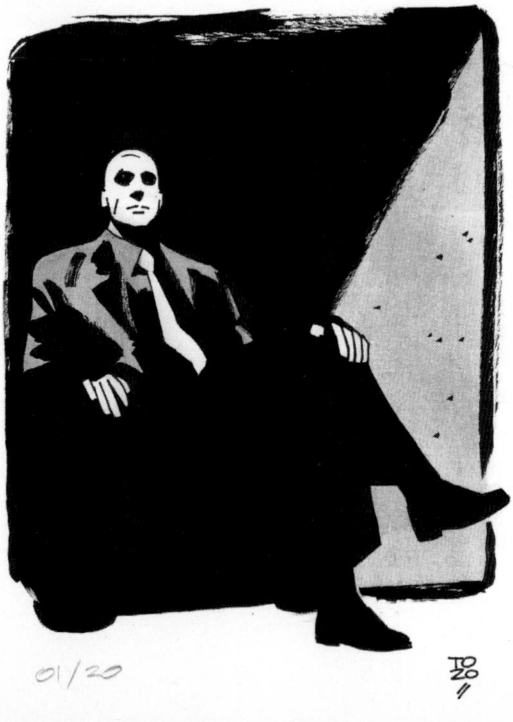

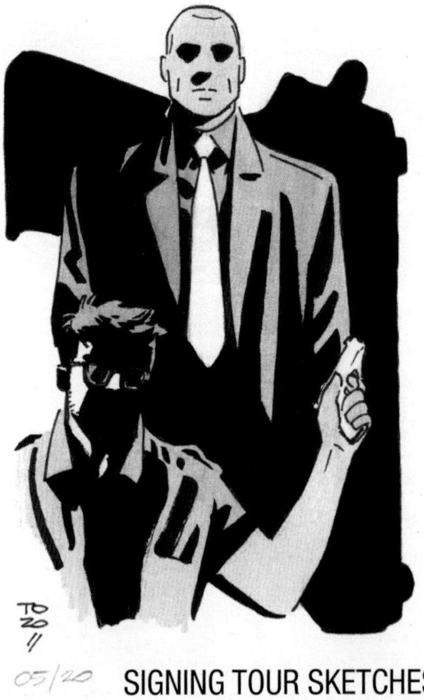

SIGNING TOUR SKETCHES

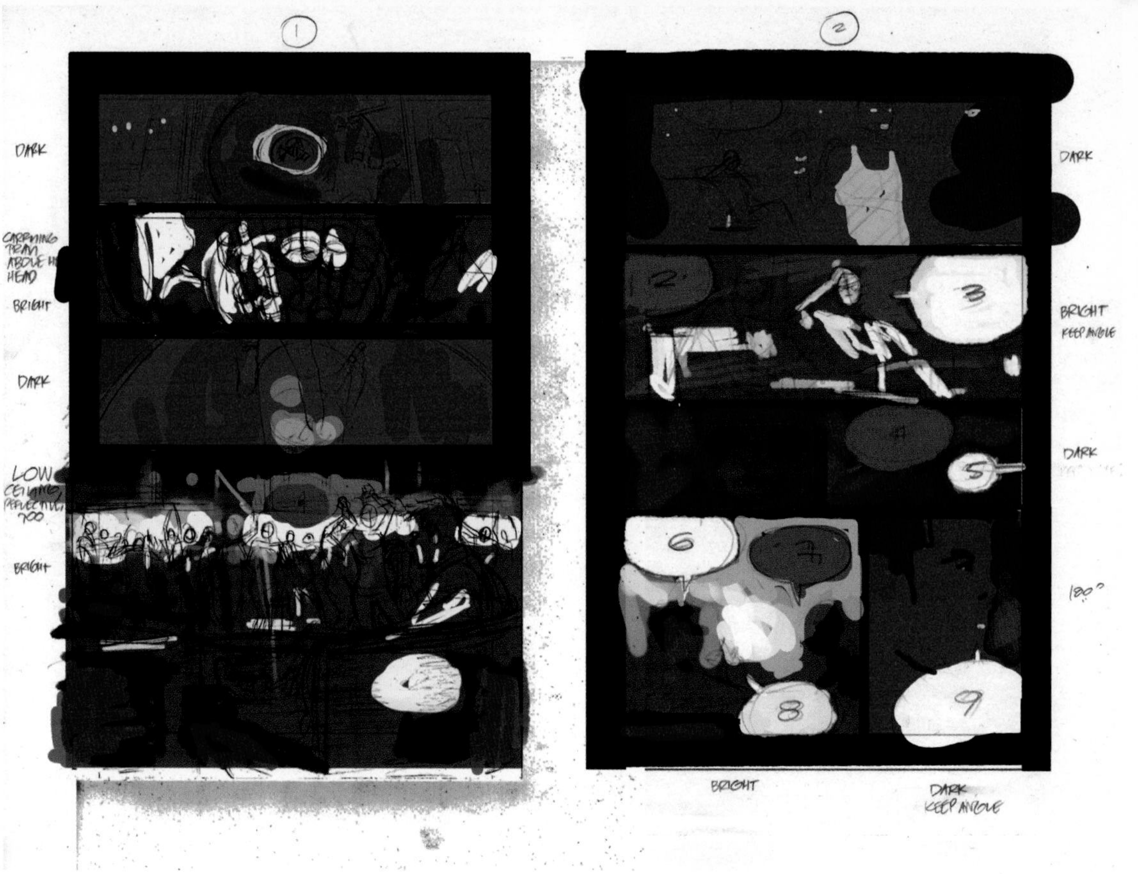
DARK
BRIGHT
DARK
LOW CEILING REFLECTING, TOO
BRIGHT
DARK
BRIGHT
KEEP ANGLE
DARK
180°
BRIGHT
DARK
KEEP ANGLE

ISSUE 3, PAGES 1-2 COLOR GUIDE

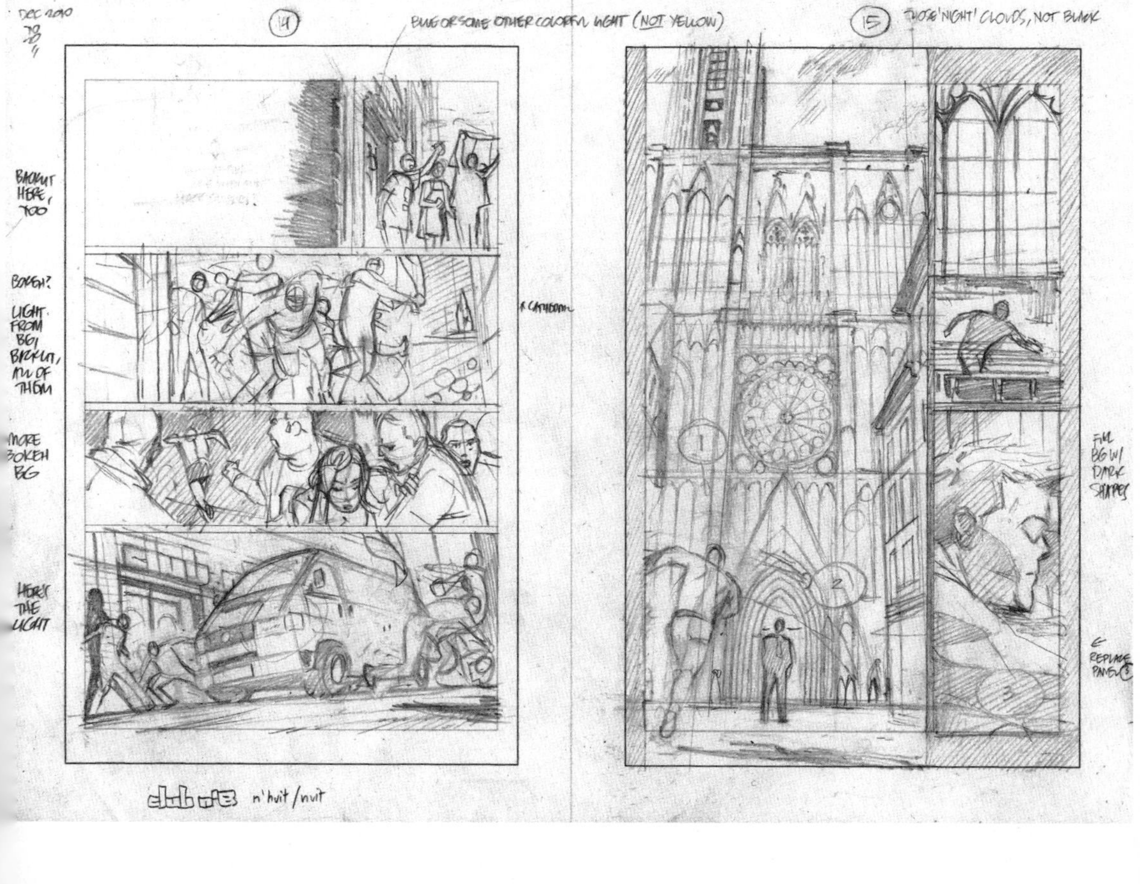
DEC 2010
BLUE OR SOME OTHER COLORFUL LIGHT (NOT YELLOW)
BACKLIT HERE, TOO
BOKEH?
LIGHT FROM BG, BACKLIT, ALL OF THEM
MORE BOKEH BG
HERE'S THE LIGHT
THOSE 'NIGHT' CLOUDS, NOT BLACK
FILL BG W/ DARK SHAPES
REPLACE PANEL 3
n' huit / nuit

ISSUE 1, PAGES 14-15 LAYOUTS

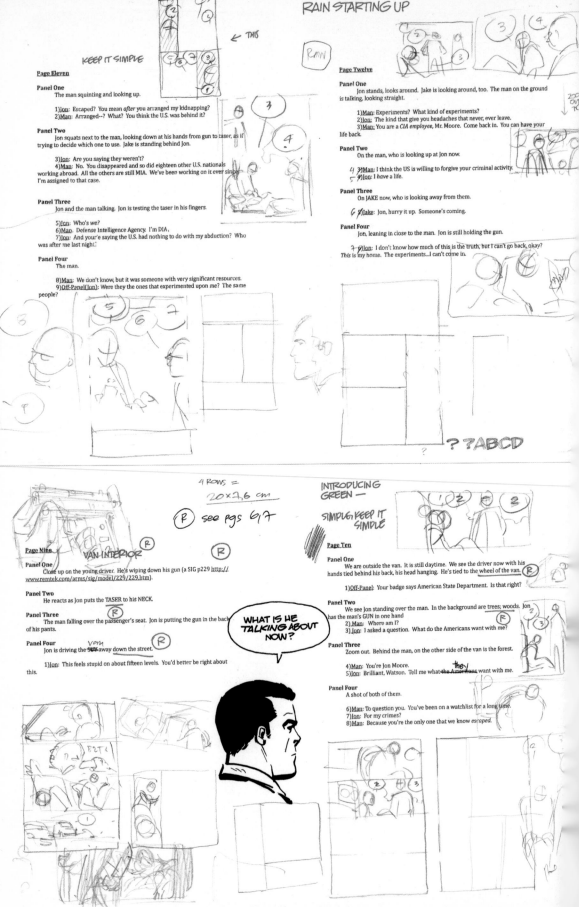

RAIN STARTING UP

KEEP IT SIMPLE ← THIS

Page Eleven

Panel One

The man squinting and looking up.

1)Jon: Escaped? You mean *after* you arranged my kidnapping?
2)Man: Arranged--? What? You think the U.S. was behind it?

Panel Two

Jon squats next to the man, looking down at his hands from gun to taser, as if trying to decide which one to use. Jake is standing behind Jon.

3)Jon: Are you saying they weren't?
4)Man: No. You disappeared and so did eighteen other U.S. nationals working abroad. All the others are still MIA. We've been working on it ever since I'm assigned to that case.

Panel Three

Jon and the man talking. Jon is testing the taser in his fingers.

5)Jon: Who's *we*?
6)Man: Defense Intelligence Agency. I'm DIA.
7)Jon: And your'e saying the U.S. had nothing to do with my abduction? Who was after me last night?

Panel Four

The man.

8)Man: We don't know, but it was someone with very significant resources.
9)Off-Panel(Jon): Were they the ones that experimented upon me? The same people?

Page Twelve

Panel One

Jon stands, looks around. Jake is looking around, too. The man on the ground is talking, looking straight.

1)Man: Experiments? What kind of experiments?
2)Jon: The kind that give you headaches that never, ever leave.
3)Man: You are a *CIA employee*, Mr. Moore. Come back in. You can have your life back.

Panel Two

On the man, who is looking up at Jon now.

3)Man: I think the US is willing to forgive your criminal activity.
4)Jon: I have a life.

Panel Three

On JAKE now, who is looking away from them.

5)Jake: Jon, hurry it up. Someone's coming.

Panel Four

Jon, leaning in close to the man. Jon is still holding the gun.

7)Jon: I don't know how much of this is the truth, but I can't go back, okay? *This* is my home. The experiments...I can't come in.

? ?ABCD

4 ROWS =
20×7.6 cm

(R) see pgs 6,7

INTRODUCING
GREEN —

SIMPLY KEEP IT
SIMPLE

Page Nine VAN INTERIOR (R)

Panel One

Close up on the young driver. He's wiping down his gun (a SIG p229 http://www.remtek.com/arms/sig/model/229/229.htm).

Panel Two

He reacts as Jon puts the TASER to his NECK.

Panel Three (R)

The man falling over the passenger's seat. Jon is putting the gun in the back of his pants.

Panel Four

Jon is driving the ~~car~~ van away down the street. (R)

1)Jon: This feels stupid on about fifteen levels. You'd better be right about this.

WHAT IS HE TALKING ABOUT NOW?

Page Ten

Panel One

We are outside the van. It is still daytime. We see the driver now with his hands tied behind his back, his head hanging. He's tied to the wheel of the van. (R)

1)Off-Panel: Your badge says American State Department. Is that right?

Panel Two

We see Jon standing over the man. In the background are trees; woods. Jon has the man's GUN in one hand. (R)

2)Man: Where am I?
3)Jon: I asked a question. What do the Americans want with me?

Panel Three

Zoom out. Behind the man, on the other side of the van is the forest.

4)Man: You're Jon Moore.
5)Jon: Brilliant, Watson. Tell me what ~~the Americans~~ they want with me.

Panel Four

A shot of both of them.

6)Man: To question you. You've been on a watchlist for a long time.
7)Jon: For my crimes?
8)Man: Because you're the only one that we know *escaped*.

SCRIPT NOTES AND THUMBNAILS

Panel One

Jake is now crouching by Jon. The first time we've seen Jake crouch. It should feel natural, until you really think about it.

    1)Jake: I told you something happened to me two months ago.
    2)Jake: It was when you were on a job. The Berlin job, pulling those files.

Panel Two   *HOW DO WE SET IT AS A FLASHBACK? ROUND CORNERS?*

A FLASHBACK. In it, Jon is in BLACK TACTICAL GEAR, a flashlight in his mouth as he (R) flips through files in a dark office. In the background, barely visible is JAKE.

    3)Jake(tailless): I waited, and watched, like I always do. But something happened.

Panel Three

Zoom in on Jake in the dark.

    4)Jake(tailless): I had a *memory*.

Panel Four   *GONITH SPECIFIC FACES!*   *?, IS SHE WRAPPED IN A FLAG?*

Suddenly a flash of a BEAUTIFUL BRUNETTE WOMAN, an American. Blurry, stylized. Unreal. If you want to someone use the image of jake in this, superimposed or something, you can try that--I'm sure you can do it without making it cheesy :).

    5)Jake: I have no idea who she was. But I *remembered* her.
    6)Jon(tailless): My memory. Must have been *my* memory.

INTIMATE, FIRST PERSON - AS CLOSE AS YOU'D BE BEFORE KISSING SOMEONE

Panel Five

Jake back in Marrakech. He's looking down. Somehow DOUBTFUL. But his emotion is only slight.

    7)Jake: I don't know, Jon. I felt an emotional connection. Do you understand me? I felt *emotion*.

Panel Six

Jon, looking doubtful himself, shaking his head.

    8)Jon: You were put in my head. I think you're confusing it with my memories.
    9)Jake(off-panel): I know what I saw, and felt.

BLEED; NO REAL PANEL BORDERS

WHITE →

SAME ANGLE

  - and scene

Panel One

Jake is standing again. The reverie is gone. He looks all business.

    1)Jake: That's why I led you here. That's why I wanted you to do this.
    2)Jake: I just need to know. Just to know how I found myself one day standing over you. I need to know who *she* was, why I felt anything at all.

Panel Two   *2.1 - 1,2* / *4*

Jon looks over the low wall again.

    3)Jon: Well...
    4)Jon: It's not that I'm not curious about this place. I am.
    5)Jon: Just...promise me you'll get me out of there. It's alot to risk, you know, for the voice in my head.
    6)Jake(off-panel): I will.

Panel Three   *BUT STILL BELOW*

Jon, now getting up a bit. He's putting the gun in one pocket and the grenades in the other of his suit coat.

    7)Jon: Okay. We're here. I'll do this. We just need to find some wire cutters.

Panel Four

Jon, crawling down a series of boxes and trashcans he used to get up to the roof.

    8)Jon: The voice in my mind has developed a mind of its own. You can't make this stuff up.

Panel Five

Jake, still on the roof, looking serious while he looks at The Facility.

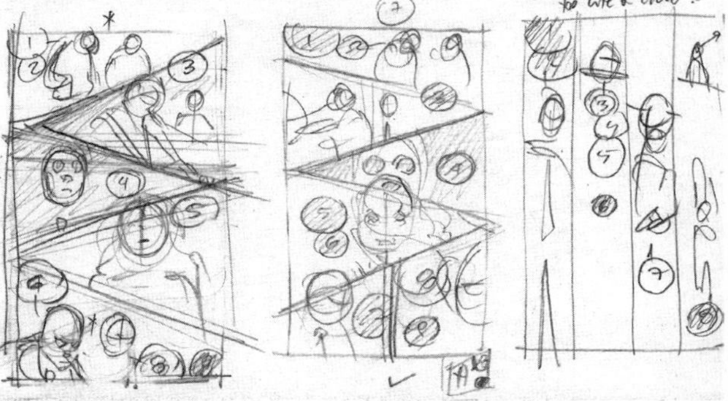

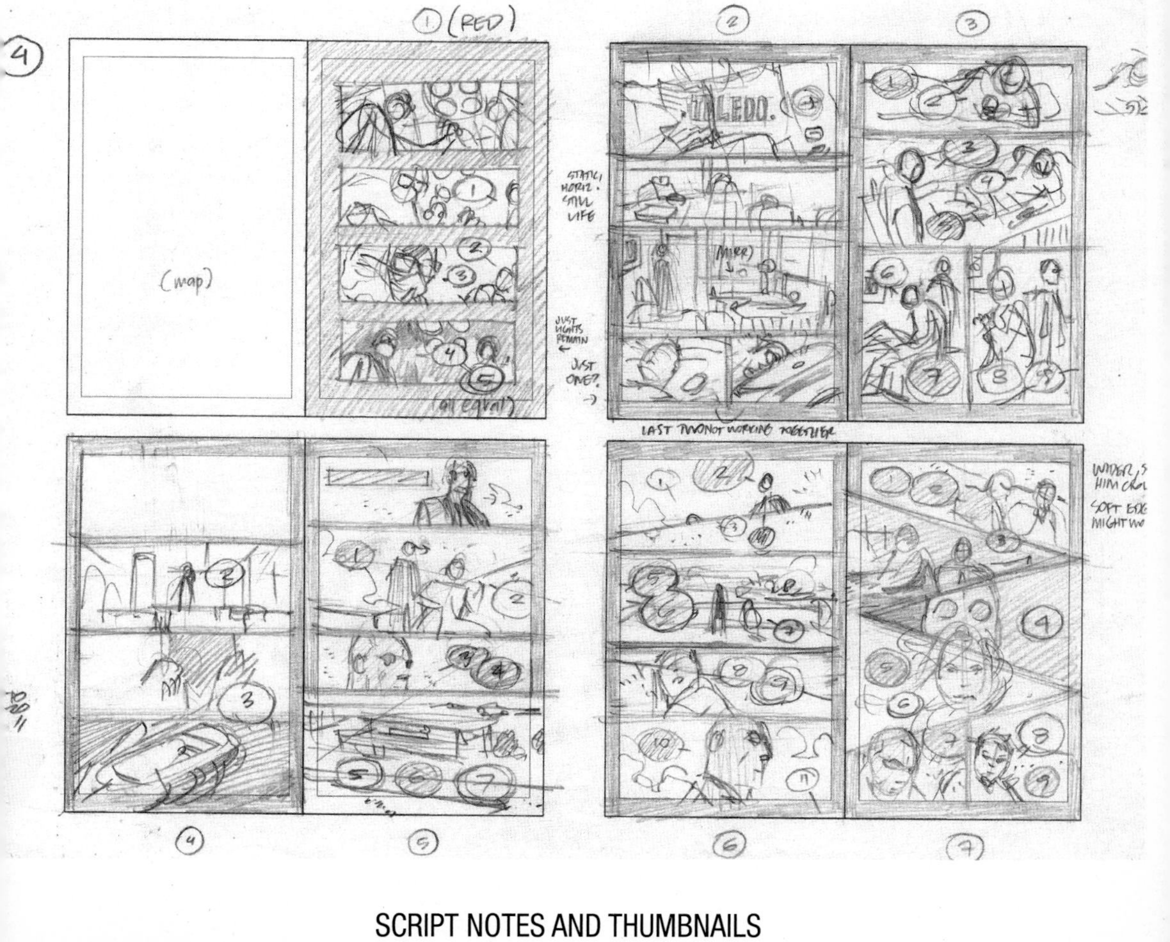

too cute & clean!

① (RED)

④

②   ③

STATIC/ NORM. STILL LIFE

MIRR

JUST LIGHTS REMAIN   *JUST ONE?* →

(map)   *(all equal)*

LAST TWO NOT WORKING TOGETHER

④   ⑤   ⑥   ⑦

UNDER IS HIM CRA... SOFT EDGE MIGHT WO...

SCRIPT NOTES AND THUMBNAILS

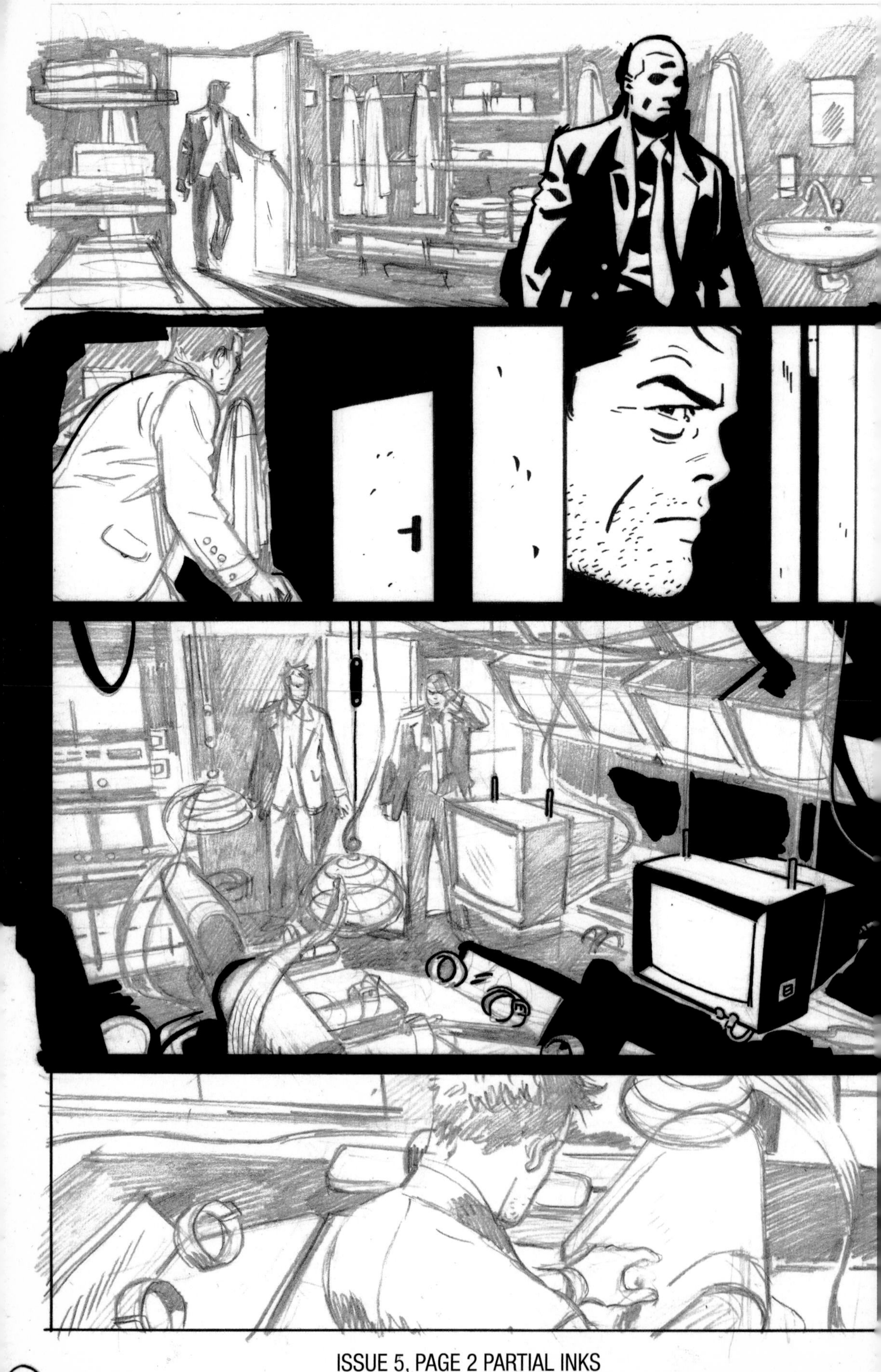

ISSUE 5, PAGE 2 PARTIAL INKS

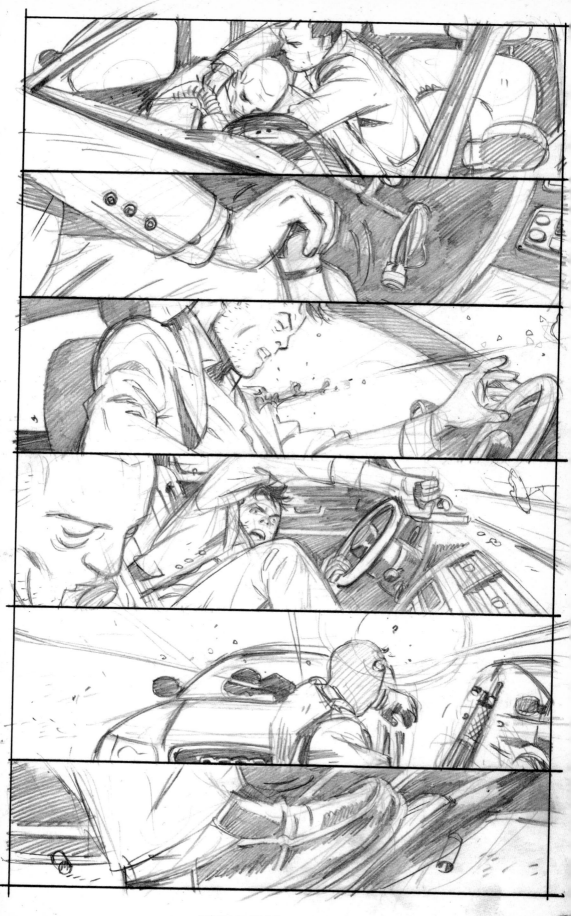

ISSUE 5, PAGE 17 PENCILS

17

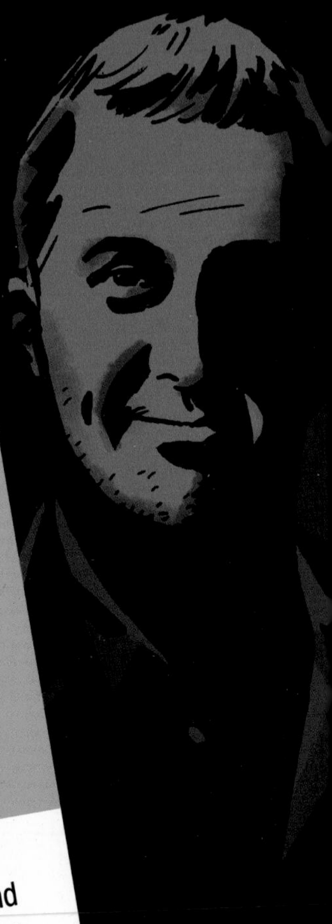

Nathan Edmondson the author of such hit Image Comics titles as *Olympus* with Christian Ward and *The Light* with Brett Weldele. He is also the writer of *Grifter* from DC Comics. He currently lives in Macon, GA with his wife where he engages in high stakes espionage when not writing or hiking. Find out more at www.nathan-e.com.

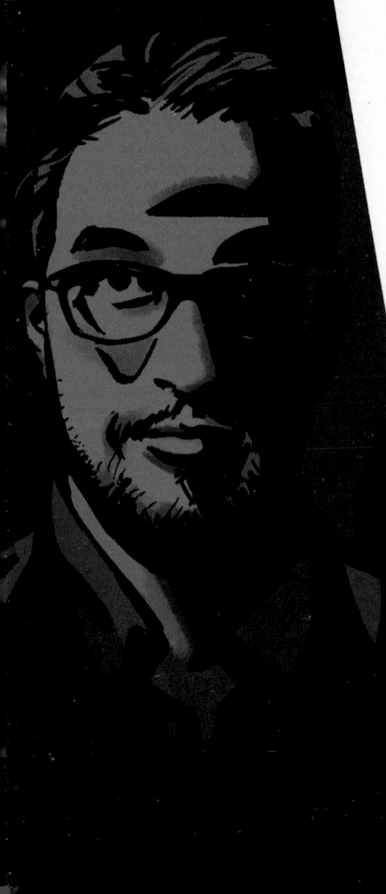

Tonči Zonjić is a celebrated and accomplished artist known for illustrating such hit comics as *The Immortal Iron Fist, Heralds*, and *Marvel Divas*. He also illustrates book covers, storyboards and hundreds of newspaper portraits. You will never pronounce his name correctly. He lives in Zagreb, Croatia with his blue-haired wife and gray-haired cat, and all three are about to move to the other end of the planet. His website is www.to-zo.com.

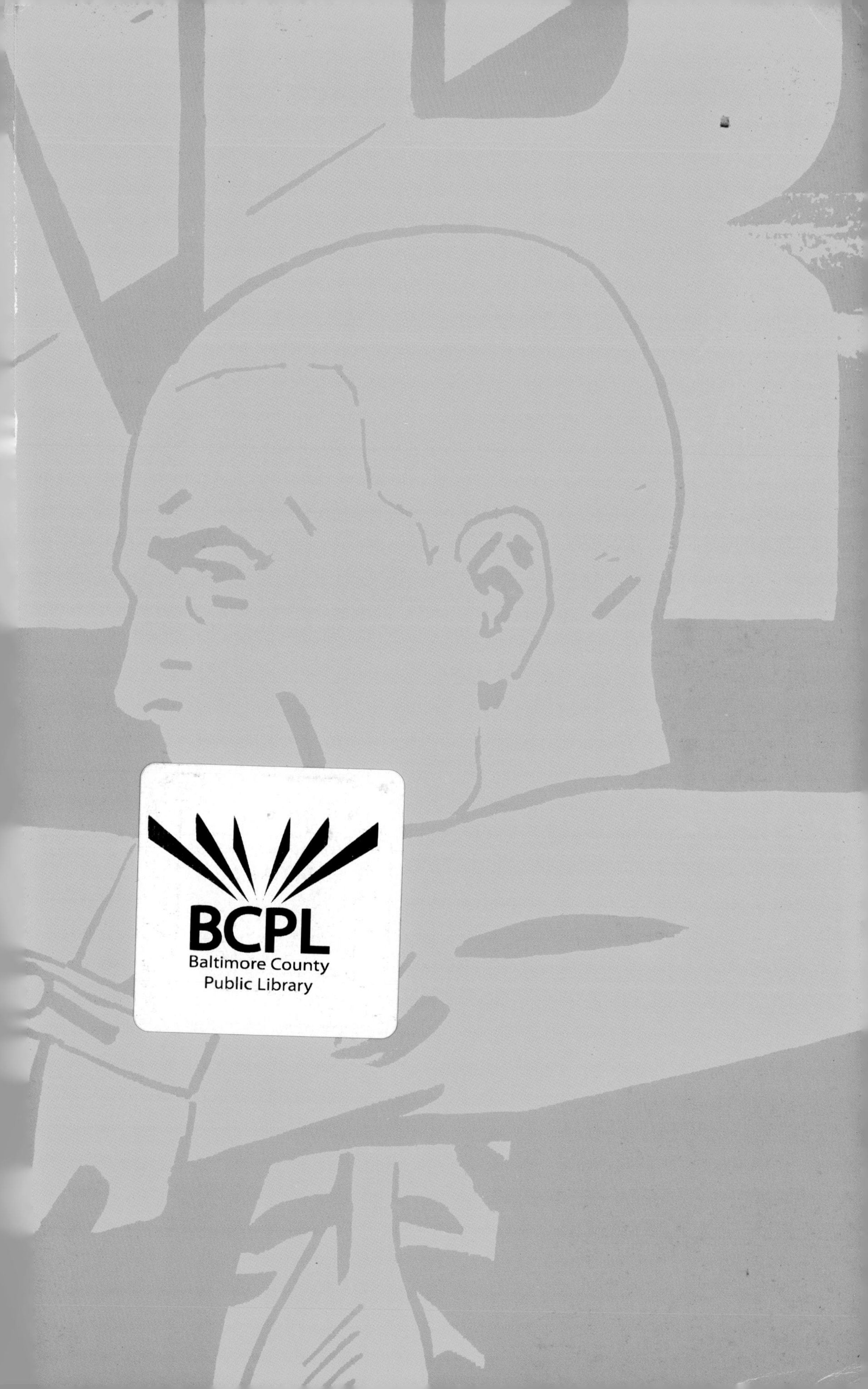

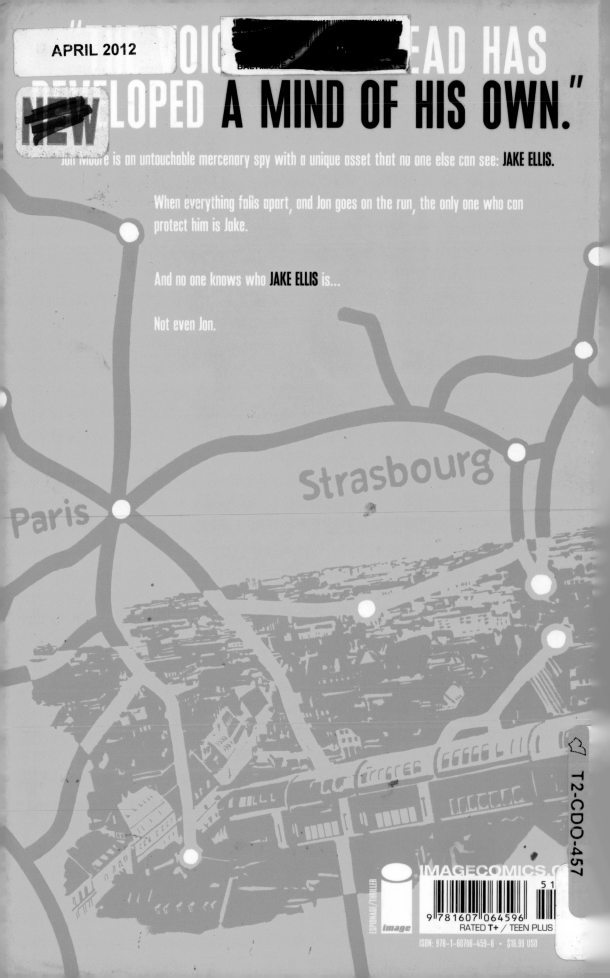

"THE VOICE IN HIS HEAD HAS DEVELOPED A MIND OF HIS OWN."

Jon Moore is an untouchable mercenary spy with a unique asset that no one else can see: **JAKE ELLIS**.

When everything falls apart, and Jon goes on the run, the only one who can protect him is Jake.

And no one knows who **JAKE ELLIS** is...

Not even Jon.

Paris

Strasbourg

IMAGECOMICS.C

ESPIONAGE/THRILLER

RATED **T+** / TEEN PLUS

ISBN: 978-1-60706-459-6 $16.99 USD

9 781607 064596   51

T2-CDO-457

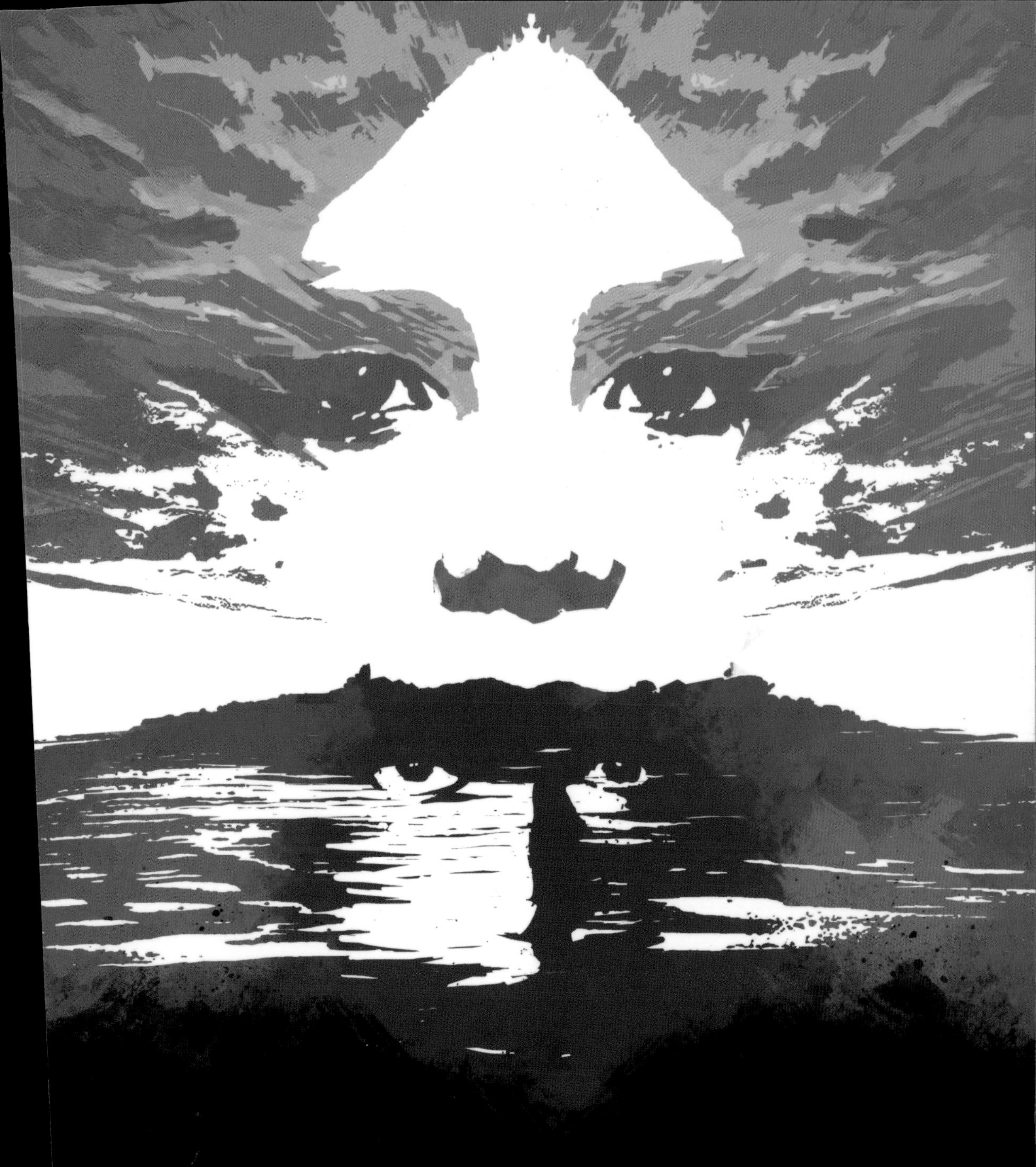

CULLEN BUNN / MARK TORRES

COLD SPOTS™